Communists and Their Victims

The Quest for Justice in the Czech Republic

Roman David

PENN

UNIVERSITY OF PENNSYLVANIA PRESS

PHILADELPHIA

Published by
University of Pennsylvania Press
Philadelphia, Pennsylvania 19104-4112
www.upenn.edu/pennpress

Printed in the United States of America on acid-free paper

10   9   8   7   6   5   4   3   2   1

Library of Congress Cataloging-in-Publication Data
Names: David, Roman, author.
Title: Communists and their victims : the quest for justice in the Czech Republic / Roman David.
Other titles: Pennsylvania studies in human rights.
Description: 1st edition. | Philadelphia : University of Pennsylvania Press, [2018] | Series: Pennsylvania studies in human rights | Includes bibliographical references and index.
Identifiers: LCCN 2017046026 | ISBN 9780812250145 (hardcover : alk. paper)
Subjects: LCSH: Transitional justice—Czech Republic. | Justice, Administration of—Political aspects—Czech Republic. | Post-communism—Czech Republic.
Classification: LCC JC599.C95 D38 2018 | DDC 323/.0440943709045—dc23
LC record available at https://lccn.loc.gov/2017046026

In memory of Vladimír Čermák and Vojtěch Cepl

Contents

Preface

For more than four decades, communist ideology divided the world. After 1989, most communist regimes collapsed but their legacies refused to disappear. Facing their history, citizens of formerly communist countries sought justice for both perpetrators and victims. The Czech Republic has been a leader in dealing with the past in postcommunist Europe. It implemented far-reaching reparation and rehabilitation programs for the victims of communist rule, it returned properties to their original owners, expropriated the assets of the Communist Party, extended the statute of limitation for communist crimes, and enriched the world's vocabulary by reviving the forgotten word "lustration" as a process for dealing with secret collaborators. The implementation of these measures was unprecedented in their scale and speed; many of these measures remain unique. Yet the results are disappointing for many Czechs who observe that historical divisions persist twenty-five years after the regime change. This book therefore raises a question about the role of justice measures in overcoming the communist past. Did justice measures transform the divided society in the Czech Republic?

This book is a culmination of my research into the topic of dealing with the past that dates back to the 1990s. Since then, my research interest in what became known as "transitional justice" has taken me to Poland, Hungary, Croatia, South Africa, and South Korea. Although I found only a few of their citizens satisfied with the outcomes of dealing with the past, I was glad to learn from their experiences. In particular, the issue of "reconciliation" helped me to revisit the Czech process of dealing with the past, which has been dominated by an emphasis on retributive and reparatory justice. I believe that this study can inform academics in the fields of history, political science, sociology and law; policymakers; and civil society members about the positive and negative features of the process of dealing with the past. My recent research and consultancy trips to Ukraine and Myanmar confirm this belief: The stakeholders of other societies divided by fundamental conflict have much to draw from the Czech experience in trying to bring justice to a divided society.

The annexation of Crimea is another motivation for writing this book. Continuing Russian interference in Ukraine and a growing Russian appetite to regain control of territories once under its occupation and influence expose the ideological vulnerability of Eastern Europe. Russian propaganda uses communism as a vehicle to attract supporters in the former Eastern bloc for its territorial drives. The membership of most Eastern European countries in the North Atlantic Treaty Organization (NATO) may be useless if Russian propaganda sways people in these young democracies against NATO. Hence, dealing with the communist past successfully continues to be politically relevant.

The book is dedicated to my teachers Vladimír Čermák and Vojtěch Cepl. Both professors belonged to the remarkable first bench of justices who served in the Constitutional Court of the Czech Republic in 1993–2003. Being professors of social philosophy and law, respectively, both acknowledged that law itself does not have answers to the dilemmas of justice after political transition. Although they searched for answers deep within themselves, they set me on a journey abroad. Justice Cepl, known for his cutting humor, then "banished" me from the country. My crime was nothing less than becoming a "part of the establishment at too young an age." Justice Čermák, a more conciliatory figure, added that I should not worry because my life during totalitarianism, transition, and democracy had provided me with a unique experience that allowed me to view the political world differently than others.

A word is due about the nomenclature used in this book. The critical notion of justice is used as a means and as an objective: I refer to "justice measures" when I speak about a means, a set of methods, laws, and other legal measures and informal societal responses devised or taken to deal with the past. "Justice measures" encompass measures of retributive, reparatory, revelatory, and reconciliatory justice, which serve as four clusters for all justice measures (see Chapter 2). When I refer to justice as an objective of dealing with the past I speak of "justice" or the "perception of justice."

The nomenclature of reconciliation is simpler because "reconciliation" has a noun and an adjective, "reconciliatory." When speaking of "reconciliation" or the "perception of reconciliation," I refer to an objective of dealing with the past. When speaking about "a reconciliatory measure" or its synonyms "a measure of reconciliatory justice" and "a reconciliatory justice measure," I refer to the means of dealing with the past. For instance, an apology is a measure of reconciliatory justice but it needs to be investigated to see whether it actually leads to reconciliation.

The term "Czech Lands" is a historical name for the territory of today's Czech Republic. It is a more accurate term than "the Czech Republic" because it also refers to the Czech part of the Czechoslovak Federation that ceased to exist in 1992. "Restituee" refers to a person whose property was returned during the restitution process. "Lustrator" refers to a person who searches secret police archives, that is, performs lustration. Since the archives have been put into the public domain, every person can search the archives for any name. I do not capitalize communism, which is an ideology such as fascism. Even Nazism does not linguistically elevate communism, since Nazism comes from *Nationalsocialism*, a word in the German language that capitalizes all nouns. As a matter of curiosity, in the Czech language both "komunismus" and "nacismus" appear in the lower case.

ČSFR	Czech and Slovak Federative Republic
ČSSD	Czech Social Democratic Party
ČSSR	Czechoslovak Socialist Republic
ČSÚ	Czech Statistics Office
ČTK	Czech Press Agency
CVVM	Center for Public Opinion Research
KDU-ČSL	Christian Democratic Union–Czech People's Party
KPV	Confederation of Political Prisoners
KSČ	Communist Party of Czechoslovakia
KSČM	Communist Party of Bohemia and Moravia
ODS	Civic Democratic Party
OF	Civic Forum
OH	Civic Movement
SBS	Association of Freedom Fighters
SBPV	Association of Former Political Prisoners
SSM	Socialist Union of the Youth
StB	State Security (secret police)
ÚDV	Office for Documenting and Investigating Communist Crimes
USSR	Union of Soviet Socialist Republics
ÚSTR	Institute for the Study of Totalitarian Regimes
ÚV KSČ	The Central Committee of the Communist Party of Czechoslovakia

Introduction

The entry of allied forces from five socialist countries into Czechoslovakia [in 1968] was an act of international solidarity, which
corresponded with the common interests of the Czechoslovak
working people as well as . . . the class interests of the world
communist movement.

—Communist Party of Czechoslovakia (1970)

Hopes to start building a more democratic, freer, just social order
were bitterly dashed on the night of 20th to 21st August [1968], when
five armies of the Warsaw Pact, allied with several local conspirators,
attacked our country.

—Václav Havel (1990)

It was about the principle of socialist internationalism. It means not
only a possibility but also an obligation for socialist states to provide
mutual help if socialism is under threat.

—Rossiya 1 TV (2015)

For more than forty years, communist regimes had engineered the souls of
Central and Eastern Europe.[1] Behind, they left the lengthy statistics of losses,
broken families, ruined careers, tainted characters, animosities, mistrust,
and painful memories, which underscored the sad history of injustices. The
regimes also created a few proud and happy faces, which remind us that history and justice have always had at least two sides. Driven by a blend of
convictions and interests, new democratic representations tried to make the
history even.

One of them, Czechoslovakia, and, since 1993, its successor, the Czech Republic, has adopted one of the most far-reaching policies of dealing with historical injustices in the world. In order to deal with the legacy of the communist regime, it implemented a rehabilitation program for victims of human rights abuses; approved a law on the restitution of nationalized property; pushed through a lustration law to disqualify members of the former regime; lifted the statute of limitations to allow the prosecution of communist crimes; opened the archives of the secret police; and symbolically declared the previous regime illegitimate. Being aware that injustices are not merely criminal and tangible, the country also pursued a range of informal measures that honored the resistance to the regime, acknowledged the suffering of the victims, renamed the streets, built monuments, and named the new heroes.

Research Questions and Their Relevance

In view of the comprehensive program of justice after transition, one would reasonably expect that the Czech Republic provided an exemplar for dealing with the legacy of human rights violations committed during the era of the communist regime. But did it? Were these measures able to rebuild a sense of justice in society? Did they restore trust? Did they help heal the victims of human rights violations? Did the perpetrators acknowledge the human rights violations? Have historical divides been surmounted? What is the scorecard for the Czech process of dealing with the past?

I believe that answers to these questions will benefit political scientists, sociologists, historians, area studies experts, lawyers, and the transitional justice community in their understanding of one of the most absorbing and complex phenomena in recent history. Answers to these questions are critical for, first, the social understanding of the postcommunist period of the modern history. Second, on the theoretical level, they would contribute to the interdisciplinary field of historical or transitional justice. Third, on the practical level, they would offer a corpus of knowledge that could provide an antidote to exploiting the past for political purposes, especially in view of the populist wave that threatened to grip Europe at the end of the second decade of the twenty-first century and the simultaneous, if not interlinked, rise of Russian territorial ambitions in Eastern Europe. Before I proceed to characterize the objectives of the book and its approach, I briefly explain my intellectual motivation, theoretical interests, and political context, which inspired me to write the book.

Social History of Dealing with the Communist Regime

My intellectual motivation for this research project is to provide readers with the testimony of modern social history by capturing people's opinions about the process of dealing with injustices of the communist regime. The search for answers for the above questions among the individual victims, communists, and society members can complement and enrich the prevalent approaches in postcommunist and democratization studies, which frequently focus on elite-level actors and macro-political processes. What people thought about the communist regime, how they viewed the process of dealing with its injustices, and whether the society still bore the consequences of the past some twenty-five years after its collapse are themes that have been rather neglected in mainstream academia. Our understanding of the history of the era would be incomplete without understanding the people and their preferences, relations, and judgments, which interplay with the collective memory of the past.

Theoretical and Policy Relevance for Transitional Justice

My theoretical aspiration is to contribute to the studies of transitional, or historical, justice.[2] Transitional justice can be defined as a set of measures and processes adopted to deal with the consequences of mass human rights violations in the aftermath of regime changes, violent conflicts, wars, and other historical injustices that were derivatives of undemocratic regimes, colonization, and occupation. The establishment of truth commissions, international criminal tribunals, grassroots justice, and alternative lustration systems may be considered to be the most innovative institutional development of the last century. The revival of the traditional dilemmas revolving around justice, truth, forgiveness, and revenge, and their elevation into the macro-political scene, has been an intriguing intellectual development that has attracted scholars from a variety of fields, including law, political science, sociology, history, and philosophy.

So seductive has transitional justice become that clichés about the ever-booming, ever-promising field have been repeated in academic journals for more than two decades. The resistance of the field to maturity was, however, a minor issue in comparison with several fundamental problems. The undertheorization of the field, and the lack of rigorous empirical research, has allowed a proliferation of researchers' beliefs, attitudes, and opinions to seep into the assessment of transitional justice.[3] Fundamentally different measures of transitional justice have all been accepted willy-nilly as being bound to result in the desired outcome, whether democracy, human rights culture, justice, or reconciliation. Trials and truth commissions, for instance, were not often treated as alternatives on the same conceptual level but as measures that were equal and interchangeable in policy terms. Ad hoc conceptualizations and measurements of these measures have precluded researchers from reaching meaningful comparative conclusions about the utility of justice after transition.

At the time of writing this book, the interdisciplinary field was undergoing a midlife crisis. The concerns about the future that appeared in the discipline's flagship journal have been symptomatic of a crisis that has loomed over the field since the 2000s. The critics have derided transitional justice as a "bandwagon" and the *International Journal of Transitional Justice*, in an editorial, admitted as much.[4] In 2015, the journal even ran a special issue on whether the discipline had a future.[5]

But crises come and go. Examining the effectiveness of the transitional justice process in the Czech Lands will help us to fathom some of the strengths and weaknesses of justice after transition. So far, a large universe of transitional justice measures has not been empirically examined in any country. Putting transitional justice measures to a test, a rigorous empirical assessment would provide feedback to the field of transitional justice and its trainers, practitioners, and consultants who advise on, design, and implement these measures around the world.

Political Relevance

My third motivation stems from political concerns about the future and security of Europe. "National security" considerations have frequently been invoked as reasons to justify an encroachment on human rights. Whether in the United States or in the European Union (EU), security reasons have been used to justify an infringement of the right to association, a threat to the freedom of speech, and the possibility of exclusion from public employment.[6] In these cases, security threats existed, or were assumed, impacting human rights. Here, however, "national security" concerns can work in the reverse: Human rights violations can have security consequences. In this case, the inability to acknowledge human rights violations committed in the past can make society vulnerable when facing populist threats. Such threats may be magnified if a foreign power was politically involved in these violations and now uses ideological tools that relativize their very existence. The question is how real are those "threats to national security" in Central and Eastern Europe?

The silver jubilee of the fall of communist regimes offered an opportunity for some to revisit the achievements in dealing with the past in Eastern Europe.[7] Unfortunately, it was not an occasion for celebration or sentimental shoulder patting. The Russian annexation of Crimea in 2014 and the de facto occupation of Eastern Ukraine suggested that a new hybrid-war era had descended upon Europe. These events were a reminder of Western complacency in dealing with the Russian occupation of territories belonging to Georgia and Moldova.[8] Indeed, Moscow has done little to hide its territorial ambitions in the former Soviet Union and other Eastern European countries.[9] As all these countries were once subordinated to Moscow, the question arises: How successful or unsuccessful were these countries in dealing with the communist past? How invincible or vulnerable are they in facing current threats? Can Russia exploit the legacy of communist ideology to fit its foreign policy interests?

The war in Ukraine was far from being merely "cold." However, another Russian military intervention in Central Europe, similar to its invasion of Hungary in 1956 and Czechoslovakia in 1968, seemed unlikely in 2015. All these countries have since become members of the North Atlantic Treaty Organization (NATO) and the EU. In spite of that, the inclusion of the East European "periphery" in these Western clubs could not change their geographical position, their history of being contested territories, and their recent communist past. In spite of the political and security guarantees from the memberships, the risk of internal destabilization is a real possibility, one that Moscow is familiar with. Propaganda, acting behind the scenes, and sowing discord were commonplace in the old Soviet Union as well as in Putin's Russia. They did not spare the United States, the Netherlands, France, Sweden, Hungary, and other EU countries.[10]

Russian interferences in the Czech Republic date back to at least the 2012–13 presidential elections. An employee of the Czech branch of Russia's energy giant, Lukoil, funded the election campaign for the party of Miloš

Zeman, who was eventually elected president of the Czech Republic. Zeman was then openly promoting Russia's version of events in Ukraine and causing rifts within the EU.[11] On the propaganda front, in May 2015, a Russian state television channel, Rossiya 1, broadcast a "documentary" about the Soviet-led military intervention into Czechoslovakia in 1968.[12] The footage, which claimed to contain declassified materials, showed that it was actually NATO that had planned an invasion of Czechoslovakia, obviously with the help of local traitors and former Nazi collaborators associated with K231.[13] It was thus the responsibility of the Soviet Union, the documentary claimed, to assist its "brother," Czechoslovakia, in a situation in which the achievements of socialism were at risk.

Russia's revision of recent history has served its leadership in two ways. It has nurtured nationalism at home and it has sent an important signal to the Czechs and the Slovaks, who had experience at several times with the revision of events of recent history. The 1968 "invasion" and "occupation" became "brotherly help" and a "temporary stay," according to the official Communist Party guidelines published in 1970.[14] Almost half a million Czechoslovak reform communists (27 percent of all members) who saw it as an invasion were purged from the party.[15] "Brotherly help" was the foundational lie for the communist regime in the 1970s and 1980s. Only after 1989 did "brotherly help" revert to being classified as "invasion" in the original vocabulary once again. The "healthy core"[16] of the Czech Communist Party could not fail to miss the signal that Russia now intended to revise its imperial history along the same lines in 2015.[17]

It is tempting to believe that the passage of time will resolve any anxiety that remains over the past on the grounds that members of communist parties and their secret networks have long since retired. This default position is unconvincing. First, not all former communists have retired at the time of the writing of this book. Certainly not Vladimir Putin, a former lieutenant colonel of the KGB in Dresden. Second, historical divisions may reproduce themselves. Research on Spain has shown that the attitudes to the past have been transmitted from generation to generation for decades.[18] In the Czech Republic, historical divisions have even become institutionalized. For instance, the daughters of former political prisoners created an association called Dcery (Daughters), while the descendants of party members created a Communist Youth Union (KSM). The latter seeks, and campaigns for, a return to the communist regime, provoking with statements that Czech laws do not apply to them.[19]

Adding to this is the existence of successor parties in Eastern Europe, some of them reformed, some of them not, but all of them previously connected to Moscow. The Soviet Communist Party (KPSS) previously instructed, organized, trained, and, most importantly, subordinated the satellite parties. Communism, with its ideological links to Leninism and its historical links to the Soviet Union, has been used by Russia as a medium for advancing its foreign policy objectives. This has not only aggravated the need for urgency in dealing with the protagonists of the communist era and their successors, but also changed its reference frame. Loyalty to the communist regime is not the main problem; loyalty to the external enemy via the former communist parties is.[20]

Until now, there was a degree of consensus in European political circles that it was irrelevant how a country dealt with its past as long as the country ended up in the EU. The measures of justice devised to deal with the past were seen as secondary to the project of greater European integration.[21] The conflict in Ukraine and related security concerns have dramatically changed the perspective on dealing with the communist past in Eastern Europe. Now one looks at historical divisions in East European societies and ponders how ready these countries are to face up to Russia's disinformation and propaganda. Countries that were able to overcome their legacies and learn from history are in a stronger position to face the threats. Overcoming communist regimes has become a test for the countries in Eastern Europe. Eventual instability in Eastern Europe will have profound security implications for the entire EU.

Objectives of the Book

This book seeks to address a key question: How effective were the justice measures that were adopted in the Czech Lands to overcome the legacy of human rights violations committed during the communist regime? If any of the measures were successful, they could serve as a model for other countries. If the rehabilitation of victims, condemnation of perpetrators, and other measures of justice did not significantly affect the outcomes of dealing with the past, then we need to determine the reasons for their failures. All material resources and intellectual effort could have been spared and spent in a more meaningful way than being wasted on the pursuit of policies that did not, or could not, deliver. Worse still, we need to be open to the possibility that these efforts may have preserved the historical divides and were even retrogressive to democratic transition. Obviously, this does not mean replacing the optimism and enthusiasm about transitional justice with skepticism and gloom. It signifies a need for empirical investigation.

In this book I examine the ability of justice measures to contribute to the overcoming of the legacy of human rights violations committed by the communist regime. In order to do so, I classify measures of justice into four categories as retributive, reparatory, revelatory, and reconciliatory. I then empirically examine both the effects of different justice measures on victims, communists, and society as a whole, and the reception of transitional justice by these stakeholders. To pursue the empirical examination, I have analyzed original interviews, focus-group sessions, surveys, and survey experiments that I conducted in the Czech Republic between 1999 and 2015. My sources were complemented by analyses of laws, judgments, surveys, government reports, historical records, and other secondary materials.

Analytical Framework: The Classification of Justice Measures

The question of whether justice matters is a simplification. In view of the variety of justice measures, the question is too broad and needs to be refined. To honor more than two decades of transitional justice scholarship, it is prudent to ask more nuanced questions. Have all of the measures of justice contributed to dealing with the past? This unpacking of justice shifts the focus of the investigation toward examining the utility of different measures of justice. Which measure has been the most effective in dealing with the past? Was any measure redundant? For instance, did financial compensation matter? Did the opening of secret archives play a role in overcoming the legacies of the past? Did apologies affect the perception of justice at all? Any meaningful search for answers to these questions is impossible without a classification of justice measures.

Among the available approaches to classification, I prefer social science approaches to legal approaches. While the latter are useful to enable legal professionals to locate a measure within the universe of legal norms and judgments in order to challenge or review it in light of existing precedents and higher legal norms, the social science approach bears an explanatory value that helps to capture the social meaning of a particular justice measure. Based on my previous research,[22] I classify the measures as follows:

1. *Retributive measures* encompass all measures that condemn perpetrators, collaborators, or other privileged sections of society. These measures include punishments, dismissals, shaming, and condemnation of the previous regime and its protagonists; confiscation of their property; and taking away their undue privileges. These measures have been implemented via various judicial, quasi-judicial, and administrative bodies at the international, national, and grassroots levels.

2. *Reparatory measures* include all measures that empower victims individually, socially, and politically, such as financial compensation, restitution of property, and social acknowledgment.

3. *Revelatory measures* disclose the records of the previous regime, open its archives, and expose the secret collaborators. They also allow victims to share their experiences and motivate perpetrators to disclose relevant information. These measures have been most prominently institutionalized in truth commissions and offices of national memory.

4. *Reconciliatory measures* seek to overcome inimical relations among victims, perpetrators, and the rest of society. Apology and confession are the most prominent examples. Reconciliatory measures were institutionalized in the form of the Amnesty Committee and the Polish lustration system.

The presented classification concerns the primary effects of justice measures, their instrumental role. Naturally, all measures carry secondary effects. For instance, retributive and reconciliatory measures may also reveal human rights violations, and revelatory and reconciliatory measures may also constitute shaming and a self-debasing penalty, respectively.

Normative Background: Lemmas of Transitional Justice

An assessment of the effectiveness of various justice measures requires stipulating a normative background against which the assessment should be made. When can one say that a country has successfully dealt with the past? How can we find out whether all of the measures or any particular measure helped the new democracy to deal with a legacy of human rights violations? How can we determine which measure is most beneficial to the people whose lives were disrupted and destroyed?[23] These questions have been asked for almost two decades. They have justifiably been repeated because consensus about what constitutes the successful outcome of transitional justice interventions has yet to be established,[24] as have the scales for measuring that outcome. Thus, rather than a definite normative framework, the following section merely outlines three guiding principles, or lemmas, that should be met in order to make an assessment as laudable as possible.

First, transitional justice measures have been commonly assessed against their ability to facilitate a transition to democracy and peace.[25] They have also been assessed against some social preconditions for democracy and peace, such as justice, equality, truth, tolerance, trust, human rights, and reconciliation.[26] Are measures of transitional justice viewed as just? Does transitional justice hinder or advance reconciliation? Obviously, the panopticon of goals does not offer a comprehensive normative framework. The degree of "success" or "failure" of transitional justice depends largely on the particular outcome that a researcher chooses to examine. But these considerations do bring us closer. They all stem from the notion of democracy. They allow us to put forward *the first lemma*: The assessment of transitional justice needs to be linked—directly or indirectly as their preconditions—to liberal democracy and peace.[27]

To be sure, transitions are not bound to result in democracy.[28] But liberal democracy offers a normative framework for assessing transitions and their various aspects. "Liberal democracy" has been used as a normative framework for the assessment of all sorts of regimes, which are then classified as illiberal democracies and liberal autocracies based on the extent to which they approximate democracy.[29] Liberal democracy has also been used as a backdrop for assessment of institutional aspects, such as elections and constitutions,[30] and various aspects of political culture, such as trust and tolerance.[31] Likewise, various conflict-transformation strategies have been assessed against their ability to contribute to peace. Hence, democracy and peace may also be applied as an overarching framework to assess transitional justice measures.

Second, because democracy has various components and attributes, the assessment of transitional justice cannot be reduced to a single objective. Indeed, scholars routinely speak about two or more objectives of transitional justice, which may be conflicting or divergent.[32] How do societies torn apart by mass atrocities pursue justice and at the same time rebuild shattered communities?[33] The assessment and the dynamic of justice measures may differ for each objective, although they may all stem from the same conception of liberal democracy. This brings us to *the second lemma*: The comprehensive examination of transitional justice cannot be reduced to a single normative item but requires specifying at least two items from different dimensions as a background for assessment.

The question is what dimensions? In order to specify the dimensions, I shall apply the considerations proposed by Ruti Teitel in her founding study *Transitional Justice*.[34] There Teitel states that transitional justice is both prospective and retrospective as it delegitimizes the old regime and legitimizes the new one. Although both dimensions intersect at a certain point, they do run in different directions. Teitel's statement can be separated into two dimensions:

1. Transitional justice is retrospective. It addresses the legacy of gross human rights violations and other injustices committed in the past, it seeks to prevent their repetition, and it delegitimizes the old regime. The legitimacy of a political regime is interlinked with justice.[35] The absence of justice after the regime change signifies the perpetuation of historical injustices, essentially acting as a "second injustice,"[36] a "second rape,"[37] or a "second death."[38] Justice thus acts as a symbolic watershed, a means of discontinuity, and perhaps even a social ritual that marks transition.[39]

2. Transitional justice is prospective. It prepares the ground for democracy by establishing equality and transforming political culture so that the segments of divided society would be able to get along, work together, and live as neighbors.[40] In other words, they would be able to achieve a degree of trust,[41] tolerance,[42] human rights culture,[43] and reconciliation.[44]

Beyond Teitel, the tensions between backward-looking and forward-looking interests have been expressed in transitional justice literatures in various forms. For instance, they have been captured in the justice or peace dilemma: The pursuit of justice may threaten peace, whereas the interests of peace may compromise justice.[45] Similarly, lustration programs have been characterized as both retrospective and prospective measures because they concern all loyalists of the previous regime who want to retain or reenter public-sector employment.[46] Likewise, scholars often cite a former East German dissident who once famously lamented that they sought justice in the past but all they got after transition was the rule of law.[47]

Finally, third, different sections of society may be affected by justice measures differently. Transitional justice is situated in societies, which have been divided by the history of human rights violations. The interests of victims, bystanders, and perpetrators may differ. A measure that promoted a sense of justice in society may solidify the denial of perpetrators and could fail to heal victims. The background for the assessment of justice measures therefore has several dimensions for each major protagonist in dealing with the past. These considerations bring us to *the third lemma*: The assessment of the social effects of transitional justice requires taking the historical divisions of society into account.

Among the broad range of options, I decided to assess transitional justice among three categories of stakeholders: victims, the communists, and society as a whole. For the purposes of this book, I consider transitional justice successful in overcoming the legacy of human rights violations committed under the communist regime to the extent to which it (1) helped victims to overcome the consequences of human rights violations (healing) and to become socially integrated; (2) helped former or current Communist Party members to internalize human rights and prevented them from passing on the denial of human rights violations to their offspring; (3) changed the material situation of the individuals who held different positions in the past regime (being a victim or a communist);[48] and (4) changed their ideological preferences vis-à-vis the return to the communist regime. This normative framework is thus underpinned by a strong human rights component, accentuating the redress of human rights violations, overcoming the situation when the human rights violations occurred, and the internalization of human rights. At the same time, it concerns three sections of divided society, in which it combines backward-looking and forward-looking aspects.

The normative background presented here is not definite; its branches are further developed and specified in Chapters 3 through 6. Moreover, any end situation is obviously an ideal-typical category, which in reality can only be approximated in different time horizons and different intensities. Perhaps none of the advanced democracies are completely free from historical legacies. The legacies of slavery in the United States, colonization in the United Kingdom, and World War II in Germany and Japan are just a few examples of unresolved historical injustices. On the other hand, not dealing with the past is also an ideal-typical category in its own right. No transitional country has been completely free to ignore the past. Liberalization in Myanmar, transition from a totalitarian regime to authoritarianism in China, and transition to democracy in Spain were accompanied by the release of political prisoners, punishment, and programmatic amnesia, respectively. It is primarily an empirical question as to whether and which measures of transitional justice were effective in dealing with the legacy of human rights violations committed under the communist regime in the Czech Republic.

The Search for Answers: Research Site, Method, and the Plan of the Book

The Czech Lands is an optimal research site for examining the utility of transitional justice. First, the communist regime in Czechoslovakia in the period 1948–89 violated human rights on a mass scale and split the society along political lines. Second, Czechoslovakia after 1989, and the Czech Republic after 1993, implemented an extensive policy of dealing with the past. The reparation and social rehabilitation of victims, the restitution of nationalized property, the nationalization of the property of the Communist Party, a relatively broad and exclusive lustration system, the total revelation of secret collaborators, moral condemnation of the communist regime, lifting the statute of limitations to prosecute crimes of the communist regime, social acknowledgment of victims, two governmental institutions to deal with the past, and other formal and informal measures signify the scope and scale of transitional justice measures that are unprecedented in Central and Eastern Europe and are perhaps the most extensive in the world.[49] The wide range of justice measures and the persistence of historical divisions paradoxically provide us with unique variations that allow an empirical examination of the utility and impact of the different measures.

The book is divided into three parts, each of them consisting of two chapters. Part I situates the book in its historical-political and sociolegal context. A study on the process of overcoming the communist regime requires an inquiry into its nature. Have we academics missed something about the communist regime? My investigation therefore starts in Chapter 1 with the characteristics of the communist regime in Czechoslovakia. The communist regime was obviously more complex than the production of statistics about gross human rights violations would suggest. Some profited from the regime, some were victimized, and many made petty compromises to get along. This chapter adopts a historical sociology approach to examine major injustices, hidden injustices, and minor injustices experienced on a daily basis; and it seeks to determine the role of individuals in creating these injustices.

What if measures of retributive justice did not help to overcome the past because they were ill conceived, too broad or too narrow, or were poorly implemented? Chapter 2 therefore examines measures of justice, both formal and informal, which were pursued in dealing with the past after 1989. The inquiry is interdisciplinary, using social, historical, and legal resources. The emphasis is on law in its political context; on individual motives and experiences of protagonists; and on law in society and informal rituals of dealing with the past that evolved along political transitions in the Czech Lands.

Part II looks at two poles of the divided society: the victims of human rights violations and the communists who supported the violations. Chapter 3 examines the impact of justice measures on former political prisoners in the Czech Republic. It uses quantitative and qualitative data to examine the effect of a variety of justice measures on victims' healing, conceptualized as overcoming physical and psychological consequences of their imprisonment; and sociopolitical redress, conceptualized as a social integration of former political prisoners. It is based on a survey, interviews, observations, and focus-group sessions that I conducted in 1999, 2006, and 2014.

Chapter 4 examines the impact of justice measures on the transformation of former Communist Party members. The transformation is conceptualized as a two-dimensional process that includes personal and intergenerational transformation, which is manifested in the internalization of human rights violations committed by the communist regime. It is based on my survey administered by the Center for Public Opinion Research (CVVM) in 2015; and interviews conducted with the help of four research assistants in the same year.

Part III examines the society as a whole. Chapter 5 asks whether justice could matter in overcoming the past. The potential of justice measures to contribute to the perception of justice and reconciliation is testable via experimental research. I therefore designed an original experiment, which was embedded in a nationwide representative survey of 1,079 respondents in 2010 and administered by CVVM. This was the first experiment that tested the effectiveness of several measures of justice, examined side-by-side in a 3x4x2 factorial design.

Chapter 6 seeks to determine whether and how justice measures affected social transformation. Social transformation is conceptualized as a two-dimensional process that includes material and ideological transformation. The former was captured in changes in the class position since the previous regime. The latter was manifested in the refusal to return to the communist regime. This chapter uses path analysis to determine the steps and the mechanisms for overcoming the communist regime. It is based on data from the nationwide survey of 1,043 respondents that I conducted with CVVM in 2015. Interviews with former political prisoners and Communist Party members are used to interpret the data.

The Conclusion has both empirical and theoretical objectives. First, it seeks to summarize the major research findings from each chapter in order to answer the key questions of this book. Second, it seeks to explain the impact that the different measures of transitional justice had. By situating the results into a coherent narrative, I propose a transformative theory of justice.

PART I

Historical and Sociolegal Context

Chapter 1

The Communist Regime in Czechoslovakia: Were People Coerced?

In a society of working people that has removed exploitation of one person by another, the development and interests of each of its members is in accordance with the development and interests of the society as a whole. The rights, freedoms and duties of citizens thus serve the free, all-inclusive development of citizens and the realization of their full potential in the consolidation and development of the socialist society.

—Constitution of Czechoslovakia of 1960

Blood, screaming, torture and gallows are hidden behind massive walls through which no voice can penetrate, while beyond the walls merry busses drive tourists up and down and newspapers are full of articles about the brutality and lawlessness of capitalism, and we are happy to participate in the new era, which gives everyone an opportunity for moral ascent, and only occasionally have to isolate from society those who are filled with hatred, and undercut the roots of the tree of Liberty but even these are given the opportunity to confess their dark deeds, over which she-comrades in factories weep in righteous anger and sign a petition to hang the spy.

—Dagmar Šimková, *Byly jsme tam taky*

This book examines the impact of justice measures on victims, communists and other sections of the Czech society in the aftermath of the communist regime. Such a study therefore requires an inquiry into the kind of injustices committed during the regime, and an overview of justice measures taken to redress those injustices. This chapter addresses the former: it situates the communist regime in Czechoslovakia into its historical-political context and focuses on the injustices it committed.[1] Based on their nature, I distinguish three categories of injustices: open repression, which concerned gross violations of human rights; hidden repression, which included secret policing and collaboration; and minor injustices that people encountered on a daily basis. Each type of injustice can be categorized in accordance with the degree to which the agency of people in general played a role. This would imply a degree of responsibility on their part. Was the communist regime imposed on the country or chosen by the people? Were high-ranking communists alone responsible for the gross violation of human rights? Were people forced, or did they volunteer information about their fellow citizens? Can a straightforward answer to these questions be provided?

To confront the questions about people's agency in creating historical injustices, this chapter is divided into four sections. The first section examines the historical context in which communism in Czechoslovakia rose and was maintained. The following three sections deal with the three types of repression, respectively. Each section combines macro- and micro-level perspectives. The perspectives of "ordinary people" are rather neglected in the studies of democratization and transitional justice at the expense of macro-level considerations, although both are critical for an understanding of the communist regime, its social dynamic, and the process of overcoming it. Methodologically, I seek evidence against both a top-down perspective (i.e., against suggestions that communism was imposed on people in Czechoslovakia) and a bottom-up perspective (i.e., against suggestions that communism was a homegrown product and that people collaborated voluntarily). These perspectives treat human agency in opposite ways, which has implications for the choice of measures of justice after transition.

The Communist Regime: Made in Czechoslovakia?

After World War II Czechoslovakia reverted to the democratic system under the stewardship of Edvard Beneš, who succeeded Tomáš G. Masaryk as president.[2] The Communist Party won 40.2 percent of the votes in the Czech Lands in the parliamentary elections of 1946.[3] Shortly after elections Beneš, in accordance with the Constitution, appointed the Communist Party's leader, Klement Gottwald, prime minister. Gottwald, having been in Moscow during the war, was "ultra-responsive to Soviet wishes," which were to strengthen the country's orientation to the Soviet Union and to reject the Marshall Plan.[4] In spite of being in a government coalition, Gottwald was able to nominate a communist, Václav Nosek, as the minister of the interior, and a communist sympathizer, Ludvík Svoboda, who later became a communist president, as the minister of defense. In response to the police abuses and growing influence of the communists in the armed forces, pro-democracy ministers resigned from the government, seeking the resignation of the entire government and new elections. However, President Beneš—facing pro-communist demonstrations, paralegal action committees, and the paramilitary People's Militia[5]—accepted their resignation and replaced them with the Communist Party members and its loyalists. In this way, the Communist Party of Czechoslovakia took power by a combination of constitutional and unconstitutional means on February 25, 1948.

Communists established a totalitarian regime that was based on the rule of the Party's politbureau.[6] The resultant partocracy was characterized by an accumulation of party positions and the state, respectively. The secretary general was often also the president of the country, and government ministers held positions in the Party's central committee and in a Parliament.[7] The centralized power included about 15,000 *nomenklatura* cadres,[8] who gave orders to lower Party members and state bureaucrats.[9] The central committee used secret police and widespread repression, Marxist-Leninist propaganda, and systems of rewards and incentives to further its goals. The Party nationalized all private establishments, created a centrally planned economy, and assumed full control of all sections of society, including the churches, trade unions, civil society, cultural establishments, and universities. Each entity had a Communist Party cell within it. Virtually all private property, as well as 88 percent of agricultural land in Czechoslovakia, was nationalized. The scale of this nationalization was unprecedented in comparison with that which occurred in other countries in Central Europe, most notably Hungary and Poland.[10]

The total control was aimed not only at the opposition outside and within the Communist Party but also at Slovak nationalism. Communism had never been as urgent and as ideological an issue in Slovakia as it had been in the Czech Lands. Slovak communists cooperated with various democrats in the Slovak National Uprising against the clerofascist Slovak State in 1944. The predominantly Catholic and agricultural Slovak society did not boast any significant working class. With only 30.5 percent of votes in the 1946 elections, the communists lost to the Democratic Party, which won 62.0 percent of the votes. Leading Slovak communists, among them the future Party secretary and the last communist president, Gustáv Husák, were later accused of "nationalist deviation" in 1954 and sentenced by their comrades to jail.[11]

Internationally, Czechoslovakia maintained its position as one of the satellite countries of the Soviet Union. Unlike Albania, Romania, and Yugoslavia, the Czechoslovak Communist Party never broke ranks with Moscow. Even Alexander Dubček, a Moscow-educated Sovietophil, never intended to do so.[12] The tragic invasion of the Warsaw Pact armies in 1968 turned into self-administered purges and mass collaboration with the occupying forces. In the 1970s and the 1980s, Prague's servility abetted Moscow's domination, although Soviet methods changed. According to a member of the Party's Central Committee (ÚV KSČ), during that era,

> The Soviets never said that Petr or Pavel should take [a post], or we should do it this way or that. But they had, at the same time somewhat, I would say, worked out . . . civil and modern methods. They now put it this way: "We have heard that you are working on a new Constitution. We have also heard that . . ." and suddenly they would say something which they could not have heard because nobody said that. . . . The form was softer . . . nevertheless complicated for us . . . because the world was divided and we existentially, fatally, depended on them, not only for [their] raw materials but also because all our production was exported there.[13]

Apart from taking a brief stand against the Soviets in 1968, Czechoslovakia was a loyal lackey and camp follower of Moscow. It was a founding member of the Warsaw Treaty—the military pact between eight socialist countries, including Bulgaria, East Germany, Hungary, Poland, Romania, the Soviet Union, and temporarily also Albania. It was also a cofounder of Comecon, the Council for Mutual Economic Assistance, that, in addition to the treaty members, associated also with Cuba, Mongolia, and Vietnam.[14] The Czechoslovak government was not only a victim of Soviet imperialism but also an active supporter of it.[15] It was a willing exporter of heavy weaponry to the Third World and an active sponsor of international terrorism.[16]

Hence, we can observe, at the outset, that the communist regime was not merely a product of external historical circumstances but that Czechoslovaks were—as in 1938 and 1968—complicit in their own defeat.[17] Popular portrayals that communism was imposed on Czechoslovakia as a consequence of a deal struck among the Allies in the aftermath of World War II, though common, appear overly deterministic. People are not a substrate of politics, but they shape politics in every way. It would be fair to say that the ascent and maintenance of the communist regime, though expedited by historical circumstances, was the direct result of the action and inaction of the Communist Party with both the initial political support and acquiescence of society and the social inertia of the following decades.[18]

However, the corroboration of this preliminary assessment requires making analytical distinctions in at least two dimensions: time and the type of injustices. Does this assessment apply to the entire period of the communist regime? Does it apply to all types of injustices? The first question points to the stages of the communist regime, while the second concerns various kinds of injustices. The first invites a historical and macro-political inquiry about the extent to which Czechoslovaks were masters of their own fate, while the second concerns individual responsibility for injustices. The former is addressed below, while the latter is examined in the following three sections.

Stages of the Communist Regime

Three stages of the communist regime can be distinguished. The first phase started with the communist takeover of February 1948 and lasted until the revelation of the worst Stalinist crimes by Nikita Khrushchev in 1956. During that period the communist regime sought to strengthen its grip on power by eliminating "enemies" outside and within the Communist Party itself. The second stage lasted until the Soviet invasion in 1968. It was marked by a gradual alleviation of the repression and a large amnesty for many political prisoners in 1960. During this stage the communists declared the victory of socialism, passed a new constitution, and changed the name of the country to the Czechoslovak Socialist Republic. The third stage, the so-called normalization era, was initiated with massive purges of the state apparatus to deal with the Prague Spring, which was followed by two decades of stagnation and inertia until 1989. The three stages correspond with the dynamic of repression as we shall see in Figures 2 and 3 later.

While the dynamic of repression changed, many things remained constant during all three stages. During all the eras, the Communist Party held monopoly power. Elections were neither free nor fair during this time.[19] With the exception of a few occasions in 1948, 1953, 1968–69, and 1988–89 few illegal protests took place. Hence, it is not possible to determine the level of support for, and the opposition to, the regime. Although the Prague Spring, and the reformist wing in the Communist Party around Alexander Dubček, enjoyed a degree of public support, while the Soviet-led invasion mobilized a notable opposition against it in August 1968 and 1969, the year 1969 restored skepticism and the withdrawal of citizens from the public sphere.[20] The self-immolation of Jan Palach in January 1969 was a response to that development. Palach's suicide was a protest not against the military invasion but against its acceptance.[21] The former was a responsibility of the Soviets while the latter was a responsibility of the Czechs.

Since then, the Czechoslovak communists had not been willing to make any significant alterations to their regime. This was in stark contrast with developments that took place in Hungary and Poland, which experienced gradual liberalization during the 1970s and the 1980s. Even the Soviet Union, under the leadership of Gorbachev, undertook the process of glasnost (openness) and perestroika (economic reform) after 1985. The proponents of the leading opposition movement, Charter 77, initially gathered 241 signatures and fewer than 2,000 in total by the end of the regime, again in a contrast to the mass Solidarity Union movement in Poland.[22] After the massive exodus of East Germans via Czechoslovakia, the fall of the Berlin Wall, and a brutal suppression of a para-legal demonstration on November 17, 1989, only then did the regime implode in the face of massive peaceful demonstrations across the country. These events are known as the Velvet Revolution. The fate of the regime was sealed by the removal of the leading role of the Communist Party from the Constitution by the predominantly communist Federal Assembly on November 29, 1989. Czechoslovaks were thus responsible for the installation of the communist regime, as well as its maintenance and its demise.

The historical-political description has largely concealed the variety of people's experiences with the regime. In different eras, the regime enjoyed different levels of popular support and experienced various degrees of resistance. Every stage was characterized by certain intensity of repression and different levels of living standards, which brought happiness to some and misery to others.

When looking back at the milestones of modern history twenty-five years after the communist regime, Czechs tended to appraise democratic changes

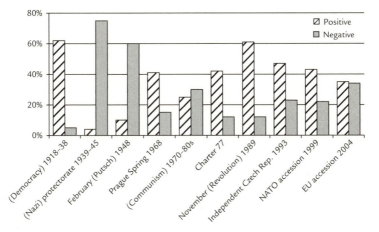

Figure 1. Popular assessment of milestones in Czechoslovak/Czech history.
CVVM, "Dvacet pět let od Sametové revoluce očima občanů ČR a SR" (2014).

more positively than changes wrought by the communist regime (see Figure 1). Although the eras of communism and Nazism were both viewed negatively, the February communist takeover was viewed less negatively than the era of Nazi occupation. During the communist era there were variations. Reform communism of the Prague Spring was rated more positively than the period during the 1980s while the beginning of the communist regime was viewed more negatively than its end.

To locate the responsibility for the injustices of the communist regime, one needs to search within the country itself. We shall look at the scale of injustices and at the issue of individual responsibility for gross human rights violations, covert repression, and minor injustice in the following three sections. However, rather than "finding the guilty," my interest is to establish the general tendencies of whether people volunteered in creating injustices or whether they were coerced into committin them. The establishment of such tendencies has an impact on the assessment of justice measures (see Chapter 2).

Open Repression: Gross Violations of Human Rights

The Communist Party of Czechoslovakia used various repressive means to establish and reinforce its hold on power, targeting hundreds of thousands of people who were, regardless of their personal beliefs, declared the "enemies of socialism." The Party was licensed to kill by Lenin, who argued that socialist revolution would require "seas of blood" and socialism "far less bloodshed."[23] Hence, after the putsch, people from all sections of society were persecuted: petit bourgeoisies, workers, and peasants; members of all political parties, including the Communist Party itself; people of various faiths and nonreligious people; people fighting the Nazis on the western and eastern fronts; and the Czechs, Slovaks, and various minorities.[24] Repression extended to family members of affected individuals; partners, children, and even grandchildren were persecuted for political opinions that had been expressed years before by their relatives.[25]

Open Repression in Numbers

The number of fatalities under communist rule in Czechoslovakia was larger than the number of deaths in Chile under Augusto Pinochet.[26] First, 262 persons were executed for political reasons, many of them on charges such as espionage and high treason.[27] Among them 244 (93.1 percent) were executed in the first stage of repression between 1949 and 1955 (see Figure 2).[28] They included the deputy chief of the General Staff of the Czechoslovak, Army General Heliodor Píka, and the former anti-Nazi resister and a member of Parliament, Milada Horáková. Among those executed in the first stage were thirteen high-ranking Communist Party exponents (5.3 percent of all executions), most of them Jewish, who may have been victims of an anti-Semitic drive within the Party and punished for their support of Israel in the late 1940s.[29] They were tried in orchestrated trials to deal with "conspiracy centers" and included, among others, the second in command of the Communist Party, its secretary general, Rudolf Slánský; the infamous orchestrator of the witch-hunt in the Czechoslovak Army, Bedřich Reicin; and a Slovak politician, Vlado Clementis, who succeeded Jan Masaryk as the minister of foreign affairs.

Second, more than four thousand political prisoners died in jail in unclear circumstances, possibly as a consequence of torture and mistreatment.[30] Third, between 1948 and 1989, at least 280 people died as a consequence of their attempts to cross the border; among them, 88 were foreign nationals.[31] Of those who died on the border, 143 (51 percent) were shot dead, 95 (33.9 percent) were electrocuted on the electric fences, 17 committed suicide before their capture, and 11 drowned.[32] It means that there were twice as many fatalities on the western border of Czechoslovakia than there were at the Berlin Wall.[33]

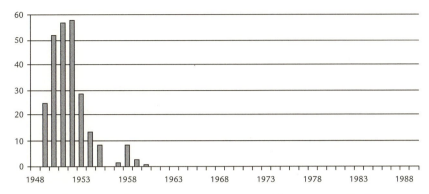

Figure 2. Numbers of persons judicially executed for political reasons. During the presidency of Klement Gottwald (1948–53), 234 death penalties were carried out, 189 of them for political criminal acts. During the era of Antonín Zápotocký (1953–57), there were 94 death penalties, 47 of them political; and during Antonín Novotný's era (1957–68), there were 78 death penalties, of which 12 were for alleged political offenses. Liška et al., *Vykonané tresty smrti*, 161; ÚDV, "Oběti komunistického režimu."

The proportion of political prisoners in the civilian population as a whole was almost the same as it was in Uruguay.[34] About 262,500 people were found guilty of political offenses in the territory of Czechoslovakia and of them 205,486 received custodial sentences.[35] Hundreds of thousands of people suffered other forms of persecution. About 20,000 people were placed in forced labor camps; they were not prisoners under the legal code of the time, but quasi-judicially persecuted "class enemies." About 60,000 men were forced to serve in the so-called Auxiliary Technical Battalions (PTP) as "politically unreliable" servicemen, 22,000 of them for political reasons. More than 6,300 monks and nuns were sent to assembly camps in 1950. Thousands of people were evicted from cities, and private property was almost all nationalized.[36]

Hundreds of thousands lost their jobs in the purges that followed the events of 1948 and 1968. The purges meant downward mobility for educated and qualified professionals who ended up in manual jobs, such as in agriculture and the mines in the 1950s and 1960s, but also as window cleaners and stokers in the 1970s and 1980s. Many of them were prosecuted or emigrated; about 170,938 citizens emigrated illegally from Czechoslovakia between 1948 and 1987.[37] Conversely, 200,000 to 250,000 workers were catapulted to technical, military, police, managerial, and political positions.[38] The result was

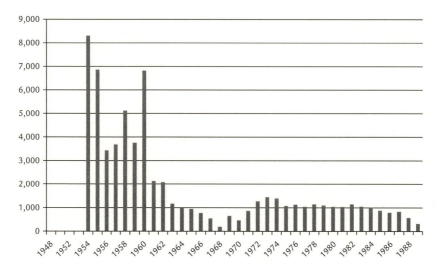

Figure 3. Numbers of secret collaborators by year of registration. Data for 1948–52 are not available. The numbers are based on my analysis of the official database of collaborators with the State Security, Ministry of the Interior (2003). I cannot refer to the database directly because my analysis included transformations and the deletion of duplicate cases.

what sociologists call a status inconsistency, a discrepancy among income, status, and power.[39]

The intensity of repression changed over time. The number of death penalties (Figure 2) suggests that the first stage in the 1950s was the most brutal era. In 1968, the liberalization intermezzo of the Prague Spring led to the alleviation of censorship and explicit repression. The open repression intensified once again during the so-called era of normalization in the aftermath of the Soviet-led invasion of Warsaw Pact armies on August 21, 1968. Hundreds of people lost their jobs in massive purges, although no show trials of the 1950s caliber were orchestrated and no death penalties for political reasons handed out. One of the reasons for the repression without executions may have been the selection of Gustáv Husák, a communist political prisoner of the communist regime in 1950s, as the general secretary of KSČ in 1969.

The decreasing intensity of the most severe repression did not mean its end. The repression continued during the 1970s and 1980s, which is demonstrated by the continued recruitment of collaborators by the secret police (see Figure 3). The repression lasted until the end of the regime, which is evidenced by the brutal suppression of peaceful political protests as late as November 17, 1989.

People and Open Repression

A macro-level perspective on the communist regime and its historical record of human rights violations are incomplete without micro-level insights. To illustrate them, I shall sketch segments of the biographies of two people who bore different relations with the regime: Miroslav Dvořáček and Milan Kundera. Their stories were widely debated in the Czech and international press in 2008 and 2009, thanks to the weekly *Respekt*. Although their stories are both extraordinary and ordinary at the same time, they illustrate the interplay between the political context and ordinary human lives. Both stories occurred at the height of repression in the 1950s. The relevant parts of the biographies can be sketched in the following way:

> Mr. Dvořáček was born in Kostelec, a town in East Bohemia in 1928. After completing his secondary education he was admitted to the elite Military Academy in Hradec Králové in 1947. After the communist takeover, he was stripped of his rank and, along with ninety-five other students and instructors, expelled for his pro-democratic stance in 1949. Shortly after, twenty-two of them emigrated to the West. One of them was his friend, Mr. Juppa, a schoolmate since secondary school. The family of Juppa's girlfriend, Ms. Militká, facilitated the escape of the two men to the West. In a refugee camp Dvořáček was recruited as a member of the independent Czechoslovak intelligence agency. He was sent to cross the border illegally into Czechoslovakia. In 1950, during his second visit, Dvořáček coincidentally met Ms. Militká. Shortly after that he was arrested, prosecuted, and by a whisker escaped the death penalty. He served fourteen years out of a twenty-two-year sentence in communist jails. A few weeks after the Soviet invasion in 1968, he emigrated to the West and settled in Sweden. He died in 2012.[40]

> Mr. Kundera was born in Brno, South Moravia, in 1929. He "shared the prevailing enthusiasm for the idea of socialism and admiration for Stalin's Soviet Union." He joined the Communist Party. In 1948, he was admitted to study film at a university in Prague. He eventually

became a writer and "penned poetry and song texts in the spirit of the socialist ardour of those days." In 1950, his friend Mr. Dlask told him about a spy who visited his future wife, Ms. Militká, in a student hostel. Kundera then reported this case to the police. However, he gradually grew disillusioned with the Soviet Union and skeptical about the communist regime in Czechoslovakia. He eventually left the country and settled in France. In 2008, a historian asked him about this report. He vehemently denied it.[41]

The question about Kundera's agency gives rise to a question about the complicity of ordinary Czechoslovaks in the perpetration of gross human rights violations. The consideration of his responsibility needs to start with his motives. Kundera may have been ideologically motivated. In 1950 the government campaign against espionage centers in the country intensified. A young enthusiast for the communist regime would report a foreign spy without any hesitation, and perhaps even without having any recollection of it, as it was just one of many ways of building a bright future, a daily routine. Kundera may have been motivated by personal interests. Journalists have suggested that he may have had problems with the Communist Party for making an inappropriate "joke" and may have needed something with which to appease his comrades in order to assuage their desire to punish him; for this reason he reported non-anonymously. His motives may have been purely personal: His reporting may have been a favor to his friend Dlask, who sought Ms. Militká; she had a relationship with Juppa, the friend of Dvořáček. By smashing the spy network, Dlask would have increased his chances of wooing Militká.

As to his legal responsibility, Kundera could defend himself as a law-abiding citizen who reported a crime to the police, while being aware of the consequences that a failure to report would have for him. The consequence of this reporting meant that Dvořáček went to jail, while not reporting carried the risk of a jail term for Kundera. Kundera did not even need to hide behind the classic civil war dilemma of "to kill or be killed," which played out in the theaters of the major ideological clashes of the twentieth century. He was protected by the laws of the time.

The question of Kundera's civil-political responsibility is more complex. Dvořáček was committed to democracy, while Kundera was committed to communism and its laws. Kundera could in theory defend himself as a believer in communism as an ideology, which was legitimate even during the first Czechoslovak Republic. The problem is that Dvořáček did not threaten Kundera. Neither did democracy threaten communism, although communists may have felt threatened by democrats. In fact, democrats tolerated communists, while communists destroyed democrats. To simplify the dilemma, Dvořáček's commitment to democracy as a possible political excuse for Kundera should be taken out of the equation; likewise, Czechoslovak democracy with its record of tolerance should not be considered as a legitimate target of destruction. After that, what remains is Kundera and his affair with communism. Could one, as Kundera asks in his *Unbearable Lightness of Being*, not know what was likely to happen as a result of his reporting? Could Kundera of the 1950s be unaware of consequences that would be wrought upon Dvořáček?

During the first stage of the communist regime, it was difficult to miss the ominous signs of repression. Unfree elections in 1948, show trials, forced nationalization of property, and violent collectivization of agriculture were done publicly with the press's support. In this context, one could hardly be unaware that reporting a "spy" would result in his punishment, if not a death penalty. The popular defense "I did not know" would not have much currency in this case. If he did not know, the consequences are upon him in accordance with his own lights. In *Unbearable Lightness*, Kundera invokes Oedipus who felt guilty about marrying Jocasta although he was not aware that she was his mother. In the Sophocles drama, Oedipus gouged his eyes out. In Kundera's novel, the main character evaded this conclusion. Kundera himself denied the whole incident about his reporting but did not sue either the historians, who produced two documents to prove his alleged reporting, or the journalists who broke the story.

Different people may have had different motives—ideological, career, and personal—for participating in the gross human rights violations, and they could have had justifiable fears about standing up against them. Nonetheless, one can hardly defend oneself by saying "I did not know." The gross injustices were apparent in their scale and publicness.

Hidden Repression: Secret Collaboration in Socialist Czechoslovakia

Communist regimes in all Eastern European countries relied heavily on secret police. The Stasi in Germany, the State Security (SB) and Security Office (UB) in Poland, III Directorate in Hungary, Securitate in Romania, and the Státní

bezpečnost (StB; State Security) in Czechoslovakia were feared secret services.[42] To ensure control over its satellites, the influence of the Soviet KGB
was critical to their establishment. Nevertheless, I resist the demonization
of any secret police as an all-powerful tool of control. Indeed, the Soviet
KGB was unable to prevent, or perhaps even spot, the warning signs of popular protests or major liberalization movements in East Germany in 1953,
Hungary in 1956, Czechoslovakia in 1968, and Poland in 1981. They were
unable to block Romania, Yugoslavia, and Albania from entirely drifting away
from the Soviet influence. Had it been such an effective force of control, the
Soviets would not have needed to send their tanks to Central Europe, which
would have saved their money and their face.

Blaming the KGB alone for the establishment of secret police in Czechoslovakia also ignores the homegrown tradition of secret policing and the experience of Nazi occupation. Historically, secret police had already operated
during the Austro-Hungarian Empire with offices in Prague, Brno, and Opava
since the late eighteenth century.[43] Jaroslav Hašek famously ridiculed the
Austrian secret police in his novel about the good soldier Švejk.[44] The
Nazi's use of the Gestapo was notorious during the era of the so-called Pro-
tectorate of Bohemia and Moravia in 1939–45. Gestapo branches in Prague
and Brno, directly subordinated to Berlin, ran a network of about 5,861
informers.[45]

To be sure, the Soviet influence, which can be traced to 1945, and which
expanded in 1949 via the system of special advisors at the Ministry of the
Interior, can be seen as *a factor* in establishing the StB and the vast network
of its collaborators.[46] The StB, as it was commonly called, was established on
June 30, 1945, as a part of regular police, which operated as a plainclothes
political police service. Since its inception it had been under the direct control of the Communist Party and had been used for its political purposes.
After the communist putsch in 1948, it started to perform tasks ranging from
investigating to liquidating opponents of the regime. The StB was dissolved
on February 15, 1990, by the order of the federal minister of the interior,
Richard Sacher.[47]

In parallel with the view of the KGB, many writers have switched to a
monochromatic vision to portray the StB as an all-powerful force equipped
with extraordinary capabilities that allowed it to outsmart the democratic
opposition. To be sure, the StB undoubtedly bears a great deal of responsibility for surveillance, smear campaigns, fabrication of evidence against regime opponents, show trials, torture and mistreatment of political prisoners

and opposition activists, as well as political murders.[48] Nonetheless, as indicated above, I am reluctant to simply accept the view that all secret police were per se an effective machine in an ineffective system. The question of which description is more appropriate is an empirical one that depends on an assessment of the recruitment of secret collaboration. This assessment then has implications for establishing individual responsibility.

Owing to the equal legal treatment they received in the lustration law, the second common perception about the secret police and its collaborators is the perception of them as a homogeneous group, all bound by the same insidious motives. However, one cannot a priori exclude the possibility that some people volunteered to collaborate, while others were forced into collaboration. The questions I am asking here are: Who were the secret collaborators? How were they recruited? To answer these questions I shall first review documents that regulated the operation of the secret police and its network. I shall then analyze the database of secret informers, which was officially published by the Ministry of the Interior in 2003. To avoid a reliance on the database and formal procedures that may be twisted in reality, I shall look at the process of recruitment from the perspective of two recruited individuals. My analytical objective in all three steps is to examine the assumptions about the homogeneity of secret collaborators that underpin the lustration and similar laws. I seek to find evidence against the assumption that all people listed as secret collaborators had the same characteristics, regardless of whether they acted as social agents who could make choices or were forced to collaborate.

The Recruitment of Secret Collaborators in Official Documents

The methods of work with secret collaborators and their ranks and of the recruitment of such collaborators evolved over the duration of the communist regime.[49] These methods were regulated by guidelines, which were issued by strictly confidential orders, given by the minister of the interior in 1948, 1954, 1962, 1972, and 1978.[50] However, the initial guidelines for recruitment, for work methods and the ranks of secret collaborators, existed on paper and apparently not in practice. According to a historian of secret services, Pavel Žáček, a security check conducted by the Ministry of the Interior in 1951 discovered that recruitment, or "binding," for secret collaboration was subject to numerous flaws.

The agency has not so far become a sharp weapon . . . in the struggle against an internal class enemy. . . . Objects bonded for secret collaboration systematically provide misleading information. . . . Persons who are completely unknown are recruited, and after a resolution of the case, thanks to another source, it is discovered that the person was a member of a subversive group. . . . A person is summoned to security [service] without prior screening and a proposal for an act of binding. During interrogation the person is forced to sign a binding oath under threat without any compromising materials. . . . Appalling cases were discovered of the use of physical force and other threats as a "means" for binding.[51]

Hence, the practice in the 1950s appeared rather more chaotic than professional. One of the possible explanations for the chaos was that a large number of secret police officers did not have any formal education. According to Williams, merely 9 percent held at least a secondary school degree.[52] This is not entirely surprising as members of the educated strata emigrated, were prosecuted, or were mistrusted.

One could say that in spite of the initial malfeasance, the StB has gradually become more rigorous over the following decades. I shall therefore examine the declassified Guidelines for Work with the Collaborators of Counterintelligence, issued by the federal minister of the interior, Jaromír Obzina, in 1978,[53] which were in place until the collapse of the communist regime in 1989. Although they were issued in response to the establishment of Charter 77, a major Czechoslovak opposition human rights movement, these guidelines did not fundamentally change the regulations that were issued in 1972, a few years after the Soviet invasions.[54]

The main objective of Obzina's guidelines was to ensure "orderly fulfillment of tasks of counter-intelligence employees in their work with its collaborators to protect socialist social and state order."[55] The guidelines contained 140 articles and four appendices, which included forms such as the "Proposal for Recruitment for Collaboration" and the "Record of Recruitment to Collaboration." It distinguished between "secret collaborators" and "confidants." Secret collaborators consisted of the categories of "resident," "agent," and "holder of a lent-out apartment"; the confidant category was merely auxiliary. A secret collaborator was defined as "a person who was recruited according to the guidelines, keeps conspirational contact with the employees of counter-intelligence, fulfills assigned tasks, provides or hands over observations and information or provides assistance or services, which need to be kept secret."[56] The guidelines considered secret collaborators as the main tool against subversion by foreign intelligence, foreign economic and ideological centers, and their "domestic helpers." The tasks of secret collaborators included disclosure, documentation, and prevention of subversive illegal activities.

The recruitment process was supposed to take into account the personal characteristics of the candidate, including his or her intellectual, psychological, and physical dispositions, and his or her predisposition to infiltrate "inimical centers" and fulfill intelligence duties. Desirable individuals were subject to background checks, including interviews. Files of persons suitable for recruitment were forwarded to a superior officer for approval. Files of persons unsuitable for recruitment were archived or canceled. The regulations distinguished between the following methods of recruitment: ideological reasons, material incentives, and compromising facts. Compromising facts, such as those that affected the reputation of the candidate and the revelation of minor criminal misconduct, were supposed to be used in justifiable cases. The regulations stated that the candidate for collaboration decided at his or her own election whether the collaboration would be a better option than facing the compromising consequences. This method could only apply to the rank of agents, not to residents and holders of lent-out apartments.

After a superior officer had approved a proposal for recruitment, the candidate had to be formally recruited by consenting and making the so-called binding act. The superior officer or his or her appointees supervised the work of secret police employees in the recruitment process. Written consent was not required in cases where the relationship with a secret collaborator could be compromised; in such cases oral consent was sufficient. The recruited collaborator then chose his or her cover name; if not, a cover name was assigned to him or her by an employee of counterintelligence. Most cover names were just ordinary Czech first names or surnames; others described a profession or an activity, such as "Electrician," "Lawyer," or "Mushroom-Picker," although I encountered eccentric names, such as "Frederic Lacoste" and "Duchess," or names that appeared to express contempt, such as "Mud" and "Sewage."

The secret police members supervised secret collaborators and corroborated their written, oral, and other reports (e.g., their recordings). The results of their work were subject to another level of control. At least once a year, the secret collaborators were subject to an appraisal, which may have led to material and moral rewards, such as state awards. The collaboration may have ended in cases of betrayal, committing a criminal act, being uncovered, rejecting collaboration, completing his or her tasks, being promoted to a higher political position, or becoming unable to meet expectations.

Based on the abstract review of the regulations, I can reject the assumption about the homogeneity of secret collaborators. First, it is possible that some secret collaborators informed about their fellow citizens for ideological, material, or personal reasons. They acted as moral agents and bear responsibility for their actions. Second, some were blackmailed into collaboration, because the regulations provided for such an alternative. Although those who were blackmailed were not forced to consent to collaborating, their refusal to do so may have carried severe consequences. During the totalitarian regime, failure to collaborate could have led to a range of work-related sanctions, such as loss of a job, demotion from a senior position, an impediment to the prospect of promotion and a bar to the practice of a profession, and discrimination regarding the allocation of housing and evictions. Sanctions could affect family members, such as a child's prospect of studying at a university, the loss of a spouse's job, or a denial of care for parents. All of these sanctions constitute various degrees of duress that invalidate the notion of voluntary agency in contractual relations. Third, some did not sign the binding act of collaboration. Although it is possible that they collaborated based on their oral consent, it is also possible to claim that this group did not collaborate at all or did not knowingly collaborate.

The result of the review appears inconclusive. But this is precisely its strength. I can formally refute the assumption about the homogeneity of secret collaborators. Agency, duress, and lack of awareness about collaboration were possible on paper. The question is, how was it in reality? We shall look at their database and then turn to a couple of individual cases.

The Recruitment of Secret Collaborators in Numbers

In 2003, the Ministry of the Interior declassified and published on its website a list of the socialist-era secret collaborators.[57] The database did not include the auxiliary category of confidant, the candidate for secret collaboration, and other categories that were removed from lustration law by the Constitutional Court in 1992.[58] This database thus provides us with a useful substrate for the analysis of the population of secret collaborators. The objective of my analysis is to explore whether any patterns existed in the recruitment. If patterns could be attributed to the interests of the regime that would suggest that recruitment was a top-down process, in which people were more likely to be forced into collaboration. If patterns were to be attributed to the interest of the people, they would reveal a bottom-up process with collaborators volunteering to inform. The absence of patterns would be manifested by a degree of randomness in recruiting people based on age, sex, and the era.[59]

My analysis of the database has shown that the recruitment of secret collaborators was not random. If it had been, one could expect that the pool of secret collaborators would mirror the sociodemographic structure of society, representing each section based on gender and age. However, several patterns, or biases, falsify the assumption of randomness.

First, different periods of the socialist era required different levels of repression and surveillance. The consolidation of power by the regime in the 1950s may have led to shifting the emphasis from the use of naked force to more subtle surveillance and reporting. How was the reality? Figure 3 shows the numbers of secret collaborators during the era of power consolidation in the 1950s. The steep rise in 1960 occurred alongside the amnesty by President Novotný, which released a number of political prisoners. Overt repression against the enemies of socialism was replaced by their covert surveillance. The lowest number in 1968 may be attributed to the liberalization era of the Prague Spring.[60] The historical pattern clearly shows the interest of the regime as a determining factor for recruitment of secret collaborators. The recruitment was distinctively a top-down process.

Indeed, unlike membership in the Association for the Friendship with the Soviet Union or other socialist organizations, it was not possible just to become a secret informant as a way to pursue career ambitions or personal motives. There was no call for applications, no recruitment counters outside of supermarkets, and no advertisements "come and join, perks attached." Obviously, some people may have had bigger ears or a greater commitment to the suppression of class enemies among their neighbors or colleagues. But they may have never been able to make it as a secret collaborator. The StB was not interested in having the best and the most loyal people but the most useful ones, in the right place and time.

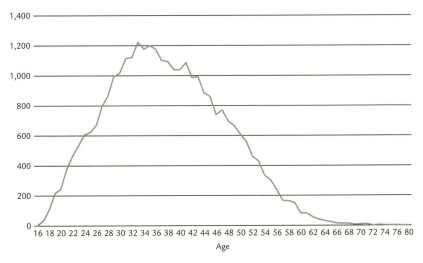

Figure 4. Numbers of secret collaborators by age at registration. The numbers here are based on my analysis of the official database of collaborators with the State Security, Ministry of the Interior (2003).

Second, if the recruitment were conducted randomly, all age categories would be equally present. However, Figure 4 shows that young and older citizens were less likely to be recruited than middle-aged groups. The most targeted group by the StB was people in their thirties. People at this stage were typically having families and sought to pursue their career ambitions. Both would make them particularly vulnerable to blackmail and susceptible to material incentives. In this cohort, the secret police did not need to risk a rejection as with younger and older people who did not have that much to lose. Conversely, people in their thirties would also likely grow up with fantasies of joining secret services. Hence, there is a clear pattern, and the pattern is not bottom up.

Third, there is an apparent gender imbalance between secret collaborators (Figure 5). About 85.8 percent of them were men, while only about 10.2 percent were women; it was impossible to determine gender in about 4 percent of cases. The proportion of new female secret collaborators did not vary much over the captured period, reaching a peak of 19 percent in 1964. The proportion of women fell to a minimum of 7 percent in 1989, but this did not really signify a meaningful decline in comparison with an overall average figure of 10 percent that was recorded in 1988 at the end of socialism.

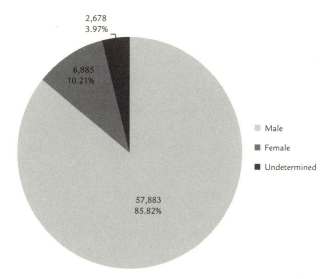

Figure 5. Numbers of secret collaborators by gender. The numbers here are based on my analysis of the official database of collaborators with the State Security, Ministry of the Interior (2003).

The gender imbalance not only falsifies the randomness but also pours cold water on the "dead souls" myth.[61] In the context of dealing with the legacy of the communist regime, secret collaborators were, according to the myth, recruited without knowing that they were collaborating because StB members needed to meet the plan and impress their bosses. The instrumental purpose of the myth was to undermine the reliability of secret archives. However, the abstract review has suggested that it would have been difficult to include "dead souls" at the level of secret collaboration, which required the participation of StB officers at various ranks. The presented data support this explanation. If dead souls were commonplace, the question would arise as to why only 14.2 percent of them were women. To be sure, gender discrimination existed in the past and persists in the present. But owing to socialist ideology, gender discrimination was not as serious as the figures for female collaboration suggest. In 1981–86 some 28 percent of de facto appointed members of the Czech National Council were women, while in 2013 only 20 percent of the elected members of the Chamber of Deputies were women.[62] The communist regime was, at least on the surface, slightly more committed to gender equality than Czech society after its collapse. If

StB members listed fictional collaborators, why did they not use female names to tally with the socialist ideology that preached gender equality?

Although these data and the general extrapolation are not strong enough to rule out the use of dead souls, it was unlikely to have been a prevalent pattern. The conclusion that recruitment appears to have been a top-down process, encompassing incentives and the blackmail of people who were likely to produce the least possible resistance, seems to be a more plausible explanation than a bottom-up process. When the StB proposed, it wanted to hear "yes."

The Recruitment of Secret Collaborators from Their Own Perspective

How did the process of recruitment for secret collaboration appear in the eyes of those who faced questions about their collaboration? The writer Zdena Salivarová-Škvorecká, the wife of the writer Josef Škvorecký, compiled an edited volume[63] of those who, like herself, appeared on the so-called Cibulka's lists of secret collaborators.[64] The book represents a unique insight into the practices of the communist secret police and into the lives of those who were rightly or wrongly accused of secret collaboration. Stories of confessions, excuses, and denials, some of them tragic, others revolting, are the actual testaments of human characters in the communist era and after it.

The recruitment for secret collaboration is often described in detail, which suggests that the recruited were aware of the seriousness of the situation. The following is the story of Mr. M., who recalls,

> Once I went to visit a known Prague actor. . . . After leaving I was boarded into a car and taken to Bartolomějská street [police station]. . . . Perhaps they often followed me and mapped the circle of friends and an optimal time for the attack. In Bartolomějská my "guardian" Mr. Svoboda introduced me to his superior who explained to me during a brief informal interview what I was asked for: a regular and perhaps even written provision of information, this time with a "broader" focus. I received a form printed on a paper with a watermark of then state symbols. . . . Unfortunately, I did not even read it, so I don't even know whether it was for remuneration and whether it included the so-called cover name—in my case "Companion," the one which was published. . . . At that time I told them "I will not be

your snitch" but if you do want something, then subject to the consent of my superior, it is my duty to inform you as [I have been doing]
until now.[65]

This statement is actually not a confession of collaboration with the secret police but its denial. Mr. M insisted that he did not do anything wrong
as he informed the StB with the consent of his superior. He told the same
story to his wife who was initially suspicious but eventually, in his words, accepted his explanation. At the time of writing this book, his name was retriev-
able from the online public archive of secret collaborators administered by
the Institute for the Study of Totalitarian Regimes.[66] He had two records of
secret collaboration, which started in 1977 and 1980, respectively, under the
cover name "Companion."

In contrast, Dr. Z. confesses his collaboration but claims that his consent
was forced under duress:

It was very simple. In 1954, there was already no beating in jails; it was
done more cunningly. Three, thoughtfully gradated, fictitious pieces
of news about the serious illness of my two-year-old son. "As a daddy
and a doctor you don't really want to help him? As soon as you sign,
you go immediately home to him." I would have signed much more
than this collaboration back then. After they did not ask me to change
and go home but took me to solitary confinement, the dupery was
clear to me.[67]

Dr. Z. then mentions several hard jails that he went through. The search
of the official database indeed confirms that Dr. Z. was listed as a secret police collaborator several times with the cover names "Doctor," "Marta,"
"Mountains of Hostýn," and "Bison."[68] This may either suggest that once the
secret police got someone, it was difficult to evade their interest, or that some
people were willing to prolong their service for the regime. An uncomfortable discovery from the archives was that a person with the same name and
surname, born in the same year as his son, was registered as a secret informant in the same town.

Both persons admitted their collaboration. Mr. M. construed his collaboration as part of his work duties, while Dr. Z. mentions duress based on a
fabricated story, although his "solitary confinement" does not make much
sense after consenting with collaboration. Both collaborated repeatedly, which

attested that they were reliable assets. Indeed, it was not easy to find persons in Salivarová-Škvorecká's book who were not listed in the official database of collaborators with the secret police. On the other hand, it would be an over-generalization to say that all listed persons collaborated voluntarily.

Petty Compromises, Minor Injustices, and the Little Czech

All communist regimes were eager to boast the success of achieving harmonious societies. The façade of a regime that granted the right to work was decorated with mass Labor Day processions, military parades, and "pioneers" greeting occasional foreign delegations. The totalitarian regime claimed control over the whole society and the whole person. The expansion of the public sphere into the private sphere meant the nationalization of the economy, the control over churches, and the liquidation of all organized enclaves of independent thinking, including education, art, literature, entertainment, the press, and civil society. The communist regime and its five-year economic plans aspired to control individuals, their thought, and their consumption.

Such ideas were dressed up in official Marxist-Leninist propaganda. A legitimate response for some Western consumers of "the evil empire" discourse could well be that most Eastern Europeans were brainwashed fanatics who would one day land in the West, just shortly after the SS-20 missiles. But less than ten years after the communist regime, the Czechs, Poles, and Hungarians joined the North Atlantic Treaty Organization (NATO) in 1999, and five years after that they voted to join the European Union. How can this dramatic "change" in attitude be explained?

The reality of totalitarian control provides a different picture than that which was presented by communist and anticommunist ideologues. Demands for political loyalty were in reality nothing more than demands for expressions of political loyalty while the New Man, *nový člověk*, actually used a "gray economy" to satisfy his material needs. Quasi-market relations operated within the centrally planned economy to overcome the shortage of everything, ranging from toothpastes to apartments, from bananas to bicycles.

In order to pursue a social inquiry into life under the communist regime, I shall apply the concept of "the Little Czech."[69] I do not aspire to engage with an elitist social critique or an exercise in moral philosophy that is typical for some protagonists of the concept. I do not intend to pass judgment about the past. I adopt a social science approach to capture life under the communist regime; I seek to explain its duration, its everyday injustices, and its collapse.

The notion of the Little Czech sounds like a cliché that has been discredited by its frequent use in the common Czech parlance. When lamenting about their fellow citizens, Czechs use the metaphor of the Little Czech to comment on attempts to circumvent the law, avoid responsibility, and engage in other less salubrious activities. The concept does not apply only to Czechoslovakia. It is not a country-specific notion. In the same way, one can speak of a Little Britain, as long as it carries an explanatory value.[70]

The social anthropologist Ladislav Holý theorized the concept so that it serves my inquiry into the nature of Czechoslovak communism appropriately: "The little Czech is not motivated by great ideals. His lifeworld is delineated by his family, work and close friends, and he approaches anything that lies outside with caution and mistrust. His attitude is down-to-earth and he is certainly not a hero."[71] In order to survive, and maintain a decent life, the Little Czech had to make compromises, swallow some injustices, and inevitably create wrongs for others. Apart from the hundreds of thousands of Czechoslovaks who ended up in jail, emigrated, or lost their livelihood, it would not be farfetched to say that there were millions of Little Czechs in Czechoslovakia. They witnessed executions, imprisonment, confiscation of properties, and purges, and they became afraid. They "muddled through" their lives without compromising access to free education for their children, the benefit of free health care, and the enjoyment of a state pension. They scrambled to get access to scarce goods and relished their weekend retreats in cottages and houses in small villages. One of them was famously described by Václav Havel as a greengrocer who placed the slogan "Workers of the world, unite!" right among onions and carrots. Why did he do it, asked Havel in his essay "The Power of the Powerless"? He offered an answer:

> I think it can safely be assumed that the overwhelming majority of shopkeepers never think about the slogans they put in their windows, nor do they use them to express their real opinions. That poster was delivered to our greengrocer from the enterprise headquarters along with the onions and carrots. He put them all into the window simply because it has been done that way for years, because everyone does it, and because that is the way it has to be. If he were to refuse, there could be trouble. He could be reproached for not having the proper

decoration in his window; someone might even accuse him of disloy-
alty. He does it because these things must be done if one is to get along
in life. It is one of the thousands of details that guarantee him a relatively tranquil life "in harmony with society," as they say.[72]

Although the parable of the greengrocer has become almost a cliché
in Eastern European studies, it vividly captures the dualism of public and
private life under communism. The dualism has become a coping strategy to
deal with efforts to instill communist ideology into people's minds. Indeed,
the education system taught children to have two faces: a false, official face
for the public, and a genuine, private face for family and friends. Families
enforced this notion, warning children not to dare to say "something" at
school.

The formal curriculum in history, civic education, defense education, defense drills, literature, and the Russian language was nominally supposed to
cover the major tools of Marxist indoctrination. However, a more significant
role was played by the informal curriculum,[73] which was essentially an exercise in learning the boundaries of the acceptable. The boundaries separated
people's behavior in private and in public. Approaching the boundaries was
discouraged by instilling fear of, and demanding respect for, the regime. Any
trespass of the boundaries, especially by expressing genuine criticism, was
punished. The informal curriculum was in effect training people to stay in
line, to not provoke, and to avoid individualism; it may have even tolerated
cheating and dishonesty as long as the transgressions were not expressly
political.[74]

Whoever studied in any university before 1989 had to pass exams in
Marxism-Leninism: The History of the International Workers' Movement,
Scientific Atheism, Marxist-Leninist Philosophy, and Scientific Communism. These subjects were part of the state graduation exam, which required
a careful recitation in order to pass. Hardly anyone believed in them. Similar questions were asked during job interviews. Getting good marks, achieving a degree, getting a good job, and not losing a good job were inevitably
forms of engagement with the regime, if not collaboration. But from the inside, each citizen saw it as a part of the ritual, the modus vivendi with the
regime. The Little Czechs were fully aware of the boundaries. Most of them
were sane, rather than ideological,[75] but supporters of communism, if needed
be. Graduating from school meant that the graduates were sufficiently social-
ized to enter their workplace. "Life in a lie," as suggested by Havel, was in

opposition to the romanticized "life in truth." Similarly, Milan Šimečka observed that

> the omnipresent lie of the state has a devastating effect on morality in general. It establishes the norm of a lie being rewarded rather than punished. The citizen accustomed to this point of view has a tolerant attitude to the lie in the non-private sphere. After all, he has been taught to lie at school, to hide his convictions; he has learnt to lie in his workplace, becoming convinced that it pays. In consequence he lies when filling in forms, in his dealing with authorities, in the court-room, to his superior—in fact, he lies wherever he can. Morally, lying to the state does not worry him; it is a lie in self-defence, for he is aware that the state cheats him too.[76]

Thus, dual behavior, morality, and norms of trust appeared. One set was intended for the public sphere, while the other for the private sphere.[77] Stealing in the private sphere was censured but it was encouraged in the public domain. "Who does not steal from the state is stealing from his family" was a saying during the communist era.

Unless a boundary was crossed, both sides of the regime coexisted relatively peacefully. Engagement with the public sphere became ritualized, as ordinary people on both sides of the line pretended anything that was required. As one saying went, people went to the work, not to work.[78] While crossing the boundary from the private to the public ran a risk of being punished by the authorities, crossing the boundary from the public to the private sphere was disapproved. Šimečka described this latter attitude as follows: "He is fully committed to the socialist order and the Communist Party, he loves the Soviet Union, he has solved the problem of religion, he participates in meetings and demonstrations, he has no doubt of any kind. . . . This same citizen at home views with horror and indescribable sadness his child lying to him for the first time and turns away with disgust from a friend who has lied to him or concealed a secret from him."[79]

There was almost no trust in public authorities. But, unlike what research on postcommunist society occasionally assumes, there was horizontal trust among friends and acquaintances. Social capital actually thrived under communism, as everybody needed a network, trust, and norms of reciprocity to acquire scarce goods. "Friendship," according to Holý, was "built on utmost trust, for if this trust was betrayed the consequences could be job loss or even imprisonment. Friendship literally meant putting one's security or even one's freedom into another's hands."[80] Indeed, social encounters with friends were frequently peppered by "golden prison-bar jokes" or singing "anti-state" and "anti-Soviet" songs. In one of the first Kundera novels, *The Joke*, "the long life to Trotsky" meant that the main hero is expelled from the university and ends up working in the mines.[81] Political jokes did not spare even the humorists from jail,[82] and the Czechs knew it.

The distinction between the public and private faces explains the fallacy of the division of society between "we" and "they." Linguistically, "they" was understood as the communists and their supporters, and "we" as the rest of society. The problem was that any "we" often appeared as "they" because of the public face the person wore. All people strove to be portrayed as "we" in private but the very nature of the communist regime with its hierarchical structure put inherent limits on the convivial self-conception. Consider an anonymous form teacher in a primary school who was doing her duties. One of them was to open a file with cadre materials, which accompanied everybody through his or her studies until employment and retirement. Cadre materials were supposed to record a person's political reliability and loyalty to communism, many of which were derived from records of family origin.[83] Missing a Labor Day procession may have been exonerated and go unrecorded in some eras, but the emigration of a family member to the West would seldom be overlooked in cadre annals. The consequence for the pupil could be a lost opportunity to study and pursue a profession of choice. Regardless of their self-conception, teachers were ultimately seen as "them."

In view of the elusive equilibrium between "we" and "they," in which everybody's position could be either on one side or on both sides of the divide, one wonders how communism collapsed. One factor was the timing. The two decades after 1968 produced a new generation that did not experience a regime change and had not tasted defeat. Indeed, students were the first to overcome their fear of the communist regime, along with actors and intellectuals who sided with a handful of dissidents. A sociologist recalls his experience in 1989: "When I learnt that in the situation when communists who barely managed to control illegal demonstrations and had to swallow the exodus of East Germans permitted a legal demonstration, I knew that [the change] starts also here. We attended the demonstration as a whole family and stayed until the end. From my viewpoint, the [violently suppressed] demonstration meant a breakthrough, I stopped being afraid."[84]

Overcoming the fear among students, intellectuals, and actors lifted the break but did not spur the critical mass of society into action. The equilibrium of stagnation that was convenient to the rulers and the ruled alike needed a motivation and a trigger. I will start with the motivation. During the 1980s, windows to the Western lifestyle gradually opened. The Czechoslovaks living along the 1,330-kilometer-long border with Poland could turn their television antennas toward Poland to pick up Hollywood productions, thrillers, horrors, and love stories alike on "their" televisions as the bankrupt Polish communists tried to appease their protesting citizens in the 1980s. Those bordering West Germany and Austria enjoyed watching the same movies in German, albeit fragmented by enticing commercials that subverted the achievements of socialism. The socialist milk sold in plastic bags could not match the imagined feeling of the freshness of milk from the Alps, and tempting German chocolate seldom had the opportunity to melt in Czech mouths. The relative deprivation of the Czechs was nerve-wrenching. The opening of several luxury Tuzex shops in major cities, which did not accept the Czechoslovak currency, brought the relative deprivation ever closer to home. The proliferation of VCR players in the mid-1980s brought Rocky, Rambo, and German porn, mostly smuggled from Yugoslavia, to well-connected households all around the country. Given the temptations of the Western lifestyle, it is hard to believe that the Little Czechs rose in 1989 merely for justice. They may well have been motivated by the need for a just society without fear, harassment, and discrimination, but many also longed for full supermarkets and a fair income with which to buy the products of Western consumption.

Justice was nevertheless the apparent trigger for the events of November 1989. It was "just anger" that stirred the critical mass of Czechs after they heard the news broadcast on Radio Free Europe (RFE) that during the paralegal demonstration of November 17 the police had killed a student.[85] A popular RFE commentator, Lída Rakušanová, noted that, if true, the communists could hardly have chosen a more symbolic day for killing a student. On that day in 1939 the Nazis had suppressed a student protest, killing a student named Jan Opletal. The idea that the communists would kill students in the same way as the Nazis was utterly unacceptable for many. It did not matter that the news, reported by the Czech dissident Petr Uhl, was later refuted: The killing had been staged by the secret police. The anger of the Little Czechs was unstoppable. Since the regime had existed unopposed for more than two decades, the massive demonstrations all over the country took the Communist Party by surprise. The communist regime was defeated by the popular protest of unexpectedly emancipated Czechs. What followed was six incredible weeks full of idealism and hope as the government of the people returned to the people. Those six weeks were followed by six months that brought calls for justice, free elections, and first disillusions with the democratic system.

For Havel, Šimečka, and other intellectuals, the greengrocer got his share of blame for communism. The Czechoslovak Greats were dreaming of a Polish electrician who would—as Lech Wałęsa did—join forces with the intellectuals and make a change. But it may have been hard for the Little Czechs to follow phenomenology philosophers, playwrights of absurd dramas, and psychedelic rockers. Their atheistic inclinations may have prevented them from believing Catholic dissidents and their memory may have made them suspicious of dissidents who clamored for communism in the 1950s. Communism did not collapse thanks to the exemplary attitude of the elites but thanks to the sanity and emancipation of the Little Czechs.

The Little Czech perspective suggested that the maintenance and collapse of the communist regime was an instance of aggregate behavior. Communism seems to have been an instance of a frequency-dependent equilibrium, in which everybody's action or inaction operates simultaneously as independent and dependent variables.[86] The action of an individual is a function of the actions of other individuals. As most people established a modus vivendi with the regime and feared to change it, it was difficult and costly for any one individual to act otherwise. Such equilibriums, as in cases of the culture of corruption, tend to be stable. People observed the public faces of others, who in turn saw other public faces. A change to an entirely different situation requires an equilibrium shift, a strong signal to society. In Czechoslovakia, it arrived with the hoax report about the killing of a student during a demonstration of November 17, 1989. People went to the streets en masse and the communist regime collapsed.

Discussion

From a historical perspective, the establishment of the communist regime along with its duration was largely a homegrown product. Obviously, the Soviets deserve their fair share of blame, but their influence would have been impossible without the input of willing local supporters in the KSČ, StB, and beyond it. In spite of its election victory in 1946, the majority of citizens did not vote for the Communist Party; and those who voted for it may not have voted for the communist regime. The KSČ thus bears not only political responsibility for the communist regime but also the failure to shield society from the Soviets. In contrast, the communist leadership in Hungary and Poland in the 1970s and the 1980s were not as ideological about communism; they never nationalized private property on the same scale as the Czechs in the 1950s and were able to pursue at least some market reforms. The variations among Eastern European countries cast a shadow over the Czechoslovak communist leadership.

However, a handful of communists could not do that alone. This chapter has shown that questions about individual responsibility can be asked in all areas of repression. Consider the case of Mr. Kundera, the case of Mr. Z., and the case of a hypothetical teacher who wrote a negative cadre report on a student. The first category of cases led to imprisonment, the second was likely to result in imprisonment or someone losing a job, and the third in the deprivation of education and labor mobility for life. Did not they know? In view of the scale and the publicity about repression, it is hard to plead ignorance. Moreover, the "dualism of faces" during the regime showed that people were aware of injustices and that they knew where the boundaries of the communist regime were. Answering questions about Marxist-Leninist ideology during a job interview was different from reporting about others.

The complexities of such conclusions were exposed in the third section, which showed that secret collaboration was predominantly a top-down process. StB recruited collaborators based on political instructions by KSČ, the changing dynamic of repression, and its operational needs. A possibility of using duress further supports the top-down hypothesis. On the other hand, StB mainly targeted people in their thirties. For people of this age, the opportunity costs of not collaborating and the costs of refusing to collaborate were the highest. The resulting collaboration was a result of individual choices in the particular opportunity structure.[87] As a Czech saying goes, an opportunity makes a thief. Yet it is not an invisible hand of opportunity that snatches and enjoys benefits. It is the thief's hand. Normally, thieves belong in jail. Are collaborators a different sort? There are no general answers to questions of individual responsibility. Each answer depends on each individual case. This has implications for the assessment of justice measures and the conclusions to this book.

This chapter did not aspire to deliver a comprehensive study of history but to provide contextual information for analyzing the social process of dealing with the past. Communism was characterized by the injustices it committed and the position of individuals in it. My approach has been reductionist, leaving aside other aspects of communism, most notably the economic system, egalitarianism, culture, and propaganda. However, my approach is broader than those that describe communism merely in terms of crime and its consequences. On the other hand, my approach included injustices that were committed on a daily basis, including those that were not addressed in the program of justice after transition.

Chapter 2

Justice After Transition: Retributive, Revelatory, Reparatory, and Reconciliatory Measures

> To understand is not to excuse, and with the exception of a few
> intellectuals, Czechoslovak people cannot freely escape their own
> portion of accountability.
> —Josef Korbel, *Twentieth Century Czechoslovakia*

This second contextual chapter provides an overview of the measures of justice, whose effects will be studied in the following chapters. What justice measures were pursued in dealing with the communist past in the Czech Lands? What kinds of measures were prevalent? What controversies surrounded these measures? How did society perceive them? Justice after regime change is not merely a legal but ultimately a social process that sends an ideological message about the past.[1] It encompasses measures, interventions, and actions, which are formal and informal, tangible and intangible, legal and social. This chapter therefore examines the process of dealing with the past, as well as its political context and its reception by the people.[2] It focuses on ten measures of justice and their purpose, scope, and limitations. Each of the justice measures can be categorized into four clusters of justice. As stipulated in the Introduction, I distinguish retributive, reparatory, revelatory, and reconciliatory measures of justice. After the brief historical inquiry into the nature of historical justice, I organize the following sections in terms of these four clusters.

History of Justice in the Czech Lands

The Czechs are experts in regime change. The years 1918, 1938, 1945, 1948, 1968, and 1989 are years in which fundamental changes took place in the country's political structure. Each change, whether democratic or undemocratic, was accompanied by the rejection of the previous regime, the tearing down of its symbols, the renaming of its streets, and the damning of old heroes.[3] Most of the political changes redefined social boundaries and national identities, and some of them triggered population changes. In 1918, Czechoslovakian nationalism withdrew from the Austro-Hungarian multicultural melting pot. In 1938, Germans expelled Czechs from Sudetenland, the Nazis killed Czechoslovak Jews during World War II, and in 1945 the Czechs expelled Germans from Sudetenland.[4] As the country turned more homogeneous,[5] expulsion turned into exclusion. Communists purged democrats in 1948, hard-line communists purged reform communists in 1968, and the 1989 Velvet Revolution purged the hard-line communists.[6]

The regime change turned winners into losers and losers into winners. Gustáv Husák, an ideological communist and a protagonist of anti-Nazi resistance in Slovakia during World War II, was a political prisoner of the communist regime in the 1950s, but he succeeded Alexander Dubček as a party secretary following the Soviet invasion in 1968.[7] Husák eventually assumed the presidency in 1975 and threw Václav Havel into jail.[8] Havel then succeeded Husák as president in 1989, while Husák was again expelled from the Communist Party and, in 1991, died in disgrace, at least in the eyes of Czechs.

The regime changed but people remained the same. Every generation of Czechs experienced regime change at least once in a lifetime. The same people may have lived on the same street, which bore different names in different systems. The centuries-old name of the Hay Market in the city of Opava changed to Franz Josef Square, to the Square of the Republic, to Goering Square, Stalin Square, the Defenders of Peace Square and has now reverted back to the Square of the Republic.[9] New eras brought new heroes who were "immortalized" in new monuments, merely to be replaced by others a few decades later. The frequent demands meant that different monuments were made by the same people. The same architect who built a gigantic Stalin monument in Prague in the 1950s previously built a monument of Tomáš Masaryk, the founder of democratic Czechoslovakia. The same sculptor who participated in the decoration of a Stalinist astronomical clock in Olomouc in the 1950s made a sculpture for former political prisoners in Prague after 1989.[10]

History taught Czechs what to do in dealing with the past. Glorifying political imprisonment dates back to the nineteenth century when Austrians jailed a Czech journalist, Karel Havlíček Borovský. Tearing down monuments followed the restoration of Czechoslovakian independence in 1918 as the Czechs destroyed the Mariensäule Column in the Old Town Square in Prague as a symbol of national humiliation. Everybody knows that medals have to be awarded to heroes and that victims need to be invited to schools to share the experience of the past with pupils. In addition, regime change leads to a change in vocabulary; not only streets are renamed. The phraseology of laws changed and people stop using "obsolete" titles. For the Czechs the fall of the communist regime meant the demise of appellations such as "comrade teacher," "comrade captain," and "comrade director."

Justice after transition emerged from historical flux as a broad category that encompassed not only criminal justice but also societal justice, which redistributed social positions and the social status of large groups of people.[11] Regime change produced new opportunities for the previously underprivileged, and justice was a vehicle in their pursuit. Painting a façade, however, does not entail a change to the floors inside the house. Turning heroes into villains and vice versa may only concern a few individuals of the elite strata in the government and the opposition. For the grassroots, there may not be any real change in their social position before and after the regime change. For those in the middle, the so-called gray zone, switching sides at the right time is a self-defense mechanism to preserve their petty privileges. Advocating and vigorously pursuing justice may have served as a means for evading their own responsibilities for the past.

Justice After Transition

While the dynamic of regime change in Huntington's terms could be considered to be transformation in Hungary and "transplacement" in Poland, Czechoslovakia's regime change was an example of replacement.[12] Unlike the communists in other Central European countries, the Communist Party in Czechoslovakia lost control of decision making at the central government level in fewer than two weeks. The constitutionally protected "leading role of the KSČ in the state and society" was abrogated on November 29, 1989,[13] and a transitional government was appointed on December 10, 1989.[14] The loss was sealed in the first elections in June 1990 when the KSČ received 13.2 percent of the votes in the Czech National Council.[15] The defeat of the KSČ signified the

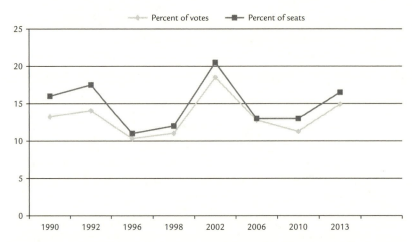

Figure 6. Election results for the Communist Party in the Czech Lands. The figure displays the results of the election of the Communist Party to the Chamber of Deputies in 1993–2013, and to its predecessor, the Czech National Council, in 1990 and 1992. The Communist Party ran as KSČ in 1990, in a coalition with the Left Blok in 1992, and has run as the KSČM since 1996. Český statistický úřad, "Výsledky voleb a referend" (2015).

rejection of communism and the desire of the people for a fair political system. Although Czechoslovakia was the last Central European country to overthrow the communist regime, regime change released the hands of the new elite to become a leader in dealing with the past.

Moreover, KSČ's successor, the KSČM, has not returned to power since 1989. It never became part of any coalition government. In 1997, the social democrats (ČSSD) approved the so-called Bohumín Memorandum that prevented them from cooperating with the KSČM at a central level.[16] The reason was that the party had been widely seen as unreformed and unrepentant about its past. On the other hand, the KSČM still enjoys solid political support. As Figure 6 indicates, its electoral support varied between 10.33 percent in the 1996 election and 18.51 percent in 2002.[17]

The color of government coalitions has not significantly affected the process of dealing with the past. The governments of 1992–98 and 2006–13 were ideologically oriented toward the center-right, while in 1998–2006 and after 2013, toward the center-left. In spite of political changes, the process has continued. The process was also not affected by international integration. In

1999, the Czech Republic joined the North Atlantic Treaty Organization, and in 2004, it became a member of the European Union.

In the history of postcommunist justice since December 1989 three stages have emerged, which *coincided* with three different presidential eras: Václav Havel (1989–92, 1993–2003), Václav Klaus (2003–13), and Miloš Zeman (2013–). The direct effects wrought by Havel and Klaus to deal with the past were not significant; the presidents have less power than the prime ministers. Havel was rather inconsistent in dealing with the past, supporting as well as opposing the process.[18] Klaus never considered justice after transition to be a priority. He usually signed measures of justice prepared by the government, but for him the real heroes were the Little Czechs who resisted the communist regime by their inefficiency.[19] The process of dealing with the past during the years listed above could be characterized by the following features: Havel's era laid the groundwork and consolidated the process for dealing with the past; this was expanded during Klaus's era; and during Zeman's era it was maintained with only minor regress.

The process of dealing with the past started with reparatory measures; at that time Havel was already the president. Shortly before the first democratic elections, the Federal Assembly passed a law that rehabilitated those who had suffered discrimination.[20] The newly elected assembly then approved the lustration law, a retributive measure that disqualified some prominent members of the regime and their collaborators from public office. In addition, the restitution law returned nationalized property to its original owners or their heirs. After a split of the Federation in 1992, Parliament approved an Act on the Illegitimacy of the Communist Regime in 1993 and the government established the Office for Documenting and Investigating Communist Crimes (ÚDV) in 1995. Revelatory measures were the last to be approved, although as early as 1991 wild lists of secret police collaborators had been published.[21] In 1997, a law allowed access to secret police files; eventually in 2003 the government was officially able to publish the names of all secret police informers.

The second stage of postcommunist justice coincided with Klaus's presidency. The period's parliamentary debates about the communist past were less emotional and more succinct. The legislative process gradually became more institutionalized and the laws were more professionally drafted than in the first stage. The legislature extended existing measures, expanded the number of claimants, and increased the institutionalization of the process.

A new office, the Institute for the Study of Totalitarian Regimes (ÚSTR), was established in 2007 and opened in 2008.[22]

The third stage was marked by the election of Miloš Zeman as president in 2013. The process of dealing with the past continued, although this stage has been characterized by the questioning of its anticommunist direction, personal quarrels between the center-right and center-left historians and dissidents, and personnel infighting in ÚSTR.[23] Zeman was the most controversial among the three presidents. He violated lustration law by appointing Andrej Babiš, the leader of the newly formed political party ANO (Yes), who was allegedly a collaborator with secret police, to the government in 2013. In addition, in 2014 Zeman signed measures to narrow the ambit of lustration law while refusing to ceremonially appoint professors due to their tainted pasts.[24]

In other aspects, the political transition yielded mixed results. Throughout the first two stages the freedom of the press had been gradually improving, and by 2015 the Czech Republic's press ranked thirteenth in the world on a freedom of the press index, scoring just below Germany and surpassing the United Kingdom and the United States.[25] On the other hand, its level of corruption, according to Transparency International, has also been increasing. In 2014 the Czech Republic was ranked as the fifty-third most corrupt country on a list of 174 countries, just behind Malaysia and Samoa.[26]

Retributive Measures

Retributive measures are the punitive measures that were imposed individually or collectively against the protagonists of the communist regime and its perpetrators and collaborators. The measures included the expropriation of the property of the KSČ and its Youth Union (SSM) in 1990, criminal trials, and lustration law in 1991. Expropriation and lustration were broad measures, while criminal trials concerned a few individuals. To facilitate the process, two government offices were established in 1995 and 2008, respectively: the ÚDV, which dealt with criminal investigations; and the ÚSTR, which was in charge of secret police files.

Expropriation of the KSČ and SSM

A few months after the first election in 1990, the Federal Assembly passed a law on the expropriation of the assets of the KSČ and SSM.[27] Speaking to the Federal Assembly on behalf of the government, Pavel Rychetský, the vice

Table 1. Assessment of Justice Measures in 2010 and 2015 (Percentage of positive and negative answers)

	2010		2015	
	Positive	Negative	Positive	Negative
Compensation	40.9	20.6	35.4	19.6
Acknowledgment	48.3	18.8	45.2	15.0
Restitution	50.9	14.1	52.9	12.4
Punishment	22.0	42.8	20.8	41.3
Condemnation	32.6	32.0	36.0	26.7
Expropriation of KSČ, SSM	28.2	36.8	27.6	35.3
Lustration	23.1	43.5	23.7	37.3
Exposure of collaborators	35.5	26.0	32.6	26.3
Access to secret archives	37.8	22.6	34.2	24.9
New textbooks	40.8	17.5	42.5	15.6
Apology	—	—	18.9	39.1

Sources: Roman David, "Twenty Years of Dealing with the Past," machine-readable data file, 2010 (on file with the author); Roman David, "Twenty-Five Years of Dealing with the Past," machine-readable data file, 2015 (on file with the author). The survey question asked: was the implementation of the following measures successful or unsuccessful?

prime minister, argued that both organizations unjustly possessed the property of the people and, for this reason, the property should be returned to the people.[28] Both organizations were in possession of enterprises, daily newspapers and magazines, publishing houses, office buildings, hospitals, entertainment venues, recreation facilities, a travel agency, and so forth. They had been able to amass these properties due to "the leading role of the Party in the state and society," which had been constitutionally protected until 1989. Rychetský validated the expropriation on the grounds of both backward-looking and forward-looking considerations of fairness. First, it was unjustifiable that an organization should be in possession of vast properties that had been procured from taxpayers' money. Second, the properties would give the Party an unfair advantage in elections. Most political parties were newly established and did not own anything other than a few uncontested ideas. The backward-looking considerations seemed to be more pressing as the name of the law suggested. In a rebuke to the communist ideologists who built and killed in the name of the people, the law was named on the return of the property of the KSČ and SSM to *the people* of Czechoslovakia.

It is one thing to expropriate property from organizations, and another to give it to the people. Many saw the property as defrauded; however, according

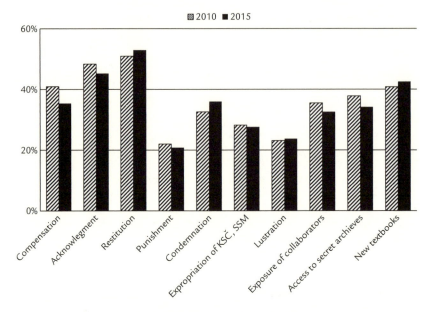

Figure 7. An assessment of justice measures in 2010 and 2015 (percentages of positive answers indicating success). David, "Twenty Years of Dealing with the Past" and "Twenty-Five Years of Dealing with the Past."

to Petr Jarolímek, the financial losses resulting from the property transfers were not significant and the property was, in fact, returned to "the people."[29] What happened to the property afterward, when it was in the hands of "non-communists," is another question.[30] This may be one of the reasons why the public viewed the process as unsuccessful. Table 1 and Figure 7 show that only around 28 percent of respondents saw the expropriation as successful, while 36.8 and 35.3 percent, respectively, saw it as unsuccessful in my surveys conducted in 2010 and 2015.

Criminal Trials

The prosecution of the perpetrators of political crimes, for which they enjoyed impunity under the communist regime, has been widely considered to be a major failure in the efforts to deal with the past (Figure 7). As Table 1 details, only 22 percent of respondents considered the punishment of communist crimes to have been successful in 2010, and this number marginally dropped to 20.8 percent in 2015.

The failure to launch prosecutions was affected by a combination of legal and institutional obstacles, personnel continuity with the past, and the nature of postcommunist mentality.[31] Legal continuity was disrupted by the Act on the Illegitimacy of the Communist Regime,[32] which excluded crimes that had not been prosecuted for political reasons from the statute of limitations. This enabled socialist-era crimes to be prosecuted without violating the prohibition against retroactive criminalization. Continuity at institutional and personnel levels was disrupted by the establishment of ÚDV, the prosecuting authority described earlier.

These measures resulted in a dismal number of criminal trials. In the period to June 30, 2000, a mere eight perpetrators were found guilty, and five of them received suspended sentences. By January 31, 2014, the ÚDV had completed investigations into 115 cases involving 213 persons; 113 of these cases, involving 138 persons, were forwarded to the state attorney. The state attorney initiated prosecution in 84 cases involving 112 persons and returned 36 cases for further investigation. The courts sentenced at least thirty persons, mostly members of the security apparatus: Nine received prison sentences (the longest was six years) and the remainder received suspended sentences (the shortest being one year suspended for eighteen months).[33] The highest-ranking official who received a jail term was a member of ÚV KSČ, Miroslav Štěpán, although his punishment predated the establishment of the ÚDV.

The dismal number of prosecutions does not appear that fruitless in comparison with the general statistics of prosecution and sentencing in the Czech Republic. In 2014, courts dealt with 126,368 criminal acts: 72,825 persons were found guilty; 9,568 of them received jail sentences, and among them 5,664 sentences were for up to one year. There were 50,203 suspended sentences.[34] A glance at these statistics suggests that the rate of convictions for general crimes does not differ much from the conviction rate for politically motivated crimes. However, it is difficult to disentangle the political bias, or affinity to the communist regime, among prosecutors and judges,[35] from the lack of professionalism and excessive training in legal positivism.[36]

In comparison with Germany, the Czech Republic appears to have failed for not prosecuting border killing. Although about twice the number of people were killed on Czechoslovakia's borders with the West than on the border with East Germany,[37] nobody was ever prosecuted for the crime in Czechoslovakia.[38] Obviously, the nature of communist crimes included other instances of gross violations of human rights and crimes against humanity. However, with the exception of an attempt to prosecute a few leaders for treason in connection with the 1968 invasion of Czechoslovakia, the border crimes were never prosecuted. This failure to prosecute does not always lie with the courts; the problem also lies with investigators. Thus, the question is whether the team of investigators in the ÚDV was strong enough to have the capacity to mount prosecutions. If not, it was a matter of political support that should have been translated into economic and personnel support for the ÚDV. The center-right governments of 1992–98, which boasted their ideological voracity in their crusades against the communist regime and the successor social-democratic governments share the responsibility for continuing impunity.

Lustration

In October 1991, fewer than two years after the fall of the communist regime, Czechoslovaks approved the lustration law.[39] The law disqualified discredited persons from having access to leading public positions in the new democracy.[40] The law effectively concerned over 23,000 secret police collaborators whose expected age[41] was under 65 in 1989 (Figure 8). Other major categories included about 165,000 members of verification committees, which facilitated purges in the aftermath of the Soviet invasion in 1968;[42] and about 100,000 members of the People's Militia, the paramilitary wing of the Communist Party.[43] The latter two categories included all the members of these organizations during the communist era. Their age was unknown. Considerably lower in numbers but significant in influence were members of the secret police itself; Communist Party secretaries at the district level and above; and students at the Soviet political and KGB universities.

The scale of this disqualification was unprecedented in Central and Eastern Europe. Yet the Czech public still considered it unsuccessful. Table 1 shows that less than 24 percent of Czechs found lustration to be successful in surveys conducted in 2010 and 2015. The studies by CVVM illustrate that about 42 percent of the public viewed lustration as helpful to democracy in 1991; 32 percent in 2000; about 47 percent in 2009; and 41 percent in 2014.[44]

How did lustration deal with secret collaboration, especially instances that may have resulted from coercion? The Czech legislators used different arguments to support lustration law in different eras. The first debate on lustration law in 1991 differed from later debates that concerned the extension of its validity in 1995 and 2000, the proposals for its abolition in 1999 and 2002, and its narrowing via the Public Employment Amendment Act in 2014.

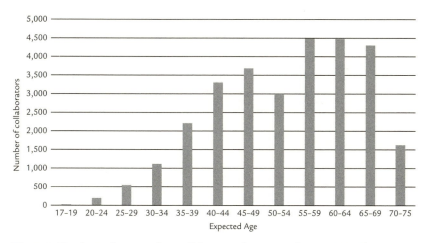

Figure 8. Numbers of secret police collaborators by expected age in 1989. The numbers here are based on my analysis of the official database of collaborators with the State Security, Ministry of the Interior (2003).

During the first parliamentary debate, some members of the Czechoslovak Federal Assembly showed a degree of empathy with the secret collaborators. They portrayed secret collaborators as those who could not withstand certain pressure, to which they and their families had been exposed.[45] The record of secret collaboration, even in cases of blackmail, may have made them vulnerable and led to new blackmail, in significant positions in the transforming state. In order to reduce the risk that blackmail posed to the nascent democracy, people with "a record of weakness" had to be removed on the grounds that they had failed. Accepting or rejecting a candidate who used to be a secret collaborator involved a judgment that stemmed from the nature of political office as a position of trust, power, and representation, rather than from the act of collaboration per se.

The forward-looking concerns about the integrity of political offices thus superseded legal concerns about secret collaboration signed under duress. The shift may have been motivated by moral, pragmatic, and ideological reasons. First, it overshadowed the moral challenge of judging secret collaborators by those legislators who were never under pressure from secret police and had no record of resistance and "strength." For other legislators, it allowed vacating positions in the state apparatus and filling them with their cronies. Still, in the Federal Assembly elected in 1990, many legislators simply did what they believed was the best for the country, although their beliefs radically differed.

Subsequent debates on the extension of the law were more ideological and partisan than the initial debates on the approval of the law. Deputies voted mainly based on their political affiliations. As a result, the second phase of lustration offered a similar resolution of the moral, legal, and political dilemmas but with a different perspective on secret collaborators. Although political considerations about the quality of democracy dominated the debates, parliamentarians expressed little concern about motives for collaboration. For the supporters of lustration it was not strategic to express any empathy and doubt. In 1995, they needed to demonstrate confidence to push the law through Parliament, not empathy that could be seen as weakness. The increasing influence of lustration law itself in debates about its extension or abrogation has become apparent since 2000. By that time, lustration law was not being read in its historical context. It was taken for granted that all people covered by it were undoubtedly collaborators. There was no provision in the law that allowed for any exemption.[46] When extending the lustration law, deputies' views stemmed from the impression that the lustration law itself conveyed rather than historical circumstances.[47]

In September 2014, deputies debated whether to limit lustration law by excluding the posts of government ministers from the lustration process. The debate bore personal overtones, which were reminiscent of the first lustration debates. At center stage was Babiš, the leader of the newly formed political party ANO, who had allegedly been a collaborator with the secret police. ANO gained 18.65 percent of the votes in the 2013 parliamentary election and the social democratic prime minister, Bohuslav Sobotka (ČSSD), needed the party's cooperation in order to form a coalition government.[48] Pursuant to Sobotka's nomination, President Zeman appointed Babiš as the vice prime minister without having him produce a clean lustration certificate. That constituted a clear violation of lustration law.[49] Babiš eventually cleared his name in Slovakia where two former secret police officers testified on his behalf.[50] This did not prevent Deputy Miroslav Kalousek, the de facto leader of the political party Top 09, from pointing to the inability of Babiš to present his lustration certificate in the first place. Kalousek also expressed annoyance that a parliamentary committee wanted him to stop using the term "communist snitch."[51]

The alleged collaborators were thus portrayed as definite collaborators who deserved public ridicule and shame. Curiously enough, the only party to express a degree of doubt about the motives of people targeted by lustration law was the KSČM: "What kind of danger for the current state is posed by a person who half a century ago, or a quarter of a century ago, signed an agreement to protect the economic interests of Czechoslovakia and, upon his return from a business trip, to report efforts by foreign services to recruit him in order to undermine economic interests of the Republic."[52] Such cases may have been perfectly plausible. However, the unwillingness of the Communist Party to renounce the communist regime and the lack of effort to reform itself prompted other deputies to point to its hypocrisy. This impression was further magnified by the fact that the sympathy with secret collaborators was expressed by Miroslav Grebeníček, former chairperson of the KSČM, whose father had allegedly been a communist torturer in the 1950s.[53]

Reparatory Measures

The Czech Republic pursued a traditional approach to mitigating the effects of the communist regime's injustice to victims. It swiftly implemented a program of financial compensation and legal rehabilitation for victims, and it returned nationalized properties to the original owners or their heirs. These programs were implemented on an unprecedented scale in comparison with other countries because they concerned hundreds of thousands of people. Although legal rehabilitation and financial compensation were not controversial programs, restitution became quite divisive as it created new injustices for émigrés and other social groups.

Judicial Rehabilitation and Social Acknowledgment

Legal rehabilitation is a precondition for effective social integration. Unless politically motivated judicial decisions are annulled, it is difficult for those affected to claim political prisoner status and be recognized by society. According to the van Boven-Bassiouni principles,[54] the starting point for reparation is restoration of the victim to his or her situation before the violation of international human rights law or humanitarian law occurred; this includes restoration of liberty, legal rights, social status, family life, and citizenship, as well as restoration of employment and return of property.[55] Conversely, the absence of formal acknowledgment contributes to a "conspiracy of silence":[56] the community does not recognize victims' suffering and continues to stigmatize and marginalize them. The experiences of South Africa and other countries show that "truth" was critical in combating denial and thereby minimizing its impact on victims.[57]

The Czechoslovak Federal Assembly passed the Rehabilitation Act of 1990 just before the first democratic elections.[58] The main objective of the Act was to nullify judicial sanctions for acts through which people exercised their fundamental rights, which had been criminalized by the judicial system between the communist takeover on February 25, 1948, and January 1, 1990, two days after the election of Havel as president, effectively delegitimizing the entire communist era. The Rehabilitation Act thus codified an important shift in judicial norms: A political regime based on the abuse of power was replaced by one that respected the rule of law. It concerned the relatives of the judicially executed, former political prisoners, and the reform communists of 1968 who were expelled from the KSČ.

The Act also sought to reverse the legal consequences of illegitimate actions. It canceled political expulsions and the dismissal of students and employees. Even relatives of deceased victims were entitled to submit requests for the formal "reinstatement" of victims to their previous roles. Every individual was entitled to make the decisions about his or her own rehabilitation public.[59] In several instances rehabilitation certificates were issued by the judges who had delivered the guilty verdicts. Those who had been rehabilitated found this process bizarre and criticized it.[60]

Further formal condemnation of previous oppression was acknowledged in parliamentary acts and governmental activities. The 1993 Act on the Illegitimacy of the Communist Regime[61] and the 2011 Act on the Third Resistance[62] referred to the illegitimacy of the old regime and honored the resistance. The latter was, however, very divisive among victims because it did not recognize political imprisonment as evidence of resistance (see Chapter 3). Informally, many victims received state awards, were honored by their town halls, and invited to schools to share their life stories with the next generation. Social acknowledgment was seen as the most successful way to rehabilitate and recognize those whose political conduct had been criminalized under the communist regime. Table 1 shows that in 2010, slightly more than 48 percent of respondents considered social acknowledgment of victims as successful, although the number marginally dropped to 45 percent in 2015.

Financial Compensation

Does money matter? Many believe that it does. Attempts to gain monetary compensation have taken center stage in international "reparation politics." Litigation against companies that profited from slave labor in Nazi Germany and apartheid South Africa is evidence of this trend.[63] Yet the emphasis on monetary compensation also sparked controversy in many countries; opponents argued that when survivors accept money it demeans the memory of deceased victims and allows perpetrators to assuage their moral guilt entirely, because they can claim that "the debt" has been repaid.[64] Martha Minow thus claimed that money was not a priority for victims.[65]

Financial compensation per se was not a contested issue in the Czech Republic, although its mechanism was highly controversial. Under the terms of the Rehabilitation Act financial compensation was paid to surviving victims or their heirs if the victims had been executed or had died in detention. Each political prisoner received a small sum of compensation to cover damage to health, legal fees, and judicial fines; political prisoners were also entitled to CZK 2,500 per month in compensation for loss of earnings during their incarceration. Many of these provisions were options that did not preclude concerned persons from using other legal means to seek redress.

The Act also sought to prevent all discriminated persons from being penalized when it came to drawing their pensions.[66] In 1990, the country was about to launch major economic reforms because its economy had been decimated by decades of central planning. People understood that compensation could only be paid to alleviate the most severe injustices.

The dispossessed groups were entitled to restitution of their personal property, which had usually been confiscated as part of their punishment. Former political prisoners also enjoyed other material support, including free public transport, subsidies for their associations (KPV and SBPV), and special medical treatment.[67] In parallel with the revisions to compensation for political prisoners between 2001 and 2009, the government gradually widened the scope of the compensation scheme to include those who had not initially been entitled to compensation, such as persons in forced labor camps, persons abducted to the USSR, and university students who had not been permitted to complete their education for political reasons.[68] The Act on the Third Resistance provided CZK 100,000 to each person, who was found to be a resister against the communist regime (see Chapter 3 about the problems with this Act).

Figure 7 shows that financial compensation was a relatively well-received measure in the Czech Republic. More than 40 percent of respondents considered compensation successful in 2010, although the number dropped to 35.4 in 2015 (Table 1).

Restitution

The major restitution laws were approved by the Parliament elected in the first free elections in 1990.[69] The restitution concerned the return of movable and immovable properties to their original owners or their heirs. The restituted properties most frequently included residential houses, small businesses, lands, and forests. Although the scale of property restitution was massive in comparison with judicial rehabilitation and financial compensation, the process was lengthier and more controversial. The motivation for the restitution law was mainly based on a belief in the liberal notion of justice that accentuates the import of private property,[70] coupled with the need to delegitimize the previous regime. The slogan "what was stolen should be returned" underpinned the process. Many deputies who voted for the restitution law did not have any material interest in it. The leader who actually benefited from the restitution was paradoxically Václav Havel, the country's prominent idealist:

> As a child from an entrepreneur's, hence bourgeoisie, family I probably lived through my childhood in abundance. Then the February putsch came, my family was deprived of all property and a class struggle was fought against our family. At that time I really did not have money. When in the sixties my dramas were played in various places in the world, the situation changed. . . . I never thought that the democracy that we sought and that was not in sight would have to return anyone his confiscated property. Even less I thought that it would concern me. Those who entertained that idea, completely absurd in my view, were only the communist propagandists. . . . And now the paradox comes: after 1989 the nationalized properties began to be returned and our family enterprises then returned to my brother and me as the heirs of our deceased parents. . . . I don't think [that we should not have launched restitution]. The desire for restitution was huge; I did not realize that it was such a painful experience, and I used to regard it with a bit of contempt. But in our country there were tens, if not hundreds of thousands of petty tradesmen for whom nationalization meant a real life catastrophe.[71]

The process was marred by controversies concerning three subjects: the tenants in the restituted flats, the churches, and restitution for émigrés. The first problem was that the residential properties were returned to the original owners along with their tenants. As a condition for return, the landlord had to take responsibility for the buildings and houses along with the tenants. The landlords could evict the tenants only if the landlords provided adequate replacement accommodation. Some landlords actually may not have had a place for their own living but they suddenly became responsible for the maintenance of their restituted buildings.

The political transition, which coincided with economic transition, led to exacerbating consequences for property restitution. During the communist regime, there was a massive shortage of flats, which were cheap and soon became a scarce commodity. Rapid appreciation in the value of properties in the market economy after 1989 aggravated the situation for tenants in rented accommodations. There was virtually no place for tenants to move into when the properties were handed back to the original owners. The rent on these properties was legally regulated but in view of the maintenance costs and opportunity costs that could have been derived from letting the flats and houses at market prices, many landlords sought to use all possible, frequently extra-legal, means to evict their tenants.

It is difficult to estimate the scale of the problem: The last communist census of 1980 recorded that 37.3 percent of the population lived in state flats, while others lived in their own or cooperative housing.[72] Some state flats were newly built but many were nationalized after 1948, and during the entire era of the communist regime in cases of emigration. The problem is likely to have affected hundreds of thousands of households. Although many tenants may have been communists or people considered loyal to that regime, many other tenants were people in need, socially disadvantaged, or the Romas who occupied city centers. The state effectively washed its hands of the housing problem when it returned expropriated property without adequately providing for alternative accommodation for the tenants. In 2014 and 2017, the European Court of Human Rights ruled against the Czech Republic by acknowledging the owners' rights and granted the complainants compensation.[73]

The second controversy arose from the return of property to the churches and religious groups. Shortly after 1989, the public was willing to support this restitution, but as transition progressed the situation changed. The political slogan "What was stolen had to be returned" remained a pronouncement by Christian parties only. It soon lost its public appeal in the predominantly atheistic society. In the census of 2011, only 14.02 percent of people mentioned a religious affiliation and an additional 6.76 were believers without affiliation, which makes the Czechs one of the most atheistic societies in the world.[74] It is not surprising that the Church Restitution Bill was supported by a mere 16 percent of Czechs and opposed by 65 percent.[75] The conservative coalition paid a price in the 2013 elections[76] for pushing through the unpopular law on church restitution in 2012.[77]

Third, not all dispossessed Czechoslovaks benefited from the restitution of property. Those who lost their citizenship due to emigration were effectively excluded from restitution, because legislation attached restitution to citizenship as well as permanent residence in Czechoslovakia.[78] These exclusions gave rise to a twofold problem. First, even in cases where they were able to regain Czechoslovak citizenship, many had to forfeit the citizenship of their new country in order to do so.[79] Second, they had to officially take up residence in Czechoslovakia, leaving their new lives and new families behind. Ironically, the democratic government gave them the same choice as the communists had: owe or leave. It was a hard choice for many. The restitution law was approved in 1991 when an attempted coup d'état in the Soviet Union took place. At that stage, return to Czechoslovakia was not entirely without risk.

Many émigrés rightly complained about the situation. In response, the Constitutional Court abrogated the requirement of the Czechoslovak residency as a condition for restitution.[80] This, however, did not mean justice for the émigrés. The deadline for submitting a restitution claim had passed by the time the permanent residence requirement had been set aside and the Court refused to review the deadline. Now the nonresident Czech citizens, who were not eligible to claim the return of their property, no longer had the right to submit their applications. The Constitutional Court washed its hands of the matter by repeatedly stating in 1999 and 2010 that restitution was a matter for the legislator to deal with.[81] Yet these obstacles were not insurmountable for the legislature. Restitution law could subsequently have been amended.

While Greeks, Poles, and Jews have maintained contact with their diasporas, the Czechs turned their back on "foreign" Czechs. How can we explain the harsh treatment of émigrés? The history of exclusions in the Czech Lands, mentioned earlier, has suggested that Czechs have increasingly attached their citizenship to both the Czech language and the territory. Another factor that contributed to the nonrestitution of property to émigrés was a feeling of injustice felt toward the émigrés from those inside the country coupled with the national conception of history. The national awakening of the nineteenth century taught Czechs that someone owed them something;[82] it is axiomatic that Czechs by the very nature of their existence have entitlements. Émigrés were seen as those who lived comfortable lives in wealth and abundance in the West. They thus had collected their historical dues and were no longer entitled to anything. Those who stayed had to suffer and needed to be recompensed. The concept of Czech identity became rigid and restrictive. Justice was not for all.

Revelatory Measures

Bringing truth commissions to the forefront of social research has been one of the main achievements of academic inquiry into transitional justice. It has been argued that truth commissions suit the needs of victims better than criminal trials and help to reconcile divided societies.[83] However, truth commissions are not without controversy.[84] This has prompted some scholars to draw attention to the limits of what truth commissions can achieve.[85]

No truth commission was established in the Czech Republic. The truth about the past was revealed via formally established government bodies, namely ÚDV and ÚSTR. Secret collaboration was disclosed via access to secret police files and official as well as unofficial publication of secret collaborators. Many victims shared their experiences informally with close friends, wrote to the media, or were interviewed by the media. New history textbooks, which abandoned the Marxist-Leninist view of history, were published.

In the public's view, the exposure of secret collaborators was reported to be successful by 35.5 percent of respondents in 2010 and by 32.6 in 2015; access to secret archives by 37.8 percent in 2010 and 34.2 in 2015; and new textbooks by 40.8 percent in 2010 and 42.5 percent of respondents in 2015 (Table 1). The revelatory measures were seen as more successful than retributive measures, but less successful than reparatory measures.

Exposing Secret Collaboration and Access to Secret Files

The secretive nature of the communist regime was a driving force behind the disclosure of information about its major protagonists and of their critical political and legal decisions. While the identities of political leaders were largely known, the calls for public revelation were particularly urgent in cases of secret collaboration. People demanded to know who among their neighbors, colleagues, and friends informed the secret police about them and why. In the context of the political system, many citizens felt entitled to exercise their right to have access to information about the past of the political leaders in order to make qualified decisions during elections. Thus, at both the individual and political levels, demands for exposure were a means for dealing with mistrust.

Most political forces were initially not keen to reveal the names of secret collaborators. Some members of parliament wanted to protect the identity of secret informers, worrying about the possibility of a wave of retribution against them.[86] Thus, the first revelations about the identities of secret informers was conducted ad hoc about individual politicians or journalists.[87] Since the Bartončík affair in 1990,[88] secret collaboration has been used as a means to discredit candidates before elections. The first wild list was published by *Rudé krávo* (Red cow) in 1992. Deriving its name from the communist mouthpiece *Rudé právo* (Red right), the weekly pursued an uncompromising anticommunist rhetoric under the editorship of the dissident Petr Cibulka. The "complete list of secret police informers" was probably leaked by one of Cibulka's colleagues from the dissident movement who worked in the Ministry of the Interior after 1989, although Cibulka himself admitted that the list was not accurate. In 1999, he amended and reprinted the list again.[89]

People wrongfully included on the 1992 list did not have many options. They could request an official lustration certificate and then turn to the courts for the protection of personality claims. They could not access their own files because access was forbidden. Thus, the initial version of the Act on the Access to Files Created Through the Activities of the State Security,[90] which was inspired by the German Stasi Records Act, was a disappointment for victims of the communist regime as well as for those who were accused of secret collaboration. That changed in 2002, when almost full access to secret police files was granted.[91] In 2003, the Ministry published the list in hard copy and online. After the establishment of the ÚSTR in 2008,[92] the database became searchable online.

However, public access to databases is not sufficient to fulfill the role expected of revelations in dealing with the past in transitional societies; for instance, they do not provide a comprehensive picture of all that occurred in the past. The lists can only provide information about the identities of those who collaborated, the time of collaboration, and their cover names. Provisions that would take into account the motives for collaboration and the collaborators' current attitude to their collaboration, if any, are missing.

Narratives, however, took place informally in the media and most prominently in an edited volume compiled by Zdena Salivarová-Škvorecká.[93] In the absence of any other public forum for dealing with the past, the book gave voice to collaborators and alleged collaborators. Their personal testimonies resemble the transcripts of truth commissions. The authentic narratives of confessions, denials, explanations, and excuses provide more insight into the process of dealing with the past than lists of names, cover names, and birthdates. The benefits of a meaningful dialogue about the past and the triangulation of materials from different sources can be illustrated in the following example.

Salivarová-Škvorecká relates, among many other stories, a story of Mr. K., who joined an anticommunist resistance group in the 1950s, which printed and distributed leaflets in parallel with a larger resistance group. Both groups were discovered, and the members of K.'s group were sentenced to several months in jail in 1952, although their sentences were more lenient than those of the larger group. K. thinks that the larger group, whose members received jail terms of five to eight years, was probably exposed by being infiltrated by an informant, but he adds that he can only speculate about it. Mr. K.'s name appeared on Cibulka's list in 1992. In response, he wrote a letter to Cibulka, sharing his feeling of devastation: "Now, shortly after we have seen the return of freedom and democracy to the center of Europe, oops! I read my name on the list of found agents of StB and suddenly become again the one whom I was before November 89—a humiliated and underprivileged member of society. This time, however, without the beautiful inner feeling of pride of my degradation, of my secondary position, which guaranteed spiritual freedom, but with the feeling of irreparable injustice, powerlessness and hopelessness."[94]

Mr. K. explained why he could possibly be on the list. He mentioned that a few years after his release from jail, he was called to the police station, resisted pressure, and avoided reporting on his friends. Instead, in his words, he reported on his colleagues who were Party members. He then signed that he would not share any information about it. In the 1980s he successfully defended his "habilitation" (an academic degree higher than a Ph.D., signifying associate professorship) and after the deliberate delay by the authorities, he was awarded the degree six years later. In 1988, he was able to travel to the West. In December 1990, he was officially cleared of the accusation. He concluded his letter to Cibulka writing, "I am asking you for advice. You became in my eyes . . . an extended hand of bolshevism, which persecuted me for 41 years. Advise me how to get out of it. If you [ignore] me, Mr. Cibulka, go to hell."[95]

The resemblance between the communist propaganda and publication of the list, and the record of imprisonment may have prompted the deputy editor of *Rudé krávo*, Petr Placák, to reply in this way: "It is clear that the lists contain the real snitches and side-by-side with them are those who were caught by the StB in very unfortunate circumstances. I do think, though, that the communist dirt can only be overcome . . . in the way that we openly stand against it. . . . You are asking about how to clear your name. The best thing is to openly speak about the whole thing."[96] In 1998, Mr. K. visited secret archives, a visit that was allowed at the time, thanks to the law providing access to the secret archives. He found information about two files: one by the Military Counter-Intelligence, which had been opened in 1955 and destroyed in 1986. The second one had been archived; it contained details of his arrest as well as a note that appeared to exonerate him dating back to 1960. It stated in his words that "in view of inimical attitudes, criminal activity, and class background," the members of the group should be "under surveillance for twenty years."[97]

If society had had to rely on the official process of dealing with the past, it would not know about K.'s representation of his motives and the whole context of his life, career, and political situation. Obviously, it is still not enough. Questions can be asked by the Communist Party members on whom Mr. K. reported. What happened to them? What about the other members of K.'s group? What about the members of the larger group? Conversely, if society had had to rely on K.'s representation, it would not have been able to corroborate his version. My search of the online archive of secret police informers in 2015 returned several hits for Mr. K. and a cover name. Five of them had an identical birthdate in 1927. This indeed suggests a collaboration that may explain the unusual fact that he was allowed to eventually get his academic degree and travel to the West in spite of the record of his imprisonment and "inimical attitudes." My search of the archives also returned positive matches, which is likely to suggest collaboration, for all three members of K.'s group.

The triangulation of Cibulka's list, Salivarová-Škvorecká's book, and an official database provides intriguing insight into the actions of individuals under the previous regime and their response to the past afterward. Their victims and the public, as Arthur Stinchcombe pointed out, gained an opportunity to evaluate the value of these excuses and explanations.[98]

School Textbooks

For the new generation of Czechs, the main source of information about the communist regime, and a factor that shapes the formation of their attitudes toward it, is the school textbook. Primary and secondary school students learn about the communist regime through subjects such as history and civic education. While there are many new history textbooks available on the market, some of them have been criticized for merely deleting the passages about the leading role of the Communist Party while retaining a Marxist-Leninist interpretation of history as a history of exploitation and class struggle.[99]

In civic education, which may alternatively be called the "basics of social sciences" at the secondary schools, the scope is broader. The recommended four-year curriculum generally covers, among other subjects, the fundamentals of political science, sociology, psychology, economics, and philosophy. The curriculum provides students with a broader perspective on political systems, economic systems, and philosophical schools. It emphasizes democracy, market economy, and philosophical pluralism, where the Marxist approach is merely one of many.[100] It is thus unsurprising that new textbooks have been considered the most successful revelatory measure in the eyes of the public (see Table 1).

Reconciliatory Measures

"To prosecute and punish or to forgive and forget" was the dilemma facing pioneering practitioners and theorists of transitional justice in the early 1990s.[101] Should we punish perpetrators or reconcile with them? This debate gained unprecedented momentum from South Africa's establishment of its iconic Truth and Reconciliation Commission (TRC), which used immunity from prosecution to incentivize perpetrators to disclose the truth and face their victims before an amnesty committee. The work of the TRC led to a reexamination, though inconclusive, of the principles of retributive justice.[102]

In the Czech Republic the reconciliation process was only articulated at the outset of transition. The nonretributive slogan "we are not like them"[103] was chanted within squares during the 1989 protests. For some it soon became a reminder of disappointment with transition, and others used it to mock the transition process. Even Havel himself had to justify using it and recuse himself from some of the potential implications.[104]

The Communist Party, though initially apologetic, remains unrepentant about the past. In 1989, the extraordinary congress of the KSČ issued a statement saying,

> Because our former leadership themselves have so far not found enough honesty and courage to publicly apologize we the delegates of the extraordinary party congress do so. We apologize to our youth and all our citizens who were affected by unjustified repression, we apologize to the children of those parents who suffered disadvantages in further generations. We also apologize for all the wrongs to those party members who, due to their reformist attitudes and due to their disagreement with the unlawful entry of troops from five allied countries in 1968, had to leave the Communist Party and lost their positions as equal citizens. Also, we feel obliged to express regret over how the former party leadership in recent years roughly and unlawfully failed to respect the right to express opinions of independent civic initiatives, including Charter 77. We are also aware of the responsibility of our entire membership base, which failed to prevent it [from happening].[105]

The Party congress apologized but no leaders followed suit. Neither the previous nor the current leadership has made any effort to face up to the past. To be sure, it may be hard to apologize for the crimes of the communist regime in the face of anticommunistic discourse. But this did not deprive the leadership of the freedom to apologize. On the contrary, the Party remains defiant, disrespectful to victims[106] and provocative of society. The chairperson of KSČM, Vojtěch Filip, even became angry when he faced claims that the Party did not apologize for the past.[107] In a press release to mark the twenty-fifth anniversary of the fall of the communist regime, KSČM admitted "repression" and "power abuses" in the past but failed to express any apology or regret for it. Instead, KSČM highlighted the existence of social security in the past and dismissed the post-1989 capitalistic changes.[108]

Reconciliatory measures differ from other measures of justice because the state cannot mandate them. None of the major reconciliatory measures,

such as apologies by leaders, confessions by perpetrators, and a reconciliation commission, took place in the Czech Republic. Gestures of apologies
and regret over the past were rare and expressed by individuals. For instance, an ordinary member of the KSČM apologized for the injustices of
the communist regime, while a daughter of a communist torturer shared
her inheritance with victims of the communist regime.[109] It is therefore not
surprising that only 18.9 percent of respondents considered apology by the
KSČM as successful, while 39.1 percent saw it as unsuccessful, making it one
of the most unsuccessful measures of justice (Table 1).

Discussion

A few features of the process of dealing with the past in the Czech Lands have
emerged. Each of the features may play a role in an assessment of the effectiveness of the justice measures. First, retributive and reparatory measures
of justice have played a dominant role. Although prosecutions largely failed,
lustration, nationalization of the communist property, rehabilitation, financial compensation, and restitution were all extensive measures. Although not
without problems in their scopes and designs, these measures were quite effectively implemented. In contrast, revelatory measures have had a limited
reach. Official revelation included the compilation of lists of secret police collaborators, the publication activities by the ÚDV and ÚSTR, and access to
secret police archives. There was no effort to compile lists of other groups
under the lustration law, such as members of the purge committees in the
aftermath of the Soviet invasion; and there was no effort to give voice to those
who were affected by these measures, depriving the society of an opportunity to engage in dialogue about the past. There were no official reconciliatory measures instituted on a formal level, although the Communist Party
on one occasion expressed an apology for the past. The apology was selective and never all-embracing and unequivocal. The Party rejected demands
for apologies on other occasions. The macro-level analysis suggests that the
country strove to pursue "justice without reconciliation." It sought to rectify
injustices of the past but did not consider the need to repair social relations
fractured by those injustices.

Second, most justice measures had largely collective features. The communist regime was condemned by holus-bolus acts of Parliament while those
who were individually responsible for the perpetration of its abuses were
seldom subjected to judicial scrutiny. Society was therefore deprived of

understanding the complexities of individual experiences. People did not have an opportunity to acknowledge the victims, and their names and sacrifices were never publicly listed. It was impossible to identify property that had been seized by the Communist Party and that was subsequently returned to the people. The various lists of collaborators were not entirely reliable and victims could not base their claims upon them. The Communist Party's blanket "apology" was issued once, vaguely and collectively. Thus, the range and variety of individual experiences and individual complicities in dealing with the regime were absolved by placing the blame on the nebulous communist regime, the Communist Party, and the mass of secret police collaborators.

Third, the reception of justice measures by the people (Table 1 and Figure 7) shows that reparatory measures were considered the most effective, followed by revelatory measures and retributive measures.[110] There was not much difference between the assessment of these measures in 2010 and 2015. Factor analyses statistically confirmed the conceptualization of the ten measures of justice into three dimensions: retributive, reparatory, and revelatory.[111] However, apology by the KSČM as an instance of a reconciliatory measure was seen and assessed by the people as a retributive measure. Retributive measures and an apology were also considered the least successful in the eyes of the public.

Fourth, measures of justice did not always match the historical injustice they were intended to address. Chapter 1 pointed to the existence of documents from the 1950s that suggested that at least some of the recruited secret collaborators were not insidious, unscrupulous crooks but heroes who risked their lives in the anticommunist resistance. Some of them may have been forthcoming informants while others may have been coerced into submission. But lustration law affected them all. In spite of this, lustration has been viewed in the opinion polls as unsuccessful. The collective nature of lustration either did not matter in the eyes of lustration supporters, or the benefits of sweeping lustration outweighed its possible costs. Another reason may be that lustration did not affect many Communist Party members who benefited from their positions in the past and capitalized on their positions and networks during the economic transformation that followed.

How can one explain that no amendment to the existing lustration law was adopted to provide for other types of injustice or to exclude injustices that were not injustices in the first place? In view of Chapter 1, it seems that either historians failed the legislators, or the legislators failed the historians in the Czech Republic. One can hardly resist the view that modern history has been rewritten in order to serve the law, not the other way around. This shift also allows avoiding questions about responsibility for the communist regime among many Czechs themselves. It is a convenience for evading uncomfortable questions about each individual's role in the past. Once the groundwork for justice is laid out, it is difficult to change the fundamentals. For many, it is more comfortable to stick with the defined victims, villains, and scapegoats than to reopen the debate at the risk of becoming a scapegoat oneself. By targeting "hidden repression," the measures of justice diverted attention away from major crimes, such as border killings, and essentially whitewashed hundreds of thousands of Little Czechs who had created injustices for others in order to survive themselves. It would not be entirely unfair to say that instead of justice being a function of history, history became a function of justice in the Czech Republic.[112]

PART II

Justice at the Poles of Society

Chapter 3

Did Justice Measures Heal Victims?
Compensation, Truth, and Reconciliation
in the Lives of Political Prisoners

> It is a painful history. It is an ulcer that is not cured. . . . If we do not
> deal with guilt, the curse remains. The nation is cursed twice, if they
> do not deal with those killed. Schools, courts, judges. We are the last
> survivors who cry so.
> —Antonín Huvar, priest and former political prisoner,
> interview, November 1999

Chapter 1 documented that human rights were violated on a mass scale during the era of the communist regime in Czechoslovakia. Chapter 2 provided an overview of the justice measures that were adopted to deal with that legacy. This chapter examines the impact of the justice measures on the victims of gross human rights violations. The chapter raises questions such as whether financial compensation was important in overcoming the consequences of these human rights violations or whether the lack of a forum for truth-sharing affected the victims' experience of sufficient redress. In order to examine these and other questions, I conducted an original survey, interviews, and focus-group sessions with former political prisoners between 1999 and 2014. This chapter sheds light on the lives and views of former political prisoners, most of whom were imprisoned during the 1950s and the 1960s. These data are the living testimony of many of those who are no longer among us.

The chapter is divided into four parts. The first part conceptualizes healing and sociopolitical redress as outcome variables to capture the impact of

justice measures on victims. The second part focuses on the social characteristics of former political prisoners as a group and on the historical context of their persecution. The third part looks at the reception of justice
measures by political prisoners after 1989. The fourth part examines factors
affecting the impact of justice measures on healing and sociopolitical redress, and it explores the social mechanisms through which these factors
affected the two outcomes.

Healing and Redress

In victims' studies and transitional justice literature, scholars speak of reparatory and other justice processes as means that have "the purpose of relieving
the suffering of and affording justice to victims by removing or redressing to
the extent possible the consequences of the wrongful acts and by preventing
and deterring violations."[1] Theoretical accounts of dealing with human rights
abuses recognize two dimensions that capture the impact of justice measures
on victims: sociopolitical and individual (internal).[2] In this book I refer to the
first one as sociopolitical redress,[3] and to the second one as individual healing.

Sociopolitical redress is a process that aims to restore the dignity of victims in the eyes of the public. Healing is the process of overcoming the physical and psychological consequences of oppression and imprisonment.[4] The
process of healing is primarily retrospective (backward-looking) because it
ensues from wrongdoing that occurred in the past, while redress is rather
prospective (forward-looking) since it relates to the social integration of victims. Both outcomes may be achieved through policy interventions, which
target victims' needs directly or indirectly through reparation, truth, criminal justice, democratization, and other measures for dealing with the past.

Before the inception of transitional justice as an interdisciplinary academic
field (see the Introduction), victims' needs were addressed via reparation. In
common parlance the term "reparation" refers to financial and material compensation. However, nowadays many scholars and practitioners in the field of
transitional justice use the term more generally as an umbrella concept con-
taining four components: restitution, compensation, rehabilitation, and,
fourthly, satisfaction and guarantees of nonrepetition.[5] Under this definition
a comprehensive reparation program should include all four components,[6]
which effectively encompass all plausible measures of transitional justice.

International acclaim for the South African Truth and Reconciliation
Commission (TRC) has posed another challenge to traditional thinking

about the value of financial and material reparation. The TRC provided a public forum for victims of gross human rights violations to share their painful experiences and allowed them to confront their perpetrators. In doing so it underlined how important truth-sharing and reconciliation were to victims' healing. Some scholars have reflected on the example of South Africa, questioning the priority of traditional methods of justice, such as financial compensation and criminal trials, in political transitions. Martha Minow has argued that "money remains incommensurable with what was lost. . . . Reparations fall short of repairing victims or social relationships after violence. This inevitable shortfall makes me wonder about the assumption that the most obvious need of victims is for compensation."[7]

Proponents of truth commissions assume that allowing victims to narrate their experiences of suffering in a receptive atmosphere will empower them and promote healing;[8] even so, many victims found the experience of testifying at the TRC traumatic.[9] However, truth commissions may also affect the well-being of victims indirectly, if they modify the perpetrators' behavior. One of the purported goals of truth commissions is to provide a forum where victims and perpetrators can meet and establish or reestablish a minimal civic relationship. It is assumed that the truth-commission process facilitates reconciliation by encouraging perpetrators to acknowledge their responsibility for their victims' suffering, helping to restore victims' dignity, and enabling victims to articulate their feelings and overcome their hatred of the perpetrators.[10] Although there is limited empirical evidence that truth-sharing has a direct or indirect positive impact on victims, truth commissions have been vigorously promoted as the optimal means of addressing gross human rights violations in diverse cultural environments around the world.[11]

The purported impact of criminal trials on victims has been a major point of contention between proponents and opponents of prosecution. Some see trials as therapeutic, and highlight their role in healing; others see healing as a long-term process and the performative nature of courtroom testimony as therapeutically problematic.[12] Similarly some argue that trials can help victims achieve closure while others claim that trials may reopen old wounds and revive hostilities.[13] It has been suggested that trials help to satisfy victims' desires for retribution, while others suggest they nurture the desire for retribution.[14] In their seminal article on violence and social repair, Laurel Fletcher and Harvey M. Weinstein observed that "the emphasis on criminal trials as the primary international response to mass violence does not respond to the needs of many for social repair."[15] Empirical research reveals the complexity of victims' responses and experiences. The critical finding of whether criminal trials or any other transitional justice intervention helps victims in overcoming the consequences of traumatic events is still inconclusive.[16]

The thorny issue of victims' healing and redress has enormous social policy implications and theoretical relevance to transitional justice. The continuing lack of empirical research means that current literature still includes mutually exclusive theoretical accounts of individual measures of transitional justice. "Victim needs" are used to argue both for the establishment of truth commissions and for criminal trials in preference to truth commissions.[17] The nature of victim needs remains one of the most contested areas in transitional justice studies. This chapter provide's empirical evidence on the dilemma of victims' needs.

Former Political Prisoners in the Czech Lands

Although hundreds of thousands were prosecuted during the forty-two years of communist rule in Czechoslovakia, the group most affected was that of former political prisoners. They were referred to as MUKLs, a Czech abbreviation of the phrase *Muž určený k likvidaci*, which means "man intended to be liquidated," an identity they proudly adopted to emphasize their survival. The number of prisoners was greatest in the late 1940s and 1950s, reaching a peak in 1950. The intensity and the scale of repression gradually reduced from the 1960s onward. Most ex-prisoners were released on amnesties granted in 1955, 1957, 1962, 1965, and 1968; the widest amnesty was granted by President Novotný in 1960.[18] The average time spent in prison by former political prisoners in my survey was 5.7 years; 9.6 percent had been imprisoned for less than one year, and about 15 percent served at least 10 years; about 13.4 percent were women (see Table 2).[19]

In the 1950s the prison system could barely cope with the growing number of political prisoners. The usual prison population of criminals was supplemented by a large group of inmates who had been condemned shortly after World War II for their collaboration with the Nazis. The lack of space and the intensive class struggle meant that during the 1950s and 1960s many political prisoners were held in the eighteen so-called remedy-labor camps rather than in prison. Those who had experienced the Nazi concentration camps reported that the conditions were the same, if not worse, and lasted much longer.[20] Many political prisoners were subjected to an extraordinarily

Table 2. Political Prisoners: Their Experiences and Attitudes

Social Indicators	Percentage (unless stated otherwise)
Gender (M)	85.8
Mean age	74.9 years
Education: University	11.9
Education: Secondary	43.5
Education: Apprentice	24.8
Part of church gatherings	64.6
Membership of political party or organization	35.7
Mean length of imprisonment	5.7 years
Torture, including inhuman or degrading treatment	47.8
Justice Measures	
Return to original profession	21.3
Sufficiency of financial compensation	15.1
Any punishment to perpetrators	3.5
Lack of reconciliation: Adversaries arrogant	15.5
Social acknowledgment: Invitation to discussion with students	9.7
Suspected by neighbors	4.5
Private truth-sharing	91.0
of them, people interested	87.8
Public truth-sharing	26.6
of them, story published	87.8
Satisfaction with democracy	18.2
Outcomes	
Sociopolitical redress (social rehabilitation)	41.0
Individual healing (overcoming consequences)	47.0

Source: Roman David, "Situace bývalých politických vězňů," machine-readable data file, 2000 (on file with the author).

harsh regime involving hard labor in uranium mines without any protection from radioactivity, as well as reductions in the daily food ration and other punishments; some also suffered gross violation of their human rights, including torture.[21] Some 47.8 percent of respondents in my survey reported that they had been tortured or treated in an inhuman or degrading way (Table 2). The range of mistreatment varied but included beating, pouring cold water over inmates in winter, electric shocks, foot beating, and so on.[22] Female political prisoners, including nuns and pregnant women, experienced beating, torture, and sexual assault.[23]

The 1960s did not herald the end of repression. Trials of political opponents to the regime took place throughout the era of reform that began with the Prague Spring in 1968,[24] although those released from jail briefly enjoyed freedom of association. Former political prisoners founded an organization called K231, which enrolled more than 100,000 members who had been incarcerated under Act 231 of 1948 for the Protection of the People's Democratic Republic.[25] The existence of K231 was one of the pretexts for the Soviet-led invasion of Czechoslovakia in 1968. Prison conditions improved markedly under Alexander Dubček's successor as head of the Communist Party, Gustáv Husák (head of the Communist Party, 1969–87; president of Czechoslovakia, 1975–89). It has not been often remembered in the post-1989 Czech Republic that Husák had been a political prisoner in the 1950s, one of the communist victims of the communist regime. This was perhaps the reason why the death penalty was not used for political offenses in the 1970s in spite of the massive purges, which took place in the aftermath of the Soviet invasion. Political prosecutions nevertheless continued until the very end of Husák's "normalization era" in November 1989.[26]

Imprisonment and persecution made a strong impact not only on victims but also on their families. Persecution included forced divorces, harassment, discrimination against family members in employment or study, and particularly poor or unpleasant living conditions:

> My wife, who was pregnant at that time [when I was arrested] and looking after our 1.5-year-old baby, was dismissed from her employment, broke down, and had to be taken to a hospital. Afterwards she got a very badly paid job, which was not enough to provide for the family. She was constantly harassed by the secret police, they searched the house, confiscated personal property . . . they tried to force her to divorce me, but she refused.[27]

> [After my arrest] my mother developed a psychological illness and never recovered. My husband had to change his vocation of a priest. . . . Luckily, I did not have children.[28]

The release of political prisoners of the communist regime did not signal the end of their persecution. The totalitarian regime—it controlled all sections and aspects of society, from enterprises to the media, from housing to the school curricula—ensured that their repression continued after their release. Many were publicly denounced as subversives and the omnipresent system of reporting and "cadre materials" prevented them finding suitable employment after their release.[29]

> After my release, I returned to my broken family as an alien, my children were scared of [me].[30]

> [After my release], I returned to Olomouc and could not get a job. For three months we had to live in one room, two families. . . . I came to the housing department and a bloke there told me "there are no flats for people like you."[31]

Many returning prisoners experienced painful alienation from family members. In many cases the attitude of the community contributed to their social isolation; neighbors were either hostile or secret police warned them against any expression of sympathy. Often such warnings were not necessary because many people were simply too afraid to talk to former political prisoners. They were surrounded by a "conspiracy of silence" after their release, which exacerbated their suffering.[32]

Reception of Justice Measures by Political Prisoners

Reception of Retributive Measures

Former political prisoners were extremely critical of the prosecution process. Some 96 percent were dissatisfied with the number of perpetrators who were convicted, although many victims were not particularly vengeful.[33] The former chairperson of KPV, Dr. Drobný, stated that the most important aspect of criminal justice was judicial condemnation and the guilty verdicts, not the jailing of former adversaries, many of whom were as old as the victims.[34] Only 24 percent of them considered imprisonment to be the appropriate outcome to the criminal trials of their adversaries; 28.1 percent would have welcomed their adversaries' confession and approved a suspended sentence; and 28.8 percent would have been happy with a formal apology.[35]

The Act on the Illegitimacy of the Communist Regime had enormous symbolic meaning for ex-political prisoners; it became their credo and was framed and displayed by their organizations on public boards and on their websites. In addition some former political prisoners received state awards or were invited by President Havel or President Klaus to Prague Castle in acknowledgment for their past sacrifices; others were awarded honorary citizenships by town halls. However, many of these symbolic gestures also generated adverse effects: For example, the political record of some award recipients was called into question.[36] Organizations of former political prisoners stopped nominating their members for state awards in 2013 because of President Zeman's past membership in the Communist Party.[37]

Reception of Reparatory Measures

The legal cancellation of wrongful judicial decisions proved quite effective, producing relatively rapid legal rehabilitation. Dealing with so-called residual punishments proved more complicated. Many political prisoners who had been jailed for treason or subversion may have had also been convicted of illegal possession of firearms; the crimes of treason and subversion were within the scope of the Act, but many subsidiary convictions were not automatically annulled and required judicial review. It is unsurprising that aging political prisoners were afraid that they would not see their name cleared before they passed away.

While the claims for financial compensation of most former political prisoners were modest, the claimants preferring to cherish the freedom they had regained, they were critical of the procedures for paying financial compensation. Initial compensation was paid in two installments, in 1990 and 1995, due to state budgetary constraints. Some former political prisoners felt this was reasonable; they understood that the economy had been devastated by decades of socialist planning. The problem was that people who had been imprisoned in the 1950s feared that they would not live long enough to receive all their compensation.[38] The second criticism stemmed from a comparison between the treatment of victims and their oppressors. Former members of the secret police received more compensation when they were forced to retire than many political prisoners had been granted. A police officer on a salary of CZK 10,000 who was dismissed after twenty years of service was entitled to a lump sum of CZK 80,000, plus a monthly rent of CZK 3,800.[39] All lump sum payments to secret police officers were made immediately. Some victims believed that their former oppressors were once again profiting at their expense.

Controversy also surrounded the compensation package because it was proposed by the transitional government led by the Prime Minister Marián Čalfa. Čalfa, and several other ministers in the government, had been a member of the Communist Party, defecting in early 1990. Many political prisoners were critical of Čalfa's past, although the character of the government, which was clearly pro-democracy and pro-reform, and included dissidents and technocrats, may have dispelled some of their concerns. The compensation policy was amended several times to address victim dissatisfaction. The Act on the Illegitimacy of the Communist Regime authorized the government to provide further compensation for former political prisoners; in 1997 they received a one-off payment of CZK 625 for each month of imprisonment.[40] In my survey, 15.6 percent of respondents considered their own financial compensation sufficient while 74.1 percent did not.[41]

The method of calculating entitlement to compensation—on the basis of length of imprisonment—also caused some discontent. All ex-political prisoners faced political discrimination after their release, regardless of the length of their imprisonment. The omnipresent system of "cadre materials" meant that they could not find suitable employment in the fully nationalized economy. In 2001, an attempt was made to rectify the discrimination in employment. All political prisoners who had been jailed for more than one year received a flat-rate payment of CZK 120,000 plus an additional CZK 1,000 for each month of imprisonment.[42] However, the rules governing financial compensation were inconsistent; political prisoners who had served between three and twelve months received CZK 60,000, although they may have experienced discrimination in employment as others did. In 2009, the government reverted to the initial compensation scheme, paying CZK 1,800 for each month of imprisonment.[43]

The Act on the Third Resistance of 2011 became one of the most controversial social acknowledgment programs.[44] Victims of the communist regime sought to be acknowledged as resisters in the same way that resisters during World War I and anti-Nazi resisters had been. Although the law awarded each resister CZK 100,000, it did not recognize imprisonment as evidence of resistance; imprisonment was neither a necessary nor a sufficient condition for classification as a member of the resistance.[45] According to the legislators, acts of resistance were instigating and distributing petitions, organizing assemblies against the regime, and other political and journalistic activities directed against the regime. Most of the qualifying activities set out in the law were more common in the 1970s and 1980s when repression was much less intense than in the 1950s and 1960s. The same moral attitudes, political opinions, and illegal activities had harsher consequences in the 1950s than they had in the 1980s. Those who resisted in the 1980s knew that the era of capital punishment was over. Treating the same activities carried out in different contexts as equivalent inevitably created double standards. According to a regional KPV leader, the Act created a rift in their organization because it recognized some former political prisoners but not others. Some 3,900 to 4,000 people, not all ex-prisoners, applied for resister status under the Act and between the years of 2011 and 2014 about 600 applications were successful.[46] Thus, most of those who were not broken by their imprisonment and refused to make compromises with the communist regime were not acknowledged.

Informal measures of social acknowledgment of victims played a historically important role in dealing with different pasts. One of its forms at the community level was invitations to talk to students, which overlaps with truth-sharing. In the Czech Lands it has been fairly common practice to invite witnesses to historical events to share their experiences with primary and secondary school students. Former political prisoners teamed up with the daughters of political prisoners who were associated with the nongovernmental organization Dcery (Daughters) to give the talks together.[47] Some 9.7 percent said that they had been invited to talk to students about their experiences, but 89.2 percent had not and 57.8 percent of the latter group said that they would accept such an invitation.[48] Finally, community acceptance is a critical feature of social acknowledgment. In the absence of a vibrant civic society, social acknowledgment was mediated through interaction with neighbors; some 11.4 percent of former political prisoners indicated that their neighbors held them in high regard, whereas 4.5 percent reported that their neighbors were suspicious of them.[49]

Pursuit of Revelatory Measures

Because no truth commission was established in the Czech Republic, I asked my respondents whether they had shared their life story privately and publicly. Some 26.6 percent said that they had tried to share their story publicly, and 74.4 percent of former political prisoners shared their story publicly. About 91 percent had shared their story privately, with friends and grandchildren (excluding other former prisoners in their organization); 87.8 percent of these people said their relatives expressed an interest in their story.[50]

Reception of Reconciliatory Measures

There was no formal measure of reconciliatory justice. The hostility between former adversaries has not significantly abated: Only 3.6 percent indicated that they were satisfied with the attitude of former adversaries, whereas 87.2 were dissatisfied; I expect that this has negatively impacted victims. Of those who have encountered their former adversaries in person, 15.5 percent found that perpetrators remained arrogant, 18 percent tried to avoid them, 13 percent considered themselves "victims of the system," and 3.3 percent apologized or made some other reconciliatory gesture.[51]

Democratization as a Measure of Justice

Many believe that macro-structural changes also made an impact on the victims of human rights violations. The sociopolitical context and the healing of victims and their families are strongly interrelated.[52] Gross human rights violations were usually institutionalized in the state apparatus. To secure a fully fledged transition and alleviate the fear of recurring violations, the root causes of human rights violations must be removed.[53] Unless this is done it is difficult for healing to begin.

Former political prisoners cannot simply be treated as individuals who were wrongfully convicted; they were persecuted for their political beliefs and engagement in political activities, and being a *political* prisoner became part of their identity. The perception of their healing and redress may be linked to the broader processes of democratization and their own political empowerment. I therefore asked former political prisoners whether they were satisfied with the development of democracy in the Czech Republic. Some 18.2 percent indicated that they were satisfied, while 72.9 percent were unsatisfied. It is notable that many of them refused to be passive observers of democratization; about 35.7 percent were members of a political party or a social organization other than their own KPV or SBPV.[54]

Impact of Justice Measures on Victims' Healing and Redress

Because I captured the outcome of justice measures on victims on two dimensions, sociopolitical redress and individual healing, I included two dependent variables in this study. The first was derived from the question "Do you feel rehabilitated?" for which there were five response categories on the Likert scale. In the context of dealing with the past in the Czech Republic, the word "rehabilitation" (*rehabilitace* in Czech) encompasses a variety of different types of redress, most particularly the repeal of unjust judicial decisions, reinstatement to one's original profession, and restoration of sociopolitical prestige. This

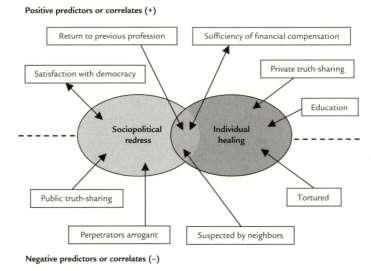

Figure 9. Predictors of sociopolitical recess and individual healing.

variable was thus intended to cater to sociopolitical redress. Some 41.0 percent of the respondents in my survey reported that they had been rehabilitated, while 50.4 percent did not feel rehabilitated. The second dependent variable, healing, was derived from an item asking whether the respondents had overcome or healed the psychological and physical consequences caused by imprisonment.[55] Again responses were given on a five-point Likert scale. Some 47.0 percent reported that they had overcome the consequences of their imprisonment, while 45.1 percent reported that they had not.[56]

Table 3 shows the variables, which predicted the extent to which victims felt they had achieved sociopolitical redress and inner healing; these results are based on multivariate analyses. Financial compensation and having been able to return to one's original profession were positive predictors of both healing and redress, whereas being the subjects of neighbors' suspicion was a negative predictor of both aspects. Satisfaction with democracy was a positive predictor of sociopolitical redress whereas public truth-sharing and lack of reconciliation were negative predictors. Private truth-sharing and education were positive predictors of inner healing, whereas having experienced torture was a negative predictor. These results are summarized in Figure 9.

The negative effect of torture seems obvious, but its persistence over decades shows how deep the wounds of the totalitarian regimes really were.

Table 3. Predictors of Healing and Sociopolitical Redress (Ordered logit models)

	Sociopolitical Redress		Individual Healing	
	B	SE	B	SE
Length of imprisonment (years)	−0.01	0.02	0.01	0.02
Tortured	−0.12	0.08	−0.32***	0.08
Returned to original profession	0.32^	0.18	0.39*	0.19
Sufficiency of financial compensation	0.87***	0.08	0.49***	0.08
Any punishment	−0.18	0.44	−0.09	0.40
Perpetrators arrogant	−0.69***	0.20	−0.19	0.20
Invitation to discussion with students	−0.30	0.27	0.11	0.26
Suspected by neighbors	−1.02**	0.36	−0.82*	0.35
Private truth-sharing	−0.06	0.28	0.91**	0.30
Public truth-sharing	−0.37*	0.18	−0.01	0.18
Satisfaction with democracy	0.26***	0.07	0.08	0.07
Gender	0.39^	0.23	−0.11	0.23
Age	−0.01	0.01	−0.01	0.01
Education	−0.02	0.09	0.31***	0.09
Took part in church gatherings	−0.19	0.16	0.23	-0.16
Member of political party or organization	−0.01	0.16	0.24	0.16
LR chi^2 (16)	234.20		128.90	
Pseudo R^2	0.13		0.07	
N	622		618	

Source: Roman David, "Situace bývalých politických vězňů," machine-readable data file, 2000 (on file with the author).
^ $p < 0.1$; * $p < 0.05$; ** $p < 0.01$; *** $p < 0.001$.

These results are in line with previous research on lifetime events and posttraumatic stress disorder in four postconflict settings. Between 1997 and 1999, Joop de Jong, Ivan Komproe, Mark van Ommeren, and others have examined the effects of multiple traumatic experiences in Algeria, Cambodia, Ethiopia, and Gaza. They found in all four countries that torture was one of the strongest predictors of posttraumatic stress disorder (PTSD).[57]

Impact of Judicial Rehabilitation: Return to One's Previous Profession

Almost all former political prisoners were judicially rehabilitated by the end of the 1990s. Although the process was lengthy for those who were aging, it was nevertheless completed faster than would have been possible if the courts had handled judicial rehabilitation on a case-by-case basis. Experiences of judicial rehabilitation have been fairly similar, so I asked about another part of the rehabilitation process: reinstatement of those who had been dismissed from their original employment for political reasons. The reinstatement policy appeared to have been implemented fairly effectively, although many were unable to benefit from it due to their age. Returning to one's previous profession enhanced both healing and redress. What mechanisms were involved in these effects?

Barring a person from reentering his or her previous profession is indicative of continuing political persecution; conversely, reinstatement symbolizes the end of it, thus promoting a sense that sociopolitical redress had been achieved. Being reinstated also helped individuals to rebuild their careers and personal lives and thus facilitated inner healing. Before 1989 only a few fortunate individuals were able to resume their previous professions immediately after release; a few more were able to do so after a certain period of time or during the relatively liberal Prague Spring period. Those who were denied the opportunity to resume their former employment considered it the most devastating consequence of their imprisonment: It meant the losses of their careers, opportunities for self-fulfillment, and earning potential:

I studied at the university (faculty of science—geology). . . . All my future and career was destroyed, I finished my working life as a miner, after thirty years in uranium mines. I do not regret it.[58]

[The most dramatic life change due to imprisonment was] the definitive loss of my profession as a journalist at the age of twenty-eight.[59]

Even after 1989, reinstatement was not always feasible for the aged, for those suffering from illness as a result of imprisonment, and for those whose workplaces no longer existed. However, reinstatement had a significant effect on those who were still of working age, as the following example illustrates:

I studied at the school of medicine and was expelled just before my graduation. After my release from the prison I worked as an autopsy assistant. After 1989, under the ordinance of the Minister of Education, I was able to continue and finish my studies in my fifties and start working as a [general practitioner].[60]

Reinstatement did not always have a wholly positive outcome. Some ex-prisoners who returned to their previous profession lamented missed opportunities for promotion and pay raises.[61] In some cases, returnees were not accepted by coworkers who saw them as unqualified after their lengthy absence or who perceived them as a threat to their personal ambitions. Sometimes hostility was openly expressed: "They are laughing at us. There was a boy who worked with me and who, after we got the compensation—a few korunas—said to me: 'Grandpa, don't laugh. You might still have to return your [compensation].'"[62] This example also illustrates the interaction between the various transitional justice interventions. In this case financial compensation overlapped with return to previous profession and, as I shall show below, with neighborhood acceptance.

Impact of Financial Compensation

Financial compensation was the most powerful predictor of a positive perception of both outcomes. Money helped to solve the pressing problems that ex-political prisoners confronted on a daily basis, particularly meeting the costs of ill health caused by imprisonment and exacerbated by old age. Although the Czech Republic provided for public health care, the health benefits from financial compensation were emphasized by respondents:

> The thing that the government should do is to make the aging of former political prisoners easier. This is mainly about health and medicine.[63]

> Thanks to [our organization] we get certain benefits [free public transport and subsidies for telephone calls]. Thanks for this! [But] all of us have come to the age when we think about where and how to spend the rest of our lives. Could we get priority when the distribution of pensions and flats with social care is decided?[64]

These quotations show the importance of financial compensation in making daily necessities affordable or accessible. The problem was that unlike a pension, compensation was not automatically inflation-adjusted. This led to dissatisfaction, particularly among victims who received their compensation in two installments separated by a gap of several years; during the wait for the second installment prices increased dramatically due to the progressive liberalization of the previously price-controlled economy.

Money also compensated ex-prisoners for some of the wider, more long-term consequences of their imprisonment, which were not limited to the direct effects of slave labor, inhuman treatment and torture, confiscation of property, reduction of wages, and loss of earnings. As mentioned earlier, the consequences of imprisonment for political offenses also included severe persecution after release, terrible social conditions, and denial of any opportunity to improve them. These experiences were often described by respondents in detail or their cost precisely calculated. Often imprisonment also had a drastic impact on the family of the prisoner. Unfortunately, the reparatory policy focused mainly on the victims without acknowledging the suffering and sacrifices of their families through, for example, awarding scholarships to their children or providing free transport for spouses. In addition budgetary constraints limited the scope of the policy. Some victims had a rigid, deontological view and felt that partial justice was still injustice.

Political prisoners' assessment of the financial compensation scheme depended not so much on the face value as on its symbolic meaning. For many, the amount of compensation was an indication of how society valued their sacrifice and past suffering. Financial compensation represented an acknowledgment that achieved more than mere words of apology or gestures ever could:

> Money cannot compensate us for our suffering or for the suffering of our families. Yet I think it is a moral gesture, which acknowledges it.[65]

> We live in a monetary society where one's social status and dignity is measured above all by money. The government should make our financial compensation equivalent to that given to prisoners of Nazism. This should be a minimum, though, because prisoners of communism were imprisoned for twice as long and continued to be harassed by secret police until the fall of communism.[66]

Just as financial compensation was a symbol of social acknowledgment, inadequate compensation was perceived to signify society's lack of concern for the prisoners' welfare. Some even concluded that by not providing them with adequate health care, society was quietly wishing that the political prisoners would die faster, thus putting an end to their effort to remember and to be the "consciences of the nation":

The Government could try to improve . . . our healthcare [e.g., in spas]. We think they are trying to make us disappear quickly—[they want us] to pass quietly away from this world.[67]

They got rid of us. They approved the law, some compensation arrived, and in doing this, they signed us off.[68]

Finally, monetary compensation acted as a proxy for justice. Dissatisfaction with financial compensation often stemmed from comparison with the treatment that perpetrators received. Most former political prisoners complained that perpetrators had received more compensation at the time of their forced retirement after the fall of the communist regime than they, the victims, had received for their suffering under the regime:

Prison wardens who tortured us were dismissed at the beginning of the 1990s, but with compensation of not less than CZK 100,000 and high pensions, while their victims continue to suffer with their pensions at the life minimum. Do you really think that these diehard communists would come to apologize to anyone? They are laughing into our faces.[69]

My wife and I went to a spa two years ago. We paid CZK 16,000 for three weeks. I got a CZK 2,000 discount as a former political prisoner . . . but former secret policemen had their spa free of charge.[70]

Many political prisoners demanded that they should have received the same pension and other benefits as perpetrators. For example, when asked what the government should do for political prisoners, a respondent suggested "transfer each political prisoner, regardless of the length of imprisonment, to the first pension category, like the one for secret policemen."[71]

As well as comparing their positions with those of perpetrators, victims also compared themselves with their "rivals," that is, high-profile dissidents, such as Charter 77 signatories and Prague Spring leaders who, as one interviewee put it, "got fame, return of property, high salaries, and especially power," after 1989.[72] The division between former political prisoners from the 1950s and 1960s and those from the 1970s and 1980s deepened after the Act on the Third Resistance was passed in 2011. The Act stated that resisters should receive a lump sum of CZK 100,000 as compensation for their acts of resistance. Many of those who had been imprisoned in the earlier part of the socialist era were not awarded the status of a "resister against the communist regime" because "they were merely in jail."[73] One interviewee contrasted the case of an ex-prisoner whose request for consideration as a member of the third resistance was declined, although he had spent fourteen years in jail, with the case of a dissident who printed an illegal journal, thus risking a jail sentence.[74]

Comparisons with perpetrators were a matter of justice, whereas comparison with dissidents was a matter of competition for social acknowledgment. The same social dynamic was apparent in their references to members of the formerly communist-sponsored anti-Nazi Association of Freedom Fighters (SBS). They felt that SBS members received wider social acknowledgment and more generous financial compensation. This frustration was reinforced because condemnation of the Nazi regime was socially uncontested whereas not everybody was ready to condemn the communist regime. Former political prisoners also compared their positions to those of current politicians who frequently claimed "astronomical" sums in compensation for defamation.[75] Hence "fair compensation" and "just satisfaction" appear not as individual categories but as broad social categories that take into account the position of an individual within the group and the position of an individual's group vis-à-vis other social groups.

Impact of Social Acknowledgment and Neighbors' Suspicion

Being regarded with suspicion by one's neighbors was negatively associated with both sociopolitical redress and individual healing. Although 11 percent of my respondents felt highly regarded by their neighbors, 4.5 percent considered that they were still regarded with suspicion. What were the reasons for this continuing hostility?

Many respondents reported that those who had informed on them in the past still lived in their neighborhood. Some felt their neighbors envied them their compensation:

They talk about hundreds of thousands in compensation[76] [or still considered them criminals who] should stay where they were.[77]

[Our neighbors were] a secret cop, [another] secret cop, [another] secret cop. A special neighborhood. They knew who I was, who we were. . . . After 1989, there was a bit of change. Some of them passed away, some of them were transferred, and some of them turned white. . . . The one who used to check my correspondence is always greeting me now, bows, cuddles my dog. The one who searched our flat . . . was begging me in 1968 not to tell the court anything; on his knees. What am I supposed to think of those people?[78]

It seems that lack of reconciliation, social ignorance about the experience of others, and disinterest in the past may have resulted in neighbors continuing to stigmatize former political prisoners. This implies that societal responses to the past were related to micro-level interactions between victims and their immediate community, and that the societal approach to dealing with the past influenced responses at the personal level. However, the healing effect of reconciliatory measures may be limited. Even when neighbors who participated in the persecution tried to change their attitude, they were not trusted.

Impact of Retributive Measures

One of the most surprising results from my survey was that criminal trials were associated with neither healing nor redress. Many respondents criticized perpetrators for showing no remorse. However, the majority did not demand that they be imprisoned. Many respondents called for symbolic justice, in the form of judicial condemnation of perpetrators, rather than retribution. They viewed Havel's slogan "we are not like them" as an attempt to draw a "thick line" under the past, a refusal to endorse prosecutions. A former political prisoner criticized Havel for his slogan yet advocated fair trials along similar lines:

After 1989, I organized three public meetings. The whole gym was cramped with people. A man was lashing out at communists. I stood up and said that I did not want that. We would be like communists. If someone is guilty because he violated laws that were in force at that time, he should be condemned in the normal way. But not in the way things were done in Hungary in 1956, where there was such [revengeful] euphoria.[79]

The absence of association between criminal justice and overcoming victimization is in line with similar research conducted in former Yugoslavia. Metin Başoğlu and others have concluded that the International Criminal Tribunal for former Yugoslavia, which was established with the expectation that the tribunal would bring to justice those responsible for human rights violations and facilitate healing of psychological wounds, would not reduce PTSD.[80]

Impact of Revelatory Measures: Public and Private Truth-sharing

One of the most fascinating findings in the survey was the ambiguous effect of truth-sharing on victims. Public truth-sharing was negatively associated with sociopolitical redress, whereas private truth-sharing was positively associated with greater inner healing.

The negative association between public truth-sharing and sociopolitical redress may have several causes. Many former political prisoners had attempted to use the media for public truth-sharing. Indeed, after the fall of the communist regime the media did report many horrific stories of victims' suffering. However, the media may not have been suitable forums for truth-sharing. Those who had tried to tell their stories in this way complained that limited space prevented them from telling their story fully and freely. Unfulfilled expectations were also a reason for the negative perception of truth-sharing of other ex-prisoners. Conscious of the constraints of old age, they saw truth-sharing as a way of compensating for their feeling of social marginalization and isolation from the political decision-making process. This may explain why the effects of truth-sharing lasted for so long. Instead of a psychological process, truth-sharing operated rather as a social process, which originated in the perceived social isolation and then turned into a political struggle. Many hoped that by increasing public awareness of the cruelty of the previous regime they would make society more vigilant against future threats. Some even viewed truth-sharing as their vocation—if those who had witnessed and experienced it firsthand did not disseminate the message, who would? The daughter of a former political prisoner, who had given talks in schools, in partnership with another ex-prisoner until he passed away, described the difficult experience of public truth-sharing:

> In spite of doing it for more than ten or fifteen years, I always feel very bad. It takes me until evening to get over it. I was too proud of myself, I thought that I was strong, but every single talk puts me off. Sometimes I read the children, as a reward, depending on the children, a letter from my father to me on my fourteenth birthday. I told my-

self that I would not do it anymore because it is about human nature, he was giving me advice about character development, which made me feel really obliged to behave in a way that would not disappoint him. But I am not sure whether it says anything to the children. . . . I told myself that I would not go anymore but now [after the death of her talk partner] I feel it is an obligation. As the communists rise, I feel it is an obligation.[81]

Some were frustrated by the general lack of interest in the past; sometimes the desire to move forward was manifested as a desire to forget the past. The lack of social acknowledgment reinforced the feeling that the rest of society wanted to forget the past. Some prisoners hoped that by telling the truth they would renew people's interest in the past. Only a handful of my respondents, mostly from the educated elite, had been able to publish an account of their experiences: "I described my fate as a co-author of a book *How to Walk in Rope*. . . . The nation should know the truth, although many are not interested in it anymore. This is the tragedy of our time."[82]

The negative association between public truth-sharing and sociopolitical redress contrasted with the positive association between private truth-sharing and healing. Private truth-sharing gave victims an opportunity to share their stories freely in a friendly, receptive atmosphere. Without this atmosphere, it is unlikely that such stories would have been shared. As well as recounting their stories verbally, some former political prisoners chronicled their experiences both to give their families a written record of their suffering and some moments of joy in jail and to record their disappointment and respect for certain inmates and their longing for their loved ones. The ambiguity of the distinction between public and private truth-sharing was apparent from the following interview.

A photographer came and he video-recorded [our meeting] and I told him everything. He spent about half a day at our home. . . . I did not feel well after that. I told myself it was a mistake. . . . I worried that I spoiled the future of my children and grandchildren. Because I am afraid . . . I told him everything, in detail; things that I don't normally share, such as who worked for us, who visited us, the people my father used to meet. . . . Then I regretted it. . . . But, inside, I was happy that I could share it. I have even written it down to leave something for my family, after I am not here anymore. They all know it anyway.[83]

Thus, the person assessed her experiences of a semiprivate truth-sharing positively but her experience shows that the difficulty of sharing details of her life persisted even twenty-five years after the end of the communist regime. Past experience of persecution had destroyed her trust in society.

As widely anticipated, truth-sharing facilitated social acknowledgment. Often neighbors were not aware that those who had returned from jail had been punished for political reasons. A former political prisoner recounted his recent experience with the local press, which had covered his life story:

> I am not anyone special. I cannot say that I desire publicity. But undoubtedly it helped in the neighborhood, because the majority of people thought that I was in jail for some mistake [on my part], some illegal act. You certainly remember that 99 percent of people voted for the [Communist] Party. Although they were not [Party] members, it had an effect. [At that time], political prisoners did not have any social credentials.[84]

The negative effect of public truth-sharing does not contradict other research. An empirical study of 134 victims conducted in South Africa has not established any significant link between the testimony at the TRC and reducing PTSD.[85] This may be due to the absence of any effect, the low sample size, and the design and implementation of that truth commission.[86]

Impact of Reconciliation

Lack of reconciliation with perpetrators, particularly perpetrators' perceived hostility, was negatively associated with perceived sociopolitical redress. Lack of reconciliation implies that the past continues to influence the present. Many victims and perpetrators reported hostile attitudes; reconciliation was rare after 1989. Although about half the respondents had met their perpetrators informally, a mere 4.5 percent had received an apology or other gesture of reconciliation. Many reported that perpetrators continued to treat them badly and were verbally offensive, arrogant, or indifferent, and made excuses for their past acts. This led former political prisoners to believe that judicial condemnation would facilitate reconciliation, although many did not demand punishment:

[S.] was a man who used to beat people because he was a sadist; he liked it. Nowadays he walks down the street. I sometimes see him. We initiated his investigation but after three years we got a reply that the case is subject to the statute of limitations. . . . I was thinking he was happy, that [S.] . . . I don't know why we forgave him. Why did we forgive the crimes? Why did we pardon them? I can't understand it until now. I cannot accept it. I am not vengeful and I don't want to see him in jail but [he should be declared guilty].[87]

General frustration that perpetrators had not acknowledged their part in past crimes generated resentment that thwarted the healing of wounds. Lack of acknowledgment may signify, in the eyes of victims, the continuing hostility of perpetrators and a view of them as a threat. This finding is consistent with research in former Yugoslavia, which has found an association between the perceived threats from those responsible for trauma and PTSD.[88] A possible solution is to try to empower victims and enhance their sense of control over their lives rather than consider the possibility of setting up a formal, carefully monitored voluntary mechanism to try to improve the outcome of interactions between perpetrators and victims. Indeed, empirical research has suggested that participation in the TRC had no effect on the survivors' level of PTSD.[89]

Sometimes there are obstacles to reconciliation on both sides. In the Czech Republic, rigid thinking and a justifiable loss of trust prevented some former political prisoners from overcoming their hostility to former adversaries. Although political prisoners lamented that communists were obdurate they would also voice contempt for those who had changed, regardless of how they behaved subsequently, seeing them as turncoats. This rigid perspective may be related to aging, to the experience of imprisonment during the formative years, and again to the fear of perpetrators and a lack of control over their lives. For this reason, a reduction in fear is likely to lead to a reduction in PTSD, followed by a change in beliefs about self, others, and the world.[90]

Impact of Democratization

Satisfaction with democratization was associated with a positive assessment of sociopolitical redress. This was easy to understand; politics was central to our respondents' lives. They had been politically active in the past; they had been punished for their political beliefs and thus became *political* prisoners.

They were *zóon politicons*, "political beings," people with an active enthusiasm for politics; this is clear from the data showing that about 36 percent were members of a political party or an association of interest after 1989. Some of them even held important roles in these organizations.[91] To my surprise, however, membership in a political party or an association of interest did not have any impact on redress.

Most had had high hopes about what transition would mean and felt betrayed when reality fell short of their expectations. They were particularly upset by the old networks' ongoing dominance over politics and the economy. As one respondent lamented,

> [In 1989] I strongly believed that genuine freedom, democracy, order, and justice would come. Now I am deeply disappointed because it is not true at all. Instead . . . gross [economic] crime, corruption, fraud of national property and banks . . . and politicians disinterested in solving the problems of the middle class. . . . I see these every day on TV and in the newspapers. I worry that the communists will win the next elections.[92]

> Another respondent said, "When I see deputies and senators who were members of the Communist Party and now they have employment, in which they do not do much but rest, drink . . . where is justice?[93]

As "political beings" some political prisoners politicized social and personal issues[94] or succumbed to conspiracy theories. Conspiracy theories were used to explain the complexity of the regime change in 1989. A few respondents made claims such as the following:

> Prague Spring leaders and [dissidents who signed] Charter 77 were in fact financed by the West via the KGB . . . to destroy the morality of the Czech nation.[95]

> I seek to warn . . . against the danger that a new generation faces. Just as Satan is cunning, communists know how to seduce the young and trusting population with their demagoguery and promises.[96]

These conspiracy theories were of two types: warnings to democrats that they must be wary of making mistakes that might be exploited by communists to regain power; and the most common category of warning, based on widespread changes of party affiliation after 1989, that communists have in fact never lost their power. Both types of warning reflected mistrust in political processes and fears that stemmed from firsthand experience of severe persecution, infiltration, and constant surveillance during the communist era.

Another obstacle to reconciliation was that the frame of reference of some of my respondents was very rigid. Many had a dualist worldview and divided people into two categories: "we" and "they"; "*mukls*" and "communists"; "good" and "bad"; those who adhered to their moral standards and those who did not. This dualism, paradoxically, mirrored the dualist perspective of their totalitarian oppressors. A dualist mentality is inconsistent with democratic principles based on the recognition of a plurality of views, which emphasize the need for compromise. Alas, political compromises were often viewed by political prisoners as a deviation from, or a betrayal of, their treasured principles. They were especially critical of political compromises made by the government if they affected measures of justice. An element of compromise involved in the preservation of much of the legal code of the repressive regime attracted criticism as did the *partial* decommunization, *alleviation* of past injustices, and reluctance to condemn the communist regime to *the same extent* as Nazism.

Discussion

In this section I summarize these findings and consider what implications they have for the practice of transitional justice.[97] My survey and qualitative data on victims' experiences demonstrate that reparatory, revelatory, and reconciliatory measures had a significant effect on victims. Retributive measures did not have any significant effect on victims in this study.

Retributive Measures Were Irrelevant for Healing and Redress

Punishment of perpetrators—perhaps because it was a rare occurrence—was not associated with either outcome. This finding is surprising in view of the anticommunist rhetoric of ex-prisoners and their demand for retributive justice. Together these findings suggest that although victims see the lack of trials as a major failure, trials did not enhance the process of healing or provide sufficient redress for them. However, their demands for trials did not automatically mean demands for punishment. Many did not want their aging adversaries to go through the same ordeal.

The findings from the Czech Republic suggest a degree of similarity with the findings of a survey of attitudes to the civil war among the Spanish general public: Paloma Aguilar, Laia Ballcels, and Hector Cebolla-Boado found that being a victim of Francoism significantly decreases the demand for criminal trials for violations of human rights.[98] However, there were not many trials in the Czech Republic and no trials in Spain. But what if there were more criminal trials? Would criminal trials heal victims?

The data only allow me to speculate about the eventual outcomes of healing and redress. Based on my observations of existing trials in the Czech Republic, a larger number of trials may have a negative effect on victims. Legally, in reality they seldom result in conviction, which is mainly due to an insufficient amount of evidence after many years; and socially, regardless of prosecution, the perpetrators are likely to remain defiant. Hence, trials may raise expectations that are likely to remain unrequited and so increase victims' frustration. My study provides evidence that the lack of condemnation and defiance by perpetrators had a negative impact on victims. On the other hand, the potential benefit of criminal trials is that they reveal the wrongdoers individually, and as such, it counteracts the unsatisfactory practice of collective condemnation. While many victims refer to particular wrongdoers by name, the collective condemnation of the communist regime, the Communist Party, and communism in general is quite prominent. Susanne Choi and I have described the process as the "collectivization of guilt."[99] The inability to prosecute individual perpetrators turns victims and perhaps also the rest of society against the collective entity responsible for the prosecution.

Lack of Reconciliatory Factors Exercised Rather Negative Effects

The lack of community acceptance (being the subject of continuing suspicion in one's neighborhood) was negatively associated with both healing and redress, while former adversaries' hostility was negatively associated with perception of sociopolitical redress. What would happen if reconciliatory methods were implemented? Qualitative evidence has suggested that overcoming imprisonment is prolonged by the loss of trust in society. However, Susanne Choi and I previously found that apology was a significant predictor of forgiveness.[100] Hence, if reconciliatory measures had been implemented in the Czech Republic, the outcomes of victims' healing and redress may have been considerably better.

Critical Role of Reparatory Measures

Financial compensation and the return to one's previous profession were positively associated with individual healing and sociopolitical redress. The strong association between financial compensation and both individual healing and sociopolitical redress may be mediated by symbolic as well as tangible factors. Financial compensation not only helped to meet the considerable economic needs of aging political prisoners; it represented a tangible acknowledgment of past suffering (when compared with the financial situation of other victims' groups) and acted as a proxy for justice (when compared with the financial situation of perpetrators). Reinstatement in one's previous profession was also a vital element of healing and redress, particularly for highly educated former prisoners of working age. Like financial compensation, formal reinstatement carries a symbolic meaning and acts as a form of social acknowledgment of the injustice suffered by victims.

In practice the symbolic significance of financial compensation proved a double-edged sword. I found cases in which compensation made it more difficult for former political prisoners to be accepted in their neighborhood and workplace. This cannot, obviously, be used as an argument against financial compensation; it makes the case for paying compensation an aspect of a broader reconciliatory policy designed to achieve social reconstruction. The practical value and symbolic significance of financial compensation seem to make it essential to any program of postconflict justice, financial constraints and administrative complexity notwithstanding. Replacing financial compensation with purely symbolic reconciliatory measures, such as social acknowledgment, apology, or truth-sharing, may not send a convincing message about the depth of political change. Hence, at least some aspects of healing can be facilitated by implementing as generous a scheme of financial compensation as economic circumstances permit.

Dual Effect of Revelatory Measures

The diverging effects of truth-sharing were another fascinating finding. Previously, supposed victims' needs to share and learn the truth had been used as an argument for two fundamentally different methods of transitional justice, namely, truth commissions and criminal trials. This argument has been part of the transitional justice literature since the early 1990s, yet the presented evidence cited in support is inconclusive; little quantitative evidence has been produced.[101] Large-sample surveys and survey experiments conducted by James L. Gibson and Amanda Gouws in South Africa suggest that the TRC had both contributed to an acceptance of amnesty and inspired reconciliation among some racial groups.[102] A panel survey of victims in South Africa conducted by David Backer linked the decline in the approval for amnesty with a change in perception about the degree to which the TRC had delivered the truth.[103]

My findings provide support for the argument that private truth-sharing has a therapeutic effect on victims. Victims who shared the story of their imprisonment privately with family members or friends were more likely to report healing whereas attempts to share the truth publicly were negatively associated with self-assessed redress. In the Czech Republic, public truth-sharing only occurred informally, when victims were interviewed or when they succeeded in sharing their experiences through the media. Many victims were dissatisfied when their narrations were edited and shortened. The accounts given by the victims were scrutinized by their fellow victims. The narrators were then criticized by their fellow victims for omitting important aspects of their shared experience, as if the narrators had been speaking on behalf of all the victims. The lack of a formal channel may account for the unsatisfactory results, in which case there is an argument to be made for the establishment of truth-sharing forums as part of a transitional justice policy. Victims' forums should provide everybody with a channel for truth-sharing. If carefully implemented so as to emulate the features of private truth-sharing, victims' forums could decrease the negative effects of public truth-sharing. Such forums are also likely to contribute indirectly to victims' healing by facilitating social acknowledgment and structural reforms. When victims share their experiences of suffering with the rest of society, it can both stimulate a greater understanding of the past and provoke sympathy and social acknowledgment, thus helping to dispel the stigma attached to victims. It can also reduce suspicion and hostility. In this way formal mechanisms for enabling victims to share their experiences can help to promote attitudinal changes in society and local communities, and correspondingly increase the social pressure on perpetrators to acknowledge their wrongdoing. Victims' testimonies about patterns of abuse can also drive and inform structural and institutional reforms. Reforms that are motivated and informed by an understanding of past abuses may also lead to social sanctions against perpetrators.

In concluding this chapter, it is important to acknowledge that the population of former political prisoners was aging and shrinking in size at the time this research was conducted. This also had a negative effect on their well-being. The statement "we are dying out" was one I heard frequently during interviews; it reflected the victims' sense of isolation and provided a clue to one of the coping strategies used by victims. It was a kind of informal motto, which helped to strengthen their togetherness and helped them to deal with the aging and passing away of many members of their fellowship. Many of the people who contributed to this study in 2000 and 2006 were no longer among us in 2014.

Chapter 4

Did Justice Measures Transform Communists?: Personal and Intergenerational Transformation

> Once [in the 1950s], on the way from a visit to some family, my granny said that communists tortured their daddy to death. I turned to a pillar of salt. I thought that I would perhaps kill her. How could she even say something so terrible?
>
> —J. Š., in Josef Alan, "Rodinné vztahy a členství v KSČ," in Zdeněk Konopásek, ed., *Otevřená minulost*

> In schools [after 1990], they teach those horrors. When my youngest grandson was perhaps in the second year in his primary school . . . he darted home all dumbfounded because his lady teacher told them that communists murdered people. And [asked] if granny also murdered anyone.
>
> —A current member of KSČM, interview, June 3, 2015

The previous chapter examined the effects of transitional justice measures on victims. This chapter turns the spotlight on the other end of the historical continuum: It examines the effects of transitional justice measures on the members of the Communist Party. It focuses on their "transformation," by which I mean the internalization of human rights and an acknowledgment that human rights violations were perpetrated in the past. Indeed, the lack of political transformation is one of the most apparent features of the successor Communist Party (KSČM) in the Czech Republic. Its hard-line stance, which contrasts with other successor parties in Eastern Europe, raises questions about the feasibility of transformation of the pre-1989 Party members and the role of transitional justice measures in facilitating or inhibiting their transformation. Did the emphasis on rehabilitation, restitution, lustration, and condemnation of the communist regime create an environment that would be conducive to the transformation of Communist Party members? Did revelatory measures provide them with an opportunity to learn from the past? Did they put former Communist Party members on the defensive and hamper their transformation? Was the lack of transformation a result of the neo-Stalinist legacy of their party, which was the most rigid and dogmatic in Central Europe? In order to examine these questions, I use original data from the survey and in-depth interviews with former and current Communist Party members, which I conducted in 2015.[1]

The chapter consists of four sections. The first section begins with illuminating the social relevance of the transformation of former Party members; it then conceptualizes the transformation of the Communist Party members as a two-dimensional process, encompassing personal and intergenerational transformation. The second section examines the Communist Party's membership before and after 1989, and it uses qualitative data to illustrate the reasons for joining and leaving the Party. The third section investigates the perception of justice measures by former and current Party members. The fourth section uses survey data to examine the role of justice measures in facilitating the transformation of party members, as well as qualitative data to investigate the social mechanisms of this effect.

Reforming Communists?

"There is no former communist." This assertion was first heard in the Czech Lands in the early 1990s.[2] It suggested that once someone was a member of the Communist Party, he or she remained a communist for life. The slogan was used by the political center-right in the ideological clash with the Prague Spring communists of 1968 who sought to reenter politics after 1989.[3] Many of the "sixty-eighters" became associated with the Civic Movement (OH), a centrist political group, which was seen as a competitor to the center-right Civic Democratic Party (ODS). By saying "there is no former communist," the sixty-eighters were put on an equal footing with all other communists. They were labeled altogether as the representatives of the communist regime who sought to derail ongoing political and economic transformation. The anticommunist rhetoric worked in the ODS's favor, and the OH lost in the elections of 1992 and 1996. The refrain that "communism is unreformable" resonates to date.[4]

The anticommunist slogans were augmented with biological characteristics. "A former communist is like a former black man," claimed some in the Czech Republic.[5] By equating an ideology with a physical feature its protagonists implied that some things are immutable.[6] In conjunction with the Act on the Illegitimacy of the Communist Regime, which condemned the communist regime as criminal, the reference implied that a communist is a criminal for life. Nothing could wash away the transgressions. A former member of a communist party could not distance him- or herself from what the Party had done. Even leaving the Party or being expelled could not eradicate the association with it. Twenty years of discrimination in professions, which was experienced by the sixty-eighters in the 1970s and the 1980s, could not change anything.[7] "One is either a communist or not a communist."[8]

The dogmatic perception of communism in turn affected the process of justice after transition. In 2010, a lawyer and activist, Tomáš Pecina, approached the Constitutional Court to obtain an order directing the Ministry of Justice to publish the names of former members of the Communist Party among judges and state attorneys. The Ministry of Justice lost the case, and in 2011 the Ministry published the names of 618 serving judges who used to be members of the KSČ. They constituted about one-fifth of the country's 3,076 judges. There were 359 former members of the KSČ among 1,272 state attorneys.[9] The lists were published for the purpose of transparency to enable the public to observe whether the judiciary was impartial. The daily *Mladá fronta Dnes*, however, automatically shifted the debate to dismissals, assuming that all former members of the KSČ were unqualified to be judges. In its online poll, readers were asked whether a pre-1989 membership in KSČ was a reason for the prohibition of judicial function. A large majority, 25,656, answered "yes," while 9,338 answered "no."[10]

To be sure, the apparent affinity of some judges to the communist regime is a cause for suspicion.[11] For instance, the infamous judge who was unable to conclude the trial of the alleged communist torturer Alois Grebeníček had been a member of the KSČ (see Chapter 2).[12] But suggestions that all judges and state attorneys, who had been KSČ members at a certain stage in their lives, were still loyal to the party were biased and unqualified generalizations.

On the other hand, the anticommunist slogans did not deprive communists and former communists of their social agency. KSČM did not do enough to dispel such generalizations. It failed to demonstrate a significant ideological difference from its totalitarian predecessor. Neither did anyone deprive the judges and state attorneys of their freedom to apologize for the human rights violations committed by the communist-era judiciary. Surely, apologies were difficult in view of hostile relations in society; the communists have been pushed into the corner and any cooperation with them has been prohibited at the central level.[13] But KSČM and its members owed an apology to those who had resisted pressure to join the Party, those who experienced injustices, those who eventually became its victims, and those who were forced to emigrate.

In view of the hostile external environment, there is currently no known reform wing within KSČM. The security risk of having an unreformed Communist Party increases as a result of Russia's growing territorial ambitions. As the third strongest party in the Czech Republic in 2013 (see Figure 6), KSČM openly supported Russia's position in the Ukrainian conflict.[14] The security risk further spread to their next generation. The Association of Young Communists of Czechoslovakia, the Communist Association of the Youth, and Young Communists are organizations for the new generation of communists. Many of them have been inspired by Marxism-Leninism, seek a return to the communist regime, and claim that the Czech laws do not apply to them.[15] According to the daily *Lidové noviny*, they planned an attack against a train transporting military material and also attacked police cars, police stations, and private property.[16] Although subversive activities of these associations were not widespread, they indicate radicalization among some communists of the second generation.

These examples raise questions about the extent to which the external environment, including a variety of measures of justice, facilitate or inhibit the transformation of the Communist Party, the members' personal transformation, and their intergenerational transformation. While personal transformation ensues from a backward-looking perspective, intergenerational transformation is prospective, relating to the conduct of the new generation in the future. Before I address the question, I am due to make a note about the nomenclature of personal change, which can be captured by the terms "transformation" and "reform." I opt for "transformation" as a process that encompasses a personal change, which mirrors a fundamental change of political system and which linguistically and conceptually corresponds with "political transformation" from the communist regime to democracy. I use "reform" when I refer to attempts to liberalize the Communist Party.

Transformative Perspective

"Who was not a communist at twenty was heartless and who was one at thirty was brainless" is one of the many paraphrases of a celebrated quote by the French revolutionary-era politician François Guizot.[17] This paraphrase epitomizes the radicalism of youth, which eventually dims as a person establishes his or her career and enters another stage in the cycle of life. The paraphrase also assumes that changes in political opinions occur. But how is such a change possible?

Political opinions are typically influenced by age, peer groups, social environment, social media, and other factors. They have been studied by political sociologists and political psychologists in the context of election campaigns and political advertising. For instance, results from a large-scale field experiment conducted by Alan Gerber and others showed that social pressure can influence citizens' willingness to vote.[18] In the social context, an eventual change of opinion may be a function of aggregate behavior; people tend to do what others do. In reality, however, it seems that people do what *some* people do, not what *all* people do.[19] If people were to do what all people do, then we would not have a problem of divided societies. People follow the groups they identify with, whether political or age groups. Such aggregate behavior may be amplified by social media, and hence its effect on the younger generation is likely to be more pronounced. An experiment with sixty-one million Facebook users conducted by Robert Bond and others found that online messages could influence offline behavior.[20]

In contrast, other scholars try to explain why people are resistant to change. For instance, Karl Mannheim argued that experiences in the formative years are the defining moments of each generation.[21] In their study of generations and collective memory, Howard Schuman and Jacqueline Scott confirmed that different cohorts remember different events that they experienced in their adolescence and early adulthood.[22] Memories resist change,[23] and people resist correcting misinformation if it fits their political beliefs.[24] This explains why, contrary to evidence, the majority of voters in the 2011

Republican primary elections in the United States believed that Barack Obama had not been born a U.S. citizen.[25]

On the intergenerational dimension, the influence of family has been scrutinized vis-à-vis other factors of political socialization. Although the family is generally considered more influential than peers, a question arises as to whether the critical role of family can be attributed to class background, lifestyle, ethnicity, race, social status, and cultural capital that are often shared by family members[26] and overlap with the broader social environment. Moreover, the classic sociological paradigms, that political behavior, values, and preferences are exclusively socially determined, have recently been challenged by advances in genetics.[27] The findings and nonfindings of genetic research are nevertheless incomplete without understanding the changing social and political context.[28] Some of the studies that have examined the experiences of twins have taken into account only the same genetic makeup but failed to also consider the same defining cultural experiences in their formative years, which are shared across regions and societies.

Very little has been done to examine the role of justice in changing political attitudes, although it has been routinely theorized that trials, amnesties, truth commissions, lustration, and apologies are likely to affect, positively or negatively, prospects for peace, reconciliation, and democracy. Most studies focus either on victims (see Chapter 3) or on societies in general; they rarely contrast the perspectives of perpetrators and victims.[29] Studies that examine any eventual change in wrongdoers, bystanders, and beneficiaries are lacking. In his survey of South Africa, James Gibson found that for white South Africans, truth leads to reconciliation and reconciliation leads to the acceptance of truth.[30] In her comparative country-level study, Kathryn Sikkink found a positive effect of trials although she could not attribute it to a deterrent effect or to socialization.[31]

In view of the gap in current research on justice and democratization, I shall examine the effects of retributive, reparatory, revelatory, and reconciliatory measures of justice on the transformation of former Communist Party members. Whether these measures transform or not is an empirical question. Little is known about the current attitudes and opinions of former members of the Communist Party and their offspring. Before I address the question, I will provide a brief list of characteristics of the Communist Party and its membership in order to disentangle the myth of their homogeneity. I will then examine their perceptions about the different measures of justice.

The Communist Party and Its Members

The Communist Party of Czechoslovakia held monopoly power in the country between 1948 and 1989.[32] As I described in Chapter 1, the politburo of the Communist Party was responsible for spearheading the repressive drive and "political management" of the secret police. The everyday implementation of the Party line was conducted by trustees of the Party and its cadre secretaries at the grassroots level. Every factory, school, and organization had a Communist Party cell, which made decisions about its leadership. Every workplace had a cadre secretary of the Party, who determined which candidates to hire or considered which employees to dismiss.

The unique position of the Party in the state apparatus, the political system, society, and the economy shaped the reasons why individuals joined its ranks. In addition to their ideological reasons for joining, many people joined the Party as a means of advancing their careers, while others sought to avoid discrimination toward themselves or their children. Some were offered material incentives to join, while others feared the consequences of refusing an offer to join. My in-depth interviews with pre-1989 members of the Communist Party, however, revealed a picture that was even more complex. Joining the Party was seldom motivated by a single reason.

For one interviewee, joining the Party was an "honest decision of a young person to make things better" and "almost a duty" if he wanted "to pursue a career."[33] The work ethics of that interviewee, rare in the past, suggested that the measure of idealism was plausible and did not serve as a disguise for his career ambitions. For other interviewees, the parents' influence seemed to be more pronounced.[34] The environment and family upbringing created a background that bolstered some interviewees, making them less susceptible to the pressure to join the Party in order to advance to better positions in the workplace:

> [In my neighborhood] there is an orthodox communist downstairs. My father-in-law was an orthodox communist—I would even say almost a chauvinist. Another neighbor is a ninety-year-old communist, a member of the Party. Here it is a hotbed. But this did not influence me. I am a son of workers; my mom and dad . . . used to work in

[a factory] but I was mainly influenced by my granddad . . . [who] was a social democrat, a big one. They debated with my mom; he was an awesome man with a great outlook. The leftwing thought was in me, always. . . . In 1978, I became a chief of the sales department and was thus a bit attacked to join. I did not like joining in this way as somebody was, in a way, dictating to me. So I zigzagged until I was about thirty-three years old, and I was told either/or, so you know how that was [at that time], so perhaps after [a] half year I nodded.[35]

The adverse family and social background was, however, sometimes defied in the face of recruiters who were regarded with respect:

[In 1958 or 1959] one professor, whom we really respected, because he was a very good painter, a very good person, though a Party member . . . came to me and my friend to tell us that he was proposing us as candidates for membership. We rejected it, both of us, very firmly. . . . And I clearly told the professor "please," because I believed that he would not talk about it: "I cannot promise it or sign it because the situation in our home is that my father was recently jailed because the communists in our village are like that." . . . And [the professor] used emotional pressure by asking whether he was the same as them. . . . At the end I succumbed to a mild deception that it was only a candidature: "You would do it for two or three years and only then join or not join the Party."[36]

Obviously, ending the candidature or not progressing to full membership would hardly be possible. The interviewee felt embarrassed about his membership, although he took the first opportunity to leave in 1968. For many others who joined later, there was no other chance to leave the Party until 1989. In 1989–90, many left because they no longer wanted to be associated with the Party, which had been discredited by its forty-two-year monopoly rule. Instead of a vehicle for furthering a career, Party membership turned into a liability. Some were even forced to leave as they had been forced to join: "My enterprise pressured me to join the Party [in 1985] and then [after 1989] it did not want us to be there."[37] Moreover, the decrease in membership led to the dissolution of some Party grassroots organizations and consequently to the further loss of members who did not have a place to register.[38] Many ambitious pre-1989 KSČ members decided to pursue their political careers in other parties. As a consequence of 1989, membership in the Communist

Party dwindled.[39] In January 1989, KSČ had 1,701,085 members in the whole territory of Czechoslovakia. In March 1990, the newly established Czech branch of the Party allegedly had 700,000 members.[40] Meanwhile, the Slovakian SDL, a successor to the Communist Party of Slovakia (KSS), voted to leave "the federation" of the two parties in December 1991 and subsequently left it in April 1992.[41] KSČM had 196,000 members in 1995; 121,000 in 2000; 88,000 in 2005; 62,000 in 2010; and 49,000 in 2015.[42] It is still the largest political party in the Czech Republic in terms of membership, and it may remain so, because membership in all the major parties has dwindled.[43]

On the other hand, many decided to stay in the Communist Party. Some stayed for ideological reasons; others did not want to be seen as opportunists. In rare cases, some were able to retain public support even during the critical years of 1989–90.

> I'm not a turncoat. [I vote for KSČM], always. Always [laughing]. . . . Neither are we, so to speak, watermelons: to be green on [the] surface and red inside.[44]
>
> I am still a member of KSČ[pause] M. . . . I come from a working-class family, and I always, I always tended toward the working class, although today it is not popular, but it's still just the way it is, and I see the social policy of KSČ that it keeps it. . . . I'm still here in the village, although there were pressures [on me to leave my position of the mayor after 1989] and I can say that of the forty-three [mayors in the district] we survived just two, everyone else was just replaced. . . . I was and remain with [our] people quite popular and liked because we had 780 citizens here before, and when I finished [as a mayor] there were 1,500 people. . . . For young people, we built six big rental [social] houses and we built the house for the elderly. . . . It's called, for seniors, well, for young people kindergarten, we expanded the entire sports facilities; today we have a stadium and a top sports hall.[45]

Such cases were, as the respondent acknowledges, relatively rare. But they defy the generalization of the membership as homogeneous.

The membership issue was linked to the reform of the Party. After losing its constitutionally protected monopoly in 1989, the Communist Party had to change its behavior as any other party in the political system would have been obliged to do. It needed to decide whether to start competing for new voters or keep its existing voters and members. At the intersection of these forward-looking and backward-looking objectives was the issue of reform. Reforming held out the possibility of attracting many of those who had been losers as a result of the transition measures and had opted to vote for democratic left-wing parties. Not reforming would mean the maintenance of the stable core of voters and members.

Initially, there was some appetite for reform. The notable attempts to reform the Party date back to 1990, when the Party elected a film director, Jiří Svoboda, as its leader. However, the reformers were defeated in 1992–93 by conservatives surrounding Miroslav Grebeníček. The subsequent attempts to establish the Party of the Democratic Left (SDL), led by Josef Mečl, and the Left Bloc (LB), led by Jaroslav Ortman, also failed.[46] The reform attempts, nevertheless, led to a further decrease in membership, as each leaving faction took some members with it. In 2015, a long-term member of the Party regretted the reluctance about reform:

> At a [recent Party] meeting I said, "Maybe you would not like to hear it, but I was the one who agreed to keep the name of the Communist Party, yeah, [. . . but] today I see that it was quite a mistake, because everyone spits on the communists. If it were called . . . otherwise, at least today it would not continue. Like Slovaks who turned it into some kind of a Left, there it is over, I do not know why or how. . . . But it is a pity that all the time they spit on communists. But the communists are not here anymore, the communists who were [at that time are not those] who are today [smile].[47]

The interviewee spoke of the anticommunist atmosphere in society, which in his view was associated with the lack of reforms within KSČM. He believed that a change in name would constitute a manifestation of reform and would be accepted by society.

Nonetheless, my interviews confirmed that an unreformed hard-line communist core remained. Some hard-liners used the vocabulary of the past with minor differences: Their vocabulary was emotionally charged with the bitterness of politically losing in 1989 and resentment toward subsequent changes. One of the interviewees admitted that "some mistakes" in the past occurred because "the leadership of the Party was unable to explain its politics to people."[48] However, the nationalization that took place after 1948 was necessary because "petty entrepreneurs went bankrupt." The hero of anti-Nazi and anticommunist resistance, "Milada Horáková, was condemned rightly," although "she should not have received the death penalty."[49] The revolution in 1989 happened not because the regime denied people their rights but because it granted them their rights.[50]

Perceptions of Justice by Communist Party Members

This section examines how the pre-1989 Communist Party members viewed justice after transition. The great variation among former Party members suggests that there was likely to be a corresponding variation in their perception of justice.

Perception of Retributive Measures

The regime change of 1989 was largely peaceful. The leaders of the Velvet Revolution successfully quelled desires for retribution and no major instances of revenge were reported in Czechoslovakia after 1989. Retributive justice measures were implemented by parliamentary acts shortly after that: the expropriation of the assets of KSČ and SSM in 1990; lustration in 1991; and condemnation of the communist regime as criminal in 1993. In parallel, individual prosecutions were launched, although with results that were disappointing for society (see Chapter 2).

Retributive measures condemned—at least symbolically—the Party and its members and collaborators. Most of them resented these measures, although some admitted that if gross human rights violations had occurred, their perpetrators should have been punished. Some pre-1989 Party members thought that they had paid for the property of KSČ and SSM from their Party contributions. Consequently, they considered the expropriation illegitimate or revengeful.[51] Others thought that the expropriation was justified, because the Party property had been stolen from the people anyway,[52] and the Party and the state were entwined.[53] Most pre-1989 members, however, lamented the consequences of the expropriation, which in their eyes led to fraud.

[The property of SSM] was absolutely devastated, looted. Really devastated, looted. It was not transferred to youth organizations. . . . It was privatized, looted and where are they [the properties]? Or they look now catastrophic . . . the hotels or travel agency. . . . In each region, there were tourist bases. . . . But the mode of transfer to "the Czechoslovak people," that was the name of the law; that is catastrophic. For it nobody was penalized. And it is the same with the property of KSČ. This was duly handed to someone who mismanaged it . . . and the Czechoslovak people got nothing from it.[54]

As Chapter 2 indicated, the communists and the rest of society may have largely shared the perception that the transfer led to property losses. However, they disagreed on whom to blame: They blamed each other.

The perception of lustration also varied. Some held realistic views of lustration, or considered it an understandable process that is conducted in any regime.[55] Others objected to its collective nature: The abusers should have been dismissed but foreign intelligence service and the economic counterintelligence service members should not have been affected. Many Party members opposed the process of exclusion entirely, although it had started in the Party itself as early as December 1989. Following its tradition of eliminating "the enemies within," the Party expelled several of its leaders, including the secretary general Miloš Jakeš and the leader of Prague communists, Miroslav Štěpán. "The party decisively parts from those who knowingly committed despotism, abused power, who became corrupt and corrupted others, from all who masked truth with falsehood, [and] committed devaluation of the ideals of socialism, fairness and justice."[56] In view of mass demonstrations that had been held across the country, this move was more a self-protective mechanism than principled. Their aim was to disassociate many from the past by expelling a few.

Perception of Reparatory Measures

Reparatory measures were beneficial not only to political prisoners but also to other disadvantaged groups. It is intriguing that some former Party members also had their property returned during the restitution process, thus benefiting from reparation directly. It is less surprising that others, who had been communist victims, who were purged from the Party, benefited from the reinstatement of their professions: They had been expelled from their employment after 1968 but could reenter it after 1990. The communists who had been victimized in 1968 thus had a chance to turn on the communists who lost in 1989.

In the army, the so-called *Obroda* [renaissance, rebirth] was set up. It was made up of officers who had had to leave the Army in '68, when they had held various civilian positions. They were then coming back into the Army. . . . We were pretty much oppressed, and they were driving. Even though from a professional perspective . . . we had learnt during those eighteen years, . . . they had never learned, and now suddenly they began to speak and advise, and so on. . . . And the second thing was that, of course, it was expected that the senior officers would have to leave and vacate their positions.[57]

There was great variation in their views about compensation and rewards for political prisoners. Some accepted the compensation, saying that it was wrong to punish people for their opinions.[58] Others supported the compensation of political prisoners but not the top-up of their pensions.[59] Some acknowledged that political prisoners should have been awarded medals because their acts had required courage.[60] Many others were dismissive of compensation, questioning the reasons for imprisonment. Some opposed "the third resistance," saying that the opposition to Nazism was not comparable with the opposition to the communist regime, while others supported the third resistance on the grounds that they considered the two oppositions to be similar.[61]

The opinions of pre-1989 Party members, however, did not vary in one aspect. Almost all interviewees, without being asked, were opposed to the restitution of church property.

Perception of Revelatory Measures

I found enormous variation in attitudes and perspectives among former members of the Party concerning revelations about the oppressive conduct of the past regime. Everyone's opinions were complex, sometimes contradictory, as each person strove to reconcile his or her changing representation of the past with historical evidence and a desire to uphold personal reputations.

For instance, a respondent maintained that knowing what happened is important in any situation. Without knowing, she claimed, she was not able to condemn Several Sentences in 1989. Several Sentences was an antigovernment petition that demanded dialogue between the opposition and the communist leadership, and it was condemned by many ordinary members of the KSČ without them ever having read it. Similarly, she considered that she lacked information on which to morally condemn Alois Grebeníček, the father of the former leader of KSČM, Miroslav Grebeníček; Alois Grebeníček had been an alleged communist torturer and had died without facing justice. These two instances appeared consistent until it emerged that she did not trust the public media, which she saw as "a massage of brains." Indeed, in my opinion, she turned from being an honest truth-seeker to being a filterer of inconvenient information. Her reference to the Several Sentences appeared to be a token attempt to instill the perception that she was an objective person.[62]

Some interviewees expressed trust in the archives of the secret police. They sometimes referred to Cibulka's lists of secret collaborators, which they acknowledged they had used to search for the names of their colleagues and acquaintances. Others doubted that the list was complete. These suspicions were unexpectedly confirmed during an interview with a female respondent who had remained a member of KSČM. She claimed that she could not trust the archives because they were "torn, plucked" because "those who held power [after 1989] plucked them," so "they [the new elite] could always remain clean." The interview was suddenly interrupted by her husband, who turned out to be a former StB officer, who passed by, uttering, "We destroyed as much as we could."[63]

Perception of Reconciliatory Measures

The need for an apology from the Communist Party for the injustices of the communist regime has been a recurring theme in post-1989 politics. Political prisoners' organizations, center-right parties and their representatives, intellectuals, and some members of civil society have demanded an apology. In response, the politicians of KSČM always reply that they have already apologized. Some ordinary members of the Party repeat the following official line: "There has already been an apology. As far as I know, an apology was made, and what do they think, they want [us] to apologize [again]?"[64]

One of the reasons for the unwillingness to apologize is that the issue has always been contentious within the Party. Initially, the progressive wing demanded an official apology, while the conservatives were against it, claiming that there was nothing to apologize for. Most reformers left the Party after their voices were not heard. However, there is no clear-cut distinction to suggest that those who left the Party stood for apology and those who stayed opposed it. One interviewee was apologetic even though he remained a member of KSČM; for another, who had not been a member before 1989, the issuing of an apology in 1989 was a reason to leave the Party:

Why were they hiding, these people [communists], when they did not do anything bad. I said, "Why you give in to everything," it's wrong after all. After all . . . I did not kill [the anticommunist resister] Horáková, yeah, neither did I tell on her, after all I was not even born. . . . I have never done anything wrong, my conscience is clear and I think that, I think the left-wing idea is not bad at all.[65]

One would expect that the respondent was a hard-line communist because he thinks that communists "did not do anything bad." But his support for the social democrats and his reformist view about the name of the Party suggested otherwise. His arguments against apology also arose as a matter of the stated fact that he and other Party members were not personally responsible for crimes committed by others and that those who apologized were not personally responsible either. He admitted that wrongs had occurred but these were committed by individual perpetrators, not the communist regime as a whole. Indeed, many other former Communist Party members during their interviews expressed an individualistic perspective to perpetrators of gross human rights violations. They tried to disassociate a few tainted individuals in their attempt to purify the group.

Transformation of Communist Party Members and Their Offspring

In this section, I examine whether different measures of justice prevented or perpetuated personal and intergenerational transformation. For the purposes of empirical analysis, I conceptualize the transformation of the Communist Party members and their descendants as a process of the internalization of human rights. It reflects an acceptance of the communist regime as one that systematically violated human rights. Human rights are thus used as a value-normative standard against which personal and intergenerational transformation is empirically assessed. In view of the heterogeneity of opinions among the pre-1989 members, and given the defiance of the KSČM officials, this fact is not obvious within the membership and is expected to vary greatly.

To empirically examine the transformation, I analyzed quantitative data from a nationwide survey I conducted in 2015 to find out whether there was an association between the perceived success of justice measures and the internalization of human rights.[66] I used the analyses of qualitative data from

Table 4. Characteristics of the Transformed and the Untransformed

	Personal Transformation		Intergenerational Transformation	
	No	Yes	No	Yes
N	68	50	57	112
Sex	44.1% Female	34% Female	45.6% Female	58% Female
Age	66.69±8.71	63.86±6.94	33±8.42	31.68±8.81
Education				
primary	25.0%	26.0%	10.5%	16.2%
apprentice	47.1%	32.0%	40.4%	28.8%
secondary	16.2%	26.0%	33.3%	41.4%
tertiary	11.8%	16.0%	15.8%	13.5%
Mean income (in CZK)	12514±5812	13776±5529	15111±11212	12393±7997
Divorced	11.8%	10%	8.8%	12.5%
Retired	72.1%	72%	—	—
Urban	73.5%	78%	73.7%	79.5%
Rehabilitated	4.4%	4%	7.0%	9.8%
Restituee	19.1%	20%	19.3%	21.4%
Evicted	5.9%	4%	8.8%	2.7%
Lustrator	17.6%	34%	14.0%	11.6%
Reparatory	7.54±2.34	7.58±2.69	7.66±2.04	7.32±2.38
Revelatory	6.03±2.69	6.94±2.10	6.64±2.34	6.91±2.40
Retributive	9.12±3.23	7.68±2.80	8.48±3.13	6.67±3.33

Source: Roman David, "Twenty-Five Years of Dealing with the Past," machine-readable data file, 2015 (on file with the author).

interviews conducted in parallel in 2015 to explain the social mechanisms underpinning the association, and to discuss whether there is any causal link between the justice measures and transformation.

Table 4 shows the variation in my sample. Some 118 respondents, which represent about 12 percent of the nationwide sample, were members of the Communist Party before 1989. Among them, 50 agreed that the former regime violated human rights, while 68 of them disagreed or held a neutral opinion. Some 418 respondents in my sample had a parent or a grandparent who had been a member of the Communist Party.[67] However, for the purposes of the analysis of intergenerational transformation, I selected respondents who were 18 or younger in 1989; intergenerational transformation would lose its research import if it concerned the retirees whose parents were communists. Table 4 does not show many apparent differences among the

Table 5. Predictors of the Personal and Intergenerational Transformation

	B	SE	B	SE
Sex	0.75^	0.44	−0.37	0.37
Age	−0.09*	0.04	−0.02	0.03
Education	−0.02	0.24	−0.01	0.20
Income	0.00^	0.00	0.00	0.00
Divorced	0.14	0.77	0.48	0.72
Retired	−1.44^	0.80	—	—
Urban	−1.70**	0.62	0.37	0.44
Catholic	−0.18	0.46	0.40	0.58
Rehabilitated	1.08	1.13	−0.27	0.66
Restituee	−0.40	0.60	−0.93^	0.48
Evicted	1.52^	0.89	0.31	0.98
Lustrator	−0.32	0.52	−0.95	0.69
Reparatory	0.28*	0.14	0.10	0.09
Revelatory	0.24*	0.11	0.34***	0.10
Retributive	−0.39**	0.12	−0.26***	0.07
LR Chi^2	40.25		28.09	
N	89		123	

Source: Roman David, "Twenty-Five Years of Dealing with the Past," machine-readable data file, 2015 (on file with the author).
$^\wedge p < .10$; $^* p \leq .05$; $^{**} p < .01$; $^{***} p < .001$.

transformed and untransformed groups. It shows, though, that the transformed were younger, better educated, and earned a larger income. There were more men among the personally transformed. The personally transformed used the lists of secret police collaborators to (lustrate) look for persons of their interest. There were apparently more people who were rehabilitated in terms of the 1990 Rehabilitation Act in the intergenerational transformation group. As to the sufficiency of transitional justice measures, revelatory measures seemed positively associated with both dimensions of transformation, while retributive measures seemed to be negatively associated with both of them.

I now turn to statistical analyses to determine the factors associated with transformation. The internalization of human rights was captured in a question about whether the previous system systematically violated human rights.[68] The examined predictors included experience with justice measures (whether a respondent was rehabilitated, received any property in restitution, was evicted from home as a consequence of restitution, and used lists of secret collaborators to search for any known name) and views about the success of three clusters of justice measures (retributive, reparatory, and revelatory), controlling for a set of sociodemographic variables (sex, age, education, income, marital status, employment status, and urban residency).

Table 5 shows the result of the statistical analyses of the two aspects of transformation.[69] All else being equal, the former communists who were older were less likely to be transformed. Those who resided in urban areas, which allowed respondents to evade personal scrutiny, were also less likely to have been transformed. Personal transformation was also associated with those who viewed the measures of reparatory justice as sufficient. Both personal transformation and intergenerational transformation were associated with those who positively appraised the revelatory justice measures and inhibited by those who positively appraised the measures of retributive justice.[70]

In the research described in this chapter I sought qualitative evidence that would help to explain these associations and shed light on the possible causal links. I start with revelatory and reparatory measures, which help me to explain the views about retributive and reconciliatory measures.

Role of Revelatory Measures

Views of revelatory measures as successful were positively associated with personal transformation. The mechanism of their transmission can hardly be doubted: *Some* people change as they learn about the past regime.

> I did not know about Havel during totalism [*sic*] at all. Only in 1989 I learnt about him after various happenings . . . and then he was probably rightly elected. . . . I remember him saying that he got always arrested when a foreign delegation from the West [arrived]; they preventatively arrested him. What I liked about him that he did not play that card, neither complained about it.[71]

The respondent did not know about Havel and was unaware of the scale of human rights violations. But when he learned about Havel's persecution, he was ready to admit that it was wrong. He also appreciated Havel's nonretributive stance.

In spite of being able to facilitate a change, the effect of revelation on personal transformation was limited to several cases, among which we can distinguish two (not necessarily exclusive) mechanisms. First, some inter-viewees assessed the success of revelation by their own experiences of the past. A few of them saw the problems of the communist regime before 1989, or even long before they actually witnessed the violation of human rights. For these people, revelation was successful, but they did not need to be transformed. Conversely, others who never personally encountered any injustice did not trust any source of information that did not fit their experience.

Second, some interviewees judged the value of revelation in terms of a personal ideological scale. They held a priori attitudes, which filtered out information that could not be organized into a coherent set of their beliefs. Those who never believed in communism easily accepted its media represen-tation as a regime that violated human rights, while those who believed in communism rejected any negative information from noncommunist sources of the present regime. For instance, a member vigorously argued against the history textbooks that he viewed as biased against communism. But when asked he admitted that he had not seen any.

In both categories, revelation did not have an effect on personal trans-formation. Personal experiences and ideological positions determined the assessment of revelatory measures as well as respondents' views of human rights. Although they may overlap, the analytical distinction between expe-rience and ideology is significant. The individual experiences cannot be passed to their offspring.

Indeed, revelation implemented by means of new school curricula and the media seemed to be a major factor in intergenerational transformation. A man who maintained that the communist regime had not violated human rights, and that political prisoners had been rightly condemned, had his opinions scrutinized by children who attended a school:

> I had exchanges with my children when they learnt [about the past at school], but somehow luckily they still had teachers who were normal. . . . I can normally [discuss politics] with my wife but with children it's somehow half-half.
> *So, do you sometimes quarrel about it? Does anything make you angry in those debates?*
> Well . . . from time to time I lose my temper but I am already calm.
> *So they have different political opinions only, or what?*

Political. . . . That they would have different, no, but they interpret them differently, so to speak. . . .
So, your children have thus different [opinions], or they differently interpret . . .
Well, their [opinions] are influenced, unfortunately.
By contemporary . . . ?
The contemporary media, yeah. But, well, somehow . . . I am not a family outcast.[72]

Another interviewee had this to say in regard to the influence of the media on the attitudes of his children:

I have two sons. No, we don't argue. We can talk about some things. They, the young lads, see it a bit differently. . . . They are a bit more radical, they are more manipulated by the media. But in principle they are not, in principle they are the same. In some issues they may have a more critical view due to the influence of the media.[73]

The changes in school curricula and the media seem to be effective factors for intergenerational transformation. The exposure of the young generation to these sources poses a challenge to the old generation holding communistic worldviews. Revelation prompts and enhances intergenerational transformation.

Nonetheless, the large number of the untransformed second- and third-generation members also points to the limits of revelatory justice measures in facilitating change. If all offspring went to school and were exposed to the revelation, why did some transform and others not? This prompts a question about the strategies that the older generation adopted to maintain their influence over their offspring. What mechanisms did they employ to neutralize the influence of the media and schools? Quarreling and insisting on their authority and dogma could hardly have prevented the young generation from drifting away from the views of their parents. Neither would cultivated debates about the past influence the youngsters who are amply supplied with evidence about systematic human rights abuses of the communist regime. I found that pointing at the common class background ("we were always poor") and highlighting the problems of the current regime ("the present has more problems than the past") were instances of a plausible counter-rationalization.

The most effective means of control was, however, via the intimacy of family relations.

An interview with a seventy-six-old grandmother exposed the power of familial ties.[74] Although it is impossible to determine how typical the following example is, it illustrates the reproduction of the communist ideology in families. The interview showed that she had been a communist hard-liner (e.g., she held the view that the socialism with the human face during the Prague Spring was an attempt at counterrevolution), demagogic in her arguments (e.g., in her view crimes in the past occurred because many turncoats joined the Party to pursue their careers), and a dedicated Party member (e.g., she distributed leaflets, maintained a notice board, wrote articles to newsletters). These attitudes are hardly likely to persuade the young generation about the validity of reports about the judicial murders and human rights abuses of the communist regime. But the embrace of love, empathy, care, and kindness coupled with emotional blackmail (e.g., "so you think that I am a murderer") thus enabled communism to withstand the scrutiny of it. As a result, her son helped her to distribute Party leaflets and her grandson accepted that "granny did not kill anyone." One could just picture the happy family holding hands and united in their thinking that all the revelations about the crimes of the communist regime were merely slander.

Role of Reparatory Measures

Reparatory measures were positively associated with the degree of personal transformation. This association is hardly surprising since compensation, social acknowledgment, and the restitution of properties were designed to rectify the consequences of human rights violations. Although I cannot rule out reverse causality in some cases, suggesting that the awareness of human rights abuses led to the appreciation of reparatory measures, the historical conditions in the country suggested that reparatory measures brought a greater awareness of human rights abuses committed in the past. During the communist regime, even KSČ members may have been aware that *some* wrongs occurred. However, the sheer scale of these human rights violations and their systematic nature were only conveyed after the Rehabilitation and Restitution Acts were passed in 1990 and 1991, respectively. The general nature of these acts that had been promulgated to remedy injustices inflicted on whole classes of people clearly indicated that the communist regime did not commit only a few individual wrongs.[75]

Qualitative data allude to this interpretation that linked the (absence of a) collective nature of reparatory measures with (the denial of) systematic violations of human rights. Two of the interviewed persons tried to avoid the question about the rehabilitation of former political prisoners because they saw the problem as being too general. Instead, they argued for rehabilitation law that would depend on a case-by-case approach.[76] In their view, human rights were not violated systematically. Again, there appears to be strenuous insistence on the individual perspective. Unlike the above case concerning criminal responsibility, where it concerned in-group members (the Communist Party), in this case the individualization concerns out-group members, namely political prisoners and other victims of the communist regime. The plausible explanation for this individualization is the link between the scale of reparatory measures and the reputation of the Communist Party members: Systematic violation supports the anticommunist position that communism is wrong in itself. Indeed, the link appeared again in the following discussion.

Role of Retributive Measures

Retributive measures were negatively associated with both dimensions of transformation. The negative association seems intriguing at first glance. Normally one would expect a positive link between retributive justice and the internalization of human rights. Fortunately, the following analyses of the retributive measures, their historical context, and qualitative interviews can help to resolve the puzzle and shed light on the causality in this association.

The negative association between retributive justice and the internalization of human rights may produce different dynamics in different groups of people. First, there may be an association without any causal link. The nominal members of the Communist Party did not need any transformation. They may have joined the Party for career purposes, they may not have believed in communism, and they clearly saw that the regime violated human rights. They may have considered the existing retribution unsuccessful because they knew about these violations and needed to distance themselves from the taint of their membership.

Second, there may be a reverse causality and interplay with revelatory and reparatory measures among some respondents. Increasing revelation and the broad nature of the reparatory process may have led to the internalization of human rights, as documented in the above sections. Those who had, because of revelatory and reparatory measures, already been transformed— in personal and intergenerational terms—may have considered the retributive measures as unsuccessful. These links may have been influenced by higher education (see Table 4), which could make respondents more receptive to the revelatory and reparatory measures.

Third, lustration, condemnation of the regime, and expropriation of communist property may have been seen as excessive punishments against all Communist Party members, impeding their transformation. Hypothetically, retributive measures may exercise their effect via fear of reprisal, which triggers self-protective mechanisms that are manifested in defiance and lead to the denial of human rights violations, and so hampering transformation. Alternatively, retributive measures may effect transformation via the delegitimization of the regime, dishonoring its proud "builders" and disparaging their "work achievements," thus challenging the dignity of their life, which would again lead to defiance and the denial of human rights violations, thus hampering transformation. Unlike the previous two causal mechanisms, the second one is more complex and requires further investigation. In the first step, I needed to establish that the retribution was seen as excessive; in the second step, I needed to determine whether its impact on defiance about human rights is facilitated via fear or dishonoring.

I identified historical and qualitative evidence that lustration was viewed as excessive. Historically, the lustration debate culminated in the approval of the lustration law on October 4, 1991. It was accompanied by allegations raised by Alexander Dubček that lustration would lead to the dismissal of one million people, predominantly communists.[77] In the same month, KSČM launched an intraparty referendum on the name of the Party. At the center of the debate was not only a nominal change of the word "communist" but potentially also the ideological orientation of the Party. About 75.9 percent of members voted for keeping the word "communist" in the name of the Party.[78] The result of the referendum may have been a sign of unwillingness to reform, a result of a fear of being viewed as an opportunist and a turncoat, but it may have also been motivated by a fear of dispersing a group that provided a sanctuary in an increasingly anticommunist society. Thus, there is a clear historical association between justice after transition, on the one hand, and the transformation of the Communist Party and its members, on the other.

Qualitatively, interviews with pre-1989 members, analyzed in the third section of this chapter, confirmed that many did find the retributive legislation excessive. For instance, one interviewee who saw the nationalization of Party property as revenge and lustration as bullying claimed that the communist regime never violated human rights.[79] Conversely, another Party member who approved the expropriation of the Party's assets and saw the exclusion of those who were employed in political branches of the secret police as justifiable, also accepted that the previous regime violated human rights.[80]

But was the link between the perceptions of retributive measures as excessive and a lack of transformation facilitated via fear? The interviews, though conducted in 2015, did not show even slight evidence of fear. None of the interviewed pre-1989 members of the Party feared for their personal safety and no one indicated that he or she had been disadvantaged due to his or her membership in KSČ. They disagreed with the frequent reemergence of the petitions on banning the Communist Party because they considered it undemocratic; but they were not afraid that it would happen and did not feel threatened by it.

The key mechanism of transmission was the view of retributive measures as anticommunistic. Retributive measures dishonored the communist regime and debased the life achievements of the Party members. They did so to a greater extent than what many of the members saw as fair. This may have triggered a self-protective mechanism that led them to oppose any more criticism. For the same reason, admitting that the regime violated human rights signified self-debasement. Hence, there is a negative *association* between the appraisal of retributive measures, which are seen as excessive and demeaning, and personal transformation. Hence, rather than a source of protection from reprisals, the Communist Party was more seen as a sanctuary for likeminded people.

Nevertheless, it is possible that this is merely an association that is coincidental and may have been caused by factors that occurred in the past. Alternative explanations for this association are based on (1) the ideological rigidity of the Communist Party and a plausible resistance to any criticism raised against their members (some communists were dogmatic then and now), and (2) an experience of the regime change, in which they lost power and never regained it (they adopt self-protective mechanisms because they are no longer protected by the power of its repressive apparatus). Hence, the causal link about the effect of retributive measures cannot be established with certainty. What can be said is that the adopted retributive measures—lustration laws, the Act on the Illegitimacy of the Communist Regime, and the expropriation of the party—were not helpful in facilitating the transformation of former Communist Party members.

Role of Reconciliatory Measures

A "dishonoring" mechanism was also detected between the reconciliatory measures and personal transformation. The appraisal of apology, as an instance of a reconciliatory measure, statistically operated on the same dimension and in the same direction as the appraisal of retributive measures. In other words, when used in the statistical model instead of retributive measures, apology inhibited both dimensions of transformation. As one interviewee said, "First, I disagree with apology. Second, the apology was given, but they don't want to hear it and only increased their demands. . . . Because it is not an apology that matters but to dishonor the party."[81] The link between the sufficiency of apology for the injustices of the past and the lack of personal transformation was deeply rooted in protecting the good name of the regime. For others, views of apology as insufficient signified their personal transformation. Personal transformation was the cause and the assessment of apology as insufficient was the effect. The causality runs exclusively in this direction in intergenerational transformation. The revelatory and reparatory measures inspired intergenerational transformation, which led to the assessment of apology as insufficient.

Discussion

To go back to the beginning of this chapter, I can refute claims that there are no former communists. The pre-1989 Communist Party membership can hardly be considered a homogeneous group. Some of them transformed, while others remained hard-liners. Some felt ashamed of their membership; others remained proud. Some may have been members of the Party who never believed in communism.

Retributive measures did not facilitate personal transformation; in fact, they may have inhibited transformation. Although I have not found evidence that they created fear and deterrence, the sweeping retributive measures may have triggered self-protective mechanisms among many Communist Party members, increasing their defiance and hampering their transformation. The self-protective mechanism may have been triggered as a result of losing face and being disparaged and "morally condemned" in spite of the genuine effort to "build socialism."

Moreover, sweeping retributive measures and the anticommunist rhetoric behind them had collectively labeled as enemies even those who were not enemies and could have transformed. All of them have been portrayed as eternal members of the Communist Party and the anticommunist rhetoric did not allow them to leave. Indeed, the collective effects of retributive measures have been detected even among individual retributive measures. The studies of the International Criminal Tribunal for Former Yugoslavia suggest profound collective responses to a judicial verdict, depending on the group membership of the perpetrator and the outcome of the trial.[82] If individual measures of justice create collective effects, we can expect that such effects would be magnified in cases of collective measures. All of these findings suggest that the emphasis on retribution did not produce transformative effects.[83]

The negative association between reconciliatory measures and both dimensions of transformation was rather unexpected. In fact, I detected a reverse causality, suggesting that transformation leads to a negative assessment of apology. The reconciliatory measures were not able to produce any transformative effects because they were virtually absent for twenty-five years. More effort will need to be done for apology to inspire transformation. The initiative should start with KSČM but needs to include a broader social effort. The eventual apologies given by the KSČM leaders would not be accepted by many Party members. They saw apologies as a challenge to what they perceived to be their proud legacy. Apology in this format would not have any effect on personal transformation. The words "they don't want to hear it" in an interview suggest that unless the social environment becomes more receptive, apology is likely to be counterproductive. It could cost the leader who apologizes his office, unsettle the followers, and be dismissed by society. But, again, nobody prevents KSČM from taking the initiative to establish a forum that would negotiate the wording of an unequivocal apology with victims' associations, political parties, and other social groups.

Unlike reconciliatory measures, revelatory measures were an effective tool for achieving personal and intergenerational transformation. Revelations about the abuse of power in the past created a direct link to the internationalization of human rights. Before 1989, many people knew that there had been problems in the past but they were not aware of their scale. Learning about modern history thus became an effective tool for human development and personal transformation in general. Revelations were also effective in intergenerational transformation. The generation of parents and grandparents faced rebellious offspring who learned about the atrocities of the communist regime from textbooks at school (see Chapter 2), from the media, and from eyewitnesses. Some of the youngsters maintained the views of their families but many accepted the view that the communist regime had systematically violated human rights.

The former Communist Party members use an individualistic perspective, in particular concerning responsibility and apology. The rest of society in contrast adheres to the collectivistic perspective, which holds an indiscriminate view of the Communist Party and the communist regime. This is a paradox because one would expect that it would be precisely opposite in both cases: The communist ideology emphasizes collectivist thinking, while the liberal and social liberal ideologies are largely individualistic.

The emergence of the individualistic perspective among communists can be explained by social identity theory. Accusations are a form of attack against a valued group identity. Such attacks trigger a self-protective mechanism among in-group members, such as denial ("it did not happen"), the increase of justice standards ("show me more evidence"), or the condoning of wrongdoing committed by other in-group members ("it is moral when we do it").[84] Assigning the guilt to a few individual wrongdoers emerges as a strategy that absolves the rest of the group. A similar social dynamic underpins thinking about international criminal tribunals.[85] Punishing a few leaders (war criminals) is believed to enable the rest of the group to move on, untainted by the past. Trials, and in particular international criminal trials (had they taken place in the Czech Republic), would be a less effective way of dealing with the past than expelling the wrongdoers from their party. The difference between prosecuting leaders at criminal tribunals and their expulsion is that the former is administered by the out-group(s) and the latter is administered by the in-group. Acknowledging a few unfortunate aberrations by a few individuals in the past has allowed the communists to preserve their reputations in their own eyes. Gustáv Husák, Miloš Jakeš, Miroslav Štěpán, and other expellees have been eternalized as individually responsible for human rights violations. Individualistic thinking has emerged as a self-protection strategy for the Communist Party.

PART III

Justice in a Polarized Society

Chapter 5

Could Justice Measures Transform the Divided Society? Experimental Evidence About Justice and Reconciliation

We are all—though naturally to differing extents—responsible for the operation of the totalitarian machinery. None of us is just its victim. . . . We should not forget any of those who paid for our present freedom in one way or another. Independent courts should impartially consider the possible guilt of those who were responsible for the persecutions, so that the truth about our recent past might be fully revealed.

—Václav Havel, New Year's address to the nation, January 1, 1990

The previous two chapters, which formed Part II of this book, examined the effects of justice measures on two pivotal sections of Czech society in transition from the communist regime: victims of human rights abuses, and pre-1989 members of the Communist Party. This chapter and the next, which form Part III, examine the effects of justice measures on society as a whole. They explore the answers to the following questions: Did the four categories of justice measures—retribution, reparation, revelation, and reconciliation— have an effect on society as a whole? Did they in fact have the capacity to affect society as a whole? Indeed, the question about capacity is significant in view of problems with the design and implementation of justice measures that were discussed in Chapter 2. The outcome of the measures may not be attributed to the measures per se but to their scope and implementation. This chapter therefore employs an experimental design to examine the potential of the justice measures. Chapter 6 will then examine the effect of the justice measures as they were implemented.

More precisely, this chapter examines the potential impact of retributive, reparatory, and reconciliatory measures on the shared perceptions of justice and reconciliation in society as a whole. It is based on an experimental vignette, which was embedded in a nationwide representative survey of 1,067 respondents in the Czech Republic in 2010. This chapter is divided into four sections. First, I examine the perception of justice and reconciliation as a normative background for the assessment of justice measures. Second, I provide readers with the results of a qualitative inquiry into understanding justice and reconciliation in a divided society. Third, I review survey experiments that have been conducted in the area of transitional justice, and I describe the setting up of my transitional justice experiment. The fourth section presents the results of the experiment. In the conclusion, I discuss the impact of the measures of justice on the perception of justice and reconciliation, and I compare those results with my other experiments.

Justice and Reconciliation

What is the potential of each of the four transitional justice measures? Which of the four clusters of transitional justice measures is perceived by society as a whole as the most effective? Which measure is the most effective within each cluster? These questions beg for the assessment of a larger spectrum of justice measures by means of an experimental method, which is able to manipulate various scenarios of dealing with the past.

The question is, How can we assess transitional justice measures? What can serve as a normative background for the assessment of retributive, reconciliatory, and other measures of justice? As mentioned in the Introduction, the assessment of transitional justice needs to be couched within the parameters of democracy or its preconditions. However, questions about how to avoid a return to a repressive communist regime and how to enhance prospects for democratic transformation cannot possibly be influenced by experimental manipulation. The perceptions that people hold about democracy and totalitarianism are derived from a mixture of real-life experiences; therefore, constructing scenarios of justice, however realistic, is hardly likely to change people's preferences for one political system over another. Instead of abstract terms like "democracy" and "totalitarianism," I selected "justice" and "reconciliation" as two preconditions for democracy.[1] They can respectively serve as backward-looking and forward-looking objectives for an assessment of the success or failure of justice measures in dealing with the past.[2] They reflect the fundamental dilemma faced by transitional societies and captured in the so-called torturer's problem: "Prosecute and punish versus forgive and forget."[3] They suggest that the pursuit of retrospective justice may undermine the prospect for peace and reconciliation in the future.

However, such a one-dimensional perspective appears at times too mechanical and rather obsolete.[4] To be sure, there may be situations when the conduct of criminal trials may threaten peace, as a survey in northern Uganda suggests.[5] But in other cases, for instance, in Sierra Leone, amnesty given to rebels in the Lomé negotiations did not lead to peace.[6] Hence, justice and reconciliation are unlikely to operate on the same dimension. A lesser degree of justice does not necessarily mean greater reconciliation. The inability of one transitional justice measure to promote justice does not say anything about its ability to advance reconciliation. Likewise, the approximation toward one objective does not necessarily preclude a simultaneous approximation toward another objective.[7] No a priori theoretical interest can exclude the possibility of examining, for instance, the effect of punishment both on the perception of justice and on forgiveness.[8] Any measure of justice can affect both justice and reconciliation, or only one of them, or even neither of them. I therefore seek to assess the utility of justice measures against their ability to approximate justice and reconciliation.

Before I do so, I will conceptualize justice and reconciliation as the categories of assessment; I then explain the meaning that members of the divided society attached to justice and reconciliation in the Czech Republic. The conceptualization is essential for reaching conclusions that may serve as a basis for comparison and generalization. The delineation of the meaning of justice and reconciliation serves as a basis for interpreting the findings and explaining any eventual differences with other studies. If different social groups in a divided society attach different meanings to justice and reconciliation, then the interpretation of statistical analyses need to take these differences into account.

Justice and Reconciliation as Concepts

While there is a degree of consensus and established disagreements in approaches to justice, reconciliation has not been systematically conceptualized.

After a brief conceptualization of justice, I will therefore pay more attention to the elusive notion of reconciliation.

Justice

Justice has been traditionally conceptualized in terms of retributive justice as a "just desert." Perpetrators should receive punishments that are proportional to the crimes committed.[9] Conversely, justice can be conceived as the debt that a victim is entitled to collect.[10] For this reason, restorative justice, conceptualized as a restoration of relationships broken by crime,[11] will not be considered in this section because it largely overlaps with reconciliation. My conceptualization of justice as a background for assessment accepts the fundamental principle of retribution as the repayment of debt,[12] which enables me to accommodate both the victim- and perpetrator-centered perspectives of justice. The perpetrator has to pay for the offense and the victim collects his or her debt.[13] The distinction of paying a debt and collecting the payment does not suggest that punishment concerns a perpetrator and financial compensation concerns a victim. Punishment vindicates the victim as the payment of compensation punishes the perpetrator.[14]

However, my understanding of debt is much broader than punishment and compensation. Consequences of crime go beyond the tangible dimension. In addition to material and health consequences, victims of crime may suffer humiliation and social isolation.[15] The social marginalization of victims is aggravated in totalitarian regimes, which possess propaganda machinery and use secret informants to control entire neighborhoods. Justice for the victim requires a social intervention that is broader than mere punishment. Conversely, the punishment of perpetrators does not need to include merely a custodial sentence. Crime can be morally condemned by a judge, the termination of employment, or public shaming. All such measures may lead to the satisfaction of desires for justice.

Reconciliation

The second major objective of transitional justice is that of reconciliation. In the aftermath of violent conflict or a regime change, reconciliation between former adversaries often becomes an imperative borne out of necessity. Democracy and human rights assume inclusiveness and equality. If democratization provides us with a certain value-normative goal,[16] reconciliation can be viewed as a step toward that goal.[17] Thus, transitional justice can be assessed against its ability to foster reconciliation in society.

Reconciliation in postconflict societies differs from reconciliation in international politics, where it signifies a normalization of foreign relations.[18] It also differs from concepts that have been inspired by various religious teachings.[19] Previously I used the word "social reconciliation" to underscore its secular nature,[20] which distinguishes it from religious projects for reconciliation.[21]

I have identified two approaches to reconciliation in the literature: One is *essentially* prospective, while the other combines both prospective and retrospective perspectives. Prospective approaches typically use an established concept that detects the attributes of interpersonal relations. For instance, James Gibson and Amanda Gouws applied the concept of political tolerance to study the process of overcoming the apartheid regime.[22] Gibson later applied the concept of racial reconciliation, which encompasses avoiding prejudices and having mutual respect and understanding.[23] I previously conceptualized reconciliation as a multifaceted concept that encompasses trust, tolerance, and a reduction in social distance.[24] A robust multifaceted concept of reconciliation was developed by Phuong Pham, Harvey Weinstein, and Timothy Longman for their research in Rwanda.[25] They conceptualized reconciliation as

> the process whereby individuals, social groups, and institutions (1) develop a shared vision and sense of collective future; (2) establish mutual ties and obligations across lines of social demarcation and ethnic groups; (3) come to accept and actively promote individual rights, rule of law, tolerance of social diversity, and equality of opportunity; and (4) adopt nonviolent alternatives to conflict management.[26]

The second type of approach amalgamates the prospective and retrospective perspectives. They typically refer to reconciliation as a process of overcoming the past, decreasing animosities, and erasing historical divisions. These approaches employ concepts that take into account the crimes of the past, such as forgiving and forgetting. Indeed, the first dilemma of transitional justice was to "prosecute and punish, or forgive and forget," not "prosecute and punish, or trust and tolerate."

Both approaches have their advantages. The second approach is appropriate for studying reconciliation with wrongdoers, while the first one is suitable for studying reconciliation with their social groups. While the forgiving and forgetting approach effectively examines the attitude toward a criminal and the crime that he or she committed, trust and tolerance are applicable to examine relations with members of an adversarial social group. In this chapter, I adopt the second approach to reconciliation. I conceptualize reconciliation as a process of reducing inimical attitudes between victims and perpetrators. In this perspective, adversaries do not need to establish a positive relationship but they should be able to overcome the past and "get along."

Justice and Reconciliation in the Czech Lands

Unlike justice, reconciliation has never been articulated as an objective of dealing with the communist past in the Czech Republic. The slogans "we are not like them" (see Chapter 2) and "we are all guilty," as raised by Havel in his ambiguous first New Year's address in the epigraph for this chapter, were the only manifestations of reconciliation in the Czech Lands. Predominantly society sought to "settle accounts" with the wrongdoer and repay the debt owed to the victims. Both justice and reconciliation, however, were well-understood concepts in the divided society.

Justice as Dealing with the Past

The notion of justice overlapped with the notion of dealing with the past among my respondents.[27] Former communists typically said that the mistakes of the past regime should be corrected, while the positive legacies should be preserved. In their view, the most prevalent perception in society was that everything that had taken place before 1989 was bad.

> What do they want to deal with? I say one thing, well, let's do things that were wrong, let's invent something new, better, that did not exist. What was good, so let it continue, let it carry on and further develop. This is dealing with the past in my view. But not to take what was before [year] eighty nine as stupidity and what is after eighty nine, it is the most ideal. . . .
>
> People [should] stop nagging each other. . . . "We will build on what we have, we would respect it and mutually behave with decency."[28]

In the ex-communists' views, justice was understood as the correction of wrong things. This concept is similar to that of former political prisoners who also tend to see justice in terms of correcting wrongs. The use of goodness and badness as a means to delineate justice was the same for both groups. The ex-communists, however, stressed the good things of the communist regime, while the ex-prisoners stressed the misery they and their families had endured. For former political prisoners, justice started with the consideration of the communist regime as a criminal regime.

Former communists and former political prisoners, however, were opposite to each other in their understanding of the scale and dynamic of justice. For former communists, the whole process of dealing with the past went too far and should stop, while for former political prisoners it had barely begun:

> Do you know anyone who was condemned for communist crimes? I do not! . . . Our "independent" judiciary will take care of Mr. Grebeníček [an alleged communist torturer] not to be bothered with such a banality as a judicial trial is. His accomplice, who tortured prisoners with electric current, has already been released. . . . None of the political prisoners wants the heads [of perpetrators] but we categorically demand that every [politically] motivated crime be punished. Unpunished crime invites perpetration of other crimes. The Communist Party was without any doubt a criminal organization with criminal objectives.[29]

> The biggest mistake was made in 1989 when we, all political prisoners, did not insist on the banning of the Communist Party as a criminal organization. [Despite] so many murders and suffering, KSČ was not punished and continues to work.[30]

The communist regime committed gross human rights violations, which made victims see them as criminals. But blaming the Communist Party collectively as a criminal organization naturally triggered a defensive response from the communists who were proud of the achievements of their regime. Protecting their reputation was perhaps the reason why the whole process of dealing with the past should stop:

> I personally would [think] that for 90 percent people to deal with the past is to make a thick line and stop being interested in it. . . . [Society

would have dealt with the past] if everyone would start somewhat to cooperate and wanted the nation to be unified, not divided.[31]

As long as we keep saying how it was last year, we'll keep lustrating, who was or was not [a secret police informant], then of course we have not dealt [with the past]. At a moment, when we don't mind [the past], then we dealt with the past.[32]

Communists and ex-prisoners thus paradoxically share the same conception of justice, although they differ in their views as to its scale and the dynamic of its use. Both groups understood justice as the remedying of wrongs. However, ex-prisoners saw justice as insufficient, while communists saw it as excessive. Moreover, in the eyes of ex-prisoners justice is necessary for overcoming the past, while in the eyes of communists justice is an obstacle to overcoming the past.

Reconciliation and Animosities

The notion of reconciliation (in Czech, *smíření*) alludes to Czech-German reconciliation[33] rather than reconciliation among Czechs over the communist regime. My inquiry about reconciliation has thus shifted to an inquiry about the relationships among the former communists, former political prisoners, and the rest of society.

The apparently inimical relationship between former communists and the rest of society did not indicate that reconciliation had been achieved: They called each other names, mostly behind their backs. I encountered communists who referred to members of the Civic Forum (OF) as *ofouni*, which resembles *ufouni*, or UFOs. They mocked the chairperson of the political party Top 09, Prince Karel Schwarzenberg, for his Czech-German accent as *Kadel*. Entrepreneurs are, in the eyes of communists, *grázlové* (bastards) and *hajzlové* (assholes), reminiscent of the class struggle. In everyday society communists are frequently called *komouši* (commies) and *komanči* (Comanches), but also *Rudí khmérové* (Khmer Rouge) and *komici* (comedians).

Communists hold negative views about former political prisoners, sometimes denying their very identity as political prisoners:

A lot of people even fabulize. . . . He was in jail for thievery, for instance, and then he said he thus undermined socialism, right, so actually he was on political grounds in the clink . . . perhaps because . . . they will be rewarded for it, they get even a better post or even be elected. Or get an electable spot on a party [list in elections].[34]

Such comments were extremely hurtful for former political prisoners who understood their cynicism and contempt. The overbearing and arrogant behavior of former communists then prompted further desires for retribution among former political prisoners:

I insist on the banning of the Communist Party. They have not improved yet. They still hold leading positions. That's the reason for our bad situation today. They have callous contempt for the suffering and killing [they had] caused. . . . I would ask for justice to let them realize their own guilt. Otherwise, I strongly believe in higher justice.[35]

The words "they have not improved" suggest that the interviewee contemplates reconciliation. The most telling word is "yet." He clearly harbors a hope that the Communist Party will change one day. Abandoning the contempt and "realizing" the guilt suggest that the ex-prisoner believes in the possibility of behavioral changes in offenders. In my survey of former political prisoners (Chapter 3), 52 percent of respondents indicated that they did not forgive and 42 percent indicated that they forgave a person who had harmed them in the past.[36]

I encountered a case in which a political prisoner, who was angry and exaggerated his disappointment, said that he would shoot all the communists. He was rebuked by his fellow ex-prisoners in the focus-group session who feared that I would take his words literally.[37] "Postřílel bych je všechny" (I would shoot them all) is a relatively common expression in Czech. It does cross the line when used in the public context, although here it was an expression of hopelessness and powerlessness rather than an intent to kill. Conversely, communists exaggerated the anticommunist atmosphere in society. "Do they want all people who lived before 1989 to be eliminated and put them against the wall and shoot them?"[38] Thus, feelings of hopelessness and powerlessness among former ex-prisoners were also felt by some communists. On both sides, these exaggerated statements expressing anger and despair were not understood literally but rather as a means of drawing attention to themselves.

In spite of their animosity, the former communists and former prisoners had much in common. They shared the same concerns about poor law enforcement, the theft of state property, the bankruptcy of banks, and corruption.[39] However, they differed in regard to the solutions of these problems. Communists believed that KSČM should regain power to prevent this from happening, while the former political prisoners were afraid that if the democrats were not able to fix it, the communists would regain power.[40]

In sum, there were commonalities and differences in the understanding of justice and reconciliation in society. On common ground was the notion that the concept of justice is both corrective and associated with political change, and a lack of reconciliation refers to the ongoing inimical relations. Nevertheless, historical divisions persist in other aspects of justice and reconciliation. In view of former political prisoners, the pursuit of justice should accelerate, while in the view of former communists, the pursuit of justice should stop. The similarities make the construction of the experimental design possible, while the differences require an inclusion of a control variable in the statistical models for the analysis of the experiment.

Experiments and Transitional Justice

Since the mid-1990s, sociology and political science have reinvented the experimental method. Until that time, social science experiments had been largely confined to psychological laboratories. The number of participants was limited to small groups of volunteers who were typically recruited from an undergraduate student population. The easy access to students made experimentation cost-effective but its findings could not be generalized beyond the classroom. Shortly after the start of the millennium, however, a study done by a major social science outlet signaled the revival of experimental methods.[41] The appeal of experiments was spearheaded by a revolutionary, though technically simple, methodological innovation, which rested in the merger of a nationwide opinion survey with experimental designs.[42] In other words, social scientists started to conduct attitudinal experiments with large samples representing entire nations.

Survey experiments, or experiments embedded in surveys, as they are called, have the combined advantages of both surveys and experiments. This merger makes them a powerful tool of social research. They have a strong internal validity as they enable an experimenter to attribute an effect to an experimental manipulation. They are effective tools in overcoming endogeneity, which reflects an inability to establish causal relations and plagues findings of cross-sectional survey research. At the same time, they have a strong external validity as they enable the researcher to generalize the findings across the entire population.[43] The bonus of this methodological fusion is the possibility of using the survey infrastructure and existing experimental designs that had been developed in areas as diverse as psychology and agriculture.

Furthermore, experiments allow researchers to be in control of the independent variable. They construct the experiment in such a way that it simulates the situation of their research interest. Experimenters can thus develop experimental vignettes, which are "short descriptions of a person or a social situation which contain precise references to what are thought to be the most important factors in the decision-making or judgment-making process of respondents."[44] In brief, a vignette is a story that can describe a real-life situation in an authentic fashion. Respondents can thus assess a realistic situation rather than answer to abstract and general questions in survey questionnaires.[45] On the other hand, survey research and even survey experiments are constrained by certain limitations in drawing conclusions about actual real-life situations. What some researchers see as an association between attitudinal variables and real-life actions,[46] others see as a shortfall between the two.[47]

Survey experiments are an ideal research instrument for transitional justice. They enable an effective study of attitudes and judgments toward difficult legal, moral, and political dilemmas in divided societies. They are conducted at the individual level but they enable drawing macro-level conclusions. The individual-level approach allows researchers, for instance, to gather attitudes of hundreds of respondents about different outcomes of truth-commission hearings, although only one truth commission was established in a country. A large sample of respondents also provides the scope for crafting more complex experimental designs than would otherwise be possible in a simple between-group experiment. With a large sample, researchers can thus simulate a process of transitional justice from the beginning to the end or compare the potential effects of various transitional justice measures side-by-side to a more reliable and nuanced extent.

The pioneering survey experiments in the area of transitional justice and political tolerance were conducted by Gibson and Gouws in South Africa. In fact, they were among the first survey experiments in general and their results attracted readership in leading social science journals. In their experiment concerning the Truth and Reconciliation Commission (TRC), Gibson and Gouws tested four major theories concerning the attribution of blame in the context of dealing with apartheid. They assessed how the public attributes blame to perpetrators with different motives (hatred versus ideological beliefs); affiliation in the historical conflict (the police versus the armed wing of the African National Congress [ANC]); position in the chain of command (leader versus follower); and consequences (innocent persons killed versus those involved in the struggle killed) in a 2x2x2x2 factorial design. They found that respondents were more likely to attribute blame for apartheid to members of the security branch than to members of the ANC's armed wing and to a person in a commanding position than to a follower.[48]

In his experiment on the fairness of the amnesty process of the TRC, Gibson used the same factorial design. However, instead of judging a complex situation concerning the motives and positions of an individual perpetrator, respondents in this experiment assessed the outcomes of a transitional process that included proxies for several transitional justice interventions. Compensation, an opportunity to share the truth by the victim, apology, and shaming of the perpetrator (contrasted with the absence of each of the respective items) were manipulated to gauge respondents' assessment of the fairness of amnesty for the perpetrator. Gibson found that compensation was by far the most powerful predictor of the fairness of amnesty, followed by truth-telling and an apology.[49] Although not without criticism,[50] Gibson's studies represent a major advancement in empirical transitional justice.

Building on Gibson's research, I previously studied the effects of different personnel (lustration) systems on trust in government and reconciliation in the Czech Republic, Hungary, and Poland in 2007. I examined the effects of dismissal, exposure, and confession, which represented retributive, revelatory, and reconciliatory methods of transitional justice. I found that the effect of dismissal is about three times greater than that of confession on perceptions of trust in government but that only confession could contribute to reconciliation. Exposure, which represented shaming or truth-revelation, was not a significant predictor of any of the experimental outcomes.[51]

Following this experiment, I used an experimental design to examine the effect of trials conducted by the International Criminal Tribunal for Former Yugoslavia (ICTY) in Croatia in 2008. I examined the operation of the ICTY vis-à-vis the operation of national courts, which were also mandated to prosecute war criminals. In addition, I examined perceptions about the Croatian versus Serbian nationality of the perpetrator; and custodial sentences (punishment) versus suspended sentences (amnesty). I found that the ICTY was more likely to be perceived as just, if it punished out-group offenders. The implication of the findings is that punishment generates a dual deterrent effect: one for the members of the in-group and one for the members of the out-group.[52]

In 2010, I devised a survey experiment to examine the perception of historical injustices committed by Japan in South Korea. This included the effect of punishment, compensation, apology, and their absence on the perception of justice. I found that the effect of apology was larger than the effects of punishment and compensation. This micro-level finding mirrored the prominent role of apologies in the relations between Korea and Japan, in terms of which Korea demanded an apology and Japan denied any wrongdoing.[53]

Experiments in transitional justice can thus contribute to our understanding of the potential that different measures of justice have in divided societies. They enable the assessment of a measure that has not yet been implemented or was poorly implemented, was ideologically contaminated, or has eroded in an unsettled political situation. In other words, survey experiments open a window to the future by allowing us to assess the eventual effects of transitional justice, if they have not yet been fully implemented. This feature makes them an optimal research method to examine the effect of various justice measures side-by-side at the same place and time.

A Transitional Justice Experiment in the Czech Republic

In order to empirically examine the effects of a variety of transitional justice measures, I devised a "transitional justice experiment." My main objective was to compare the effects of retributive, reparatory, revelatory, and reconciliatory measures of transitional justice, as categorized in the Introduction,[54] on perceptions of justice and reconciliation in the Czech Republic.

In designing the experiment, I first considered a traditional factorial design, such as 2x2x2x2. However, this would only have allowed me to compare a measure with its absence in each factor. This meant that I would only have been able to test four measures. My research interest was to compare the effects of several justice measures at once, and I needed to choose a larger factorial design. At the same time, I was constrained by manipulating too many factors on too many levels as the number of respondents per cell would be too small. I therefore opted for a 3x4x2 factorial design, in order to manipulate reparatory, retributive, and reconciliatory measures.

Revelatory measures were conceived as a revelation of information about the wrongdoer that leads to his shaming and hence could be, and were, merged with retributive measures. Reparatory measures included financial compensation and social acknowledgment of victims, which were contrasted with the absence of financial compensation. Retributive measures in my experiment manipulated punishment, suspended sentence, dismissal, and shaming of a perpetrator. Reconciliatory measures were limited to the examination of the most prominent measure: an apology, which was contrasted with the absence of an apology.[55]

The 3x4x2 factorial design therefore required the preparation of the questionnaire with twenty-four combinations of the experimental vignette. This in turn required twenty-four versions of the questionnaire. This design is an apparent departure from previous survey experiments, which were dichotomous in nature. Capturing four categories in a nationwide survey is nothing unusual: Respondents' religious affiliation in multifaith societies, or voting preferences in multiparty systems, are typical examples of multiple categorical variables.

The experiment was piloted among twenty-four respondents. It was then embedded in a nationwide opinion survey conducted in the Czech Republic in 2010. The survey included 1,067 respondents who were older than fifteen years. It means that it had on average about forty-four respondents per experimental cell.

Experimental Vignette

The experimental vignette presented a story about two men: Mr. Novák, who was a dissident, and Major Procházka, who was an officer of the State Security (secret police, or StB). Novák and Procházka are among the most common Czech surnames. The political system was described as communist, not socialist. Although Czechoslovakia was officially a socialist country before 1989, "communist regime" has been predominantly used since 1989. To describe it in politically neutral language, I used the words "system" and "regime" interchangeably. The affiliation of Procházka with the StB was preferred over the affiliation with the Communist Party because more retributive justice measures, such as judicial trials, lustration, and shaming, studied here, were adopted against StB than against KSČM.

The experimental vignette was divided into two parts. The first part was situated in the 1980s. Mr. Novák is said to sign a petition against the system.

Signing a petition was rather unusual in the 1970s, as the experience of Charter 77 signatories shows; those who demanded that the country uphold human rights, which it officially adopted as a consequence of the Helsinki Final Act, were imprisoned, forced into exile, or prosecuted. The courage to sign petitions picked up in the 1980s as tens of thousands signed the petition called Several Sentences in 1989, although some signatories were still prosecuted.

In response to the petition, Procházka orders that Novák is to receive a one-year jail sentence. Ordering a punishment may sound controversial. Obviously, sentencing was always a prerogative of the judiciary in the past but most judges were merely cogs in the machinery of the communist system, exercising political power as they were told. A one-year sentence was selected because it was an official threshold for reparation and enabled a comparison with the punishment to Procházka after 1989. A one-year jail term for each of them meant that a debt had been settled.

The second part of the vignette was situated after 1989. It manipulates three reparatory versions, in which Mr. Novák (1) received financial compensation; (2) was publicly acknowledged by receiving an honorary citizenship from his town hall; or (3) did not receive compensation. Four retributive measures were then manipulated. Procházka was (1) judicially condemned and punished with a one-year custodial sentence; (2) judicially condemned and received a one-year suspended sentence; (3) dismissed from his new employment; or (4) publicly exposed. In order to test the reconciliatory measures, Procházka either (1) apologized or (2) never apologized to Novák.

The first version of the vignette used the most tangible reparatory and retributive measures. It combined financial compensation with punishment and ended with an apology given.

> In the 1980s, Mr. Novák signed a petition against the then communist system. In response to it, Major Procházka, an officer of the then StB, ordered Mr. Novák to be charged and subsequently sentenced him to jail, where he spent a year.
>
> Now let's take a look how the situation was resolved after the change of the regime: Mr. Novák was financially compensated for his one-year sentence. Mr. Procházka was charged and sentenced to one year in jail. At the end, Mr. Procházka apologized to Mr. Novák.

Other versions of the vignette were manipulated accordingly. For instance, version thirteen used a symbolic reparatory measure, which was operationalized as acknowledgment by a town hall; a mild retributive measure, which was represented by dismissal; and an apology as an instance of reconciliatory measures: "Mr. Novák received an honorary citizenship in his town. Mr. Procházka was dismissed from his new employment. At the end, Mr. Procházka apologized to Mr. Novák." The last, the twenty-fourth, version of the vignette was the most negative. It read as follows: "Mr. Novák was not financially compensated for his one-year sentence. The name of Mr. Procházka appeared in the list of secret police members published by the Ministry of the Interior. Mr. Procházka never apologized to Mr. Novák."

All versions of the vignette were perfectly plausible. As overviewed in Chapter 2, a one-year jail sentence was the minimum period for political prisoners to qualify for financial compensation. One year may have meant that the sentence was just a few days short of the year or was just one year and no more, making the option of receiving and not receiving financial compensation equally believable. As to the secret police members, a few of them received mild penalties for their actions, while a few others got custodial sentences. Pressures for the release of former secret police officers from new posts, as a result of the lustration law or a public pressure, and their public exposure, were quite common. Although noncriminal sanctions were more frequent than criminal sanctions, both categories were equally conceivable. Apologies were not commonplace in Czech society (see Chapter 2) but there was always the possibility that a person could apologize of his or her own volition. Indeed, my survey of political prisoners showed that some of them received an apology from people who had harmed them in the past.[56]

Was the vignette realistic? Obviously, the goal is to construct an experimental vignette that is realistic; it is something else to see whether the experimental vignette is perceived as realistic. Researchers have often aspired to construct vignettes that accurately represent reality but the accuracy of their representation was, to my knowledge, never empirically tested. In order to determine the level to which the vignette is perceived as realistic, I asked my respondents to assess four options:

1. What happened before the year 1989 between Mr. Novák and Mr. Procházka could have easily happened in our country.
2. What happened after 1989 with Mr. Novák could have easily happened in our country.

3. What happened after 1989 with Mr. Procházka could have easily happened in our country.

4. How Mr. Procházka approached Mr. Novák could have easily happened in our country.[57]

In order to disentangle the aspects, which made the vignette less realistic than others, I examined the effect of the experimental variables on a realistic vignette scale. The parameter estimates received from the general linear model are reported in Table 6. Unlike other multivariate analyses, the best findings to attest the realistic character of my vignette would be those without any significant differences, if all versions were equally plausible. Indeed, the findings show that the reparatory measures were not significant predictors of the scale. They were seen as almost equally likely to occur in reality. However, the retributive factor was significant. A closer exploration has revealed that respondents found suspended sentences more realistic than punishments. This was perfectly understandable, given the fact that the vast majority of persons condemned for communist crimes received suspended sentences.

The effect of reconciliatory measures on the realistic vignette scale was highly significant. This suggests that an apology from Procházka to Novák was seen as significantly less likely to occur than no apology. In a country

Table 6. Between-Subject Effects of Experimental Factors and the Reality, Justice, and Reconciliation Scales

	Dependent Variables		
	Reality	Justice	Reconciliation
	F	F	F
Reparatory Measures	.950	16.990***	1.148
Retributive Measures	2.602^	5.567**	1.509
Reconciliatory Measures	17.004***	19.997***	10.762**
Former Party Member	.345**	10.100**	22.632***

Note: A higher *F* value signifies a better predictive value of the independent variable. The higher the *F* value in the justice and reconciliation, the better the predictive value. The Realistic column, however, seeks to determine whether all versions of the vignette were equally realistic. The lower the value of *F*, the more realistic is the vignette. Reconciliatory measures were seen as rather unrealistic by Czechs.
$^\wedge p < 0.10$; $^* p < 0.05$; $^{**} p < 0.01$; $^{***} p < 0.001$.

that favored a retributive policy to deal with the past, this finding was not entirely unexpected. Fortunately, the perspective that an apology is unlikely was not as important for the study as seeing other justice measures as unlikely. An apology may be a private matter, which could easily have occurred between any two people.

Could Justice Measures Affect Justice and Reconciliation?

In this section, I examine the impact of justice measures manipulated in the experimental vignette on the perceptions of justice and reconciliation. I present the operationalization and the creation of justice and reconciliation scales and the analyses of the results.

Perception of Justice

In order to empirically examine the effect of the experiment on the perception of justice, I asked my respondents five questions. They included a question about the general notion of justice, two victim-centered questions, and two perpetrator-centered questions. One victim-centered and one perpetrator-centered question asked about justice directly. In order to capture a variety of tangible and intangible (symbolic) measures of transitional justice, justice was conceived as a broader category, which included the moral condemnation of a perpetrator and social recognition of the victim. Without the broader approach, my outcome variable could have been biased toward tangible measures, such as criminal trials and financial compensation. Respondents were asked to what extent they agreed or disagreed with the following statements: (1) Justice has been served; (2) Mr. Novák received justice; (3) Mr. Novák received social recognition; (4) Mr. Procházka was morally condemned; and (5) Mr. Procházka was justly punished. The composition of the justice scale was based on the responses to these questions; the scale ranged from 0 to 20.[58]

I used statistical methods to analyze the data.[59] I will present my results in three steps. I first compare the effects of each of the three factors—reparatory, retributive, and reconciliatory measures of justice—on the justice scale. In the second step, I compare the results of the individual components of these factors, such as punishment, dismissal, and apology. In my third step I examine the mean scores of these components on the justice scale.

Turning back to Table 6, we can observe that the reparatory, retributive, and reconciliatory factors were all highly significant predictors of justice.[60]

Table 7. The Effect of Experimental Variables on the Justice Scale

	B	SE	95% Confidence Interval	
			Lower	Upper
Intercept	8.326***	.391	7.558	9.094
Financial Compensation	2.037***	.353	1.344	2.730
Social Acknowledgment	1.280***	.352	.590	1.970
No Financial Compensation	0 [a]	.	.	.
Punishment	1.659***	.409	.856	2.461
Probation	.971*	.405	.177	1.766
Dismissal	.780^	.405	−.015	1.574
Shaming	0[a]	.	.	.
Apology	1.283***	.287	.720	1.846
No Apology	0[a]	.	.	.
Party Member	1.527**	.481	.584	2.470

[a] The parameter is set to zero because it serves as a contrast category.
^$p < 0.10$; * $p < 0.05$; ** $p < 0.01$; *** $p < 0.001$.

Contrary to my expectations, the retributive measures were the least efficient predictor of justice.

Table 7 reports the parameter estimates for each component of the three factors. Starting with the reparatory measures, we can observe that the mean differences between the absence of financial compensation on the one hand, and social acknowledgment and financial compensation on the other were highly significant. It means that both tangible and symbolic reparatory measures mattered, although the effect of the former was larger than the effect of the latter. Moreover, further analysis revealed that the mean difference between the effect of financial compensation and social acknowledgment on justice was also statistically significant. The tangible reparatory measure thus had a significantly stronger effect on the perception of justice than the symbolic reparatory measure had.

Turning to the retributive measures, the effects of punishment, probation, and dismissals were contrasted against the effect of shame. Punishment had the strongest effect on justice in comparison with shame, followed by probation and dismissal (Table 7). All three tangible (punitive) measures had a considerably stronger effect on justice than the symbolic (shaming) measure. As envisaged earlier, the reconciliatory measure had a strong effect on justice. The mean difference between apology and no apology is robust

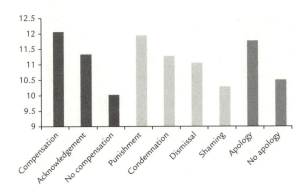

Figure 10. The mean scores of experimental variables in the justice scale.

and highly significant. The effect of apology shows that reconciliatory measures have a strong potential to affect the perception of justice in the Czech Republic.

Historical divisions still played a role in the assessment of justice. Former members of the Communist Party were more likely to see that justice had been done. This corresponds with the qualitative assessment above, which suggested that the former members of the Communist Party tended to view justice measures as excessive. The experimental finding confirms that the impact of any measure of transitional justice was more greatly magnified in their eyes than in the eyes of nonmembers.

The third step of my analysis visualizes the results of my experiment. Figure 10 presents the means of justice for the three sets of reparatory, retributive, and reconciliatory variables. Financial compensation and punishment, the two most tangible reparatory and retributive measures, respectively, exercise the strongest effect on justice. The mean score of financial compensation was 12.01, while the mean score of punishment was 11.88. Condemnation and dismissal as tangible alternatives to punishment scored 11.20 and 11.00 on the justice scale, respectively. At the same time, intangible measures were also relevant. The mean score of social acknowledgment was 11.25, which was above the mean of the justice scale and above its central value of 10.0. The mean score for apology was 11.72, compared with the mean score of 10.43 for the absence of apology.

Figure 11 then presents three plots, which "graphically cross-tabulate" the estimated marginal means between (top) reparatory and reconciliatory mea-

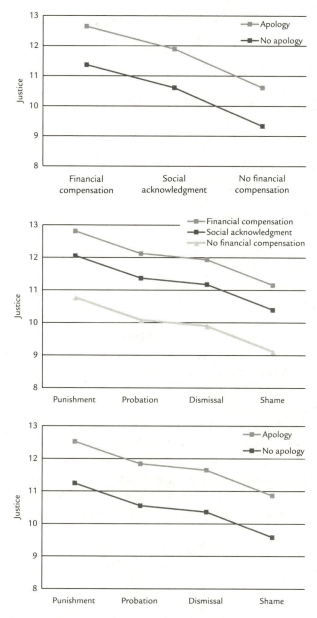

Figure 11. The plots of experimental variables in the justice scale.

Table 8. The Effect of Experimental Variables on Reconciliation

	B	SE	95% Confidence Interval	
			Lower	Upper
Intercept	10.245***	.308	9.639	10.850
Financial Compensation	.337	.279	−.211	.885
Social Acknowledgment	−.050	.279	−.597	.498
No Financial Compensation	0[a]			
Punishment	.476	.324	−.159	1.112
Probation	.406	.321	−.224	1.037
Dismissal	.660*	.320	.032	1.287
Shaming	0[a]			
Apology	.745**	.227	.299	1.191
No Apology	0[a]			
Party Member	1.810***	.380	1.063	2.557

[a] The parameter is set to zero because it serves as a contrast category.
* $p < 0.05$; ** $p < 0.01$; *** $p < 0.001$.

sures; (middle) retributive and reconciliatory measures; and (bottom) retributive and reparatory measures. The distance on the justice scale between any two points is relatively large, conveying the significance of the results; the only exception is probation and dismissal, which generate a marginal effect. We can also observe that the largest impact on justice is made by (1) financial compensation and apology; (2) punishment and apology; and (3) financial compensation and punishment. The smallest impact on justice is made by (1) the absence of financial compensation and the absence of apology; (2) shaming and the absence of apology; and (3) shaming and the absence of financial compensation. The poor performance of shaming can be explained by the absence of expressive value-normative judgment that is present in other retributive measures. Punishment, probation, and dismissal all express condemnation of past behavior, whereas shaming is essentially a revelatory measure that does not explicitly condemn.

The Perception of Reconciliation

The second concept that serves as an assessment of the experimentally manipulated measures of justice was reconciliation. To empirically examine reconciliation, my survey asked respondents five questions. The questions

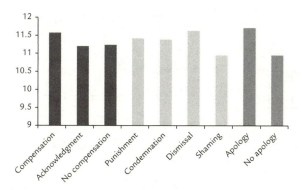

Figure 12. The mean scores of experimental variables in the reconciliation scale.

needed to be related to the experimental vignette, which narrated a story of wrongdoing and its resolution after the regime change. Like the justice scale, the first question asked generally about the prospect for reconciliation between Novák and Procházka. The second question asked about the forgiveness of Novák, who was the victim, toward Procházka, the secret police officer. In spite of its religious connotations, forgiveness was empirically examined in the same way as any other political or psychological process.[61] The third question asked about forgetting, which, together with forgiveness, formed the right tail of the first transitional justice dilemma: Prosecute and punish, or forgive and forget. The fourth and fifth questions concerned retribution as the opposite of forgiveness. I asked whether the victim should take revenge on Procházka or whether the victim should sue him.

The exact wording of the questions was as follows: "(a) Mr. Novák and Mr. Procházka should reconcile; (b) Mr. Novák should forgive Mr. Procházka; (c) Mr. Novák should forget Mr. Procházka; (d) Mr. Novák should sue Mr. Procházka; (e) Mr. Novák should take somehow revenge against Mr. Procházka. The perceptions of reconciliation scale thus consisted of five items, including 'reconcile,' 'forgive,' 'forget,' 'not sue,' and 'not revenge.'"[62] In the analysis of reconciliation, I proceed in the same way as I did in the section on justice. Table 6 has shown that reconciliatory measures—in this case, an apology—were the best predictor of the perception of reconciliation. Table 8 "elevated" the effect of apology to a significant increase in the reconciliation scale. This is perfectly understandable and is an expected finding. On the other hand, Table 8 also detected a somewhat unexpected finding

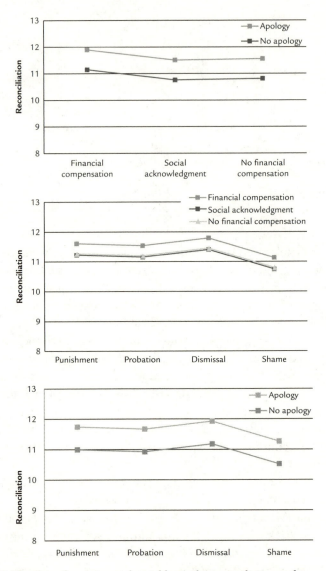

Figure 13. The plots of experimental variables in the reconciliation scale.

concerning retributive measures. It seemed to suggest that dismissal had a positive effect on the perceptions of reconciliation. Obviously, this find needs to be interpreted in relation to the contrast category, which is shaming.

The positive impact of apology versus the absence of apology and the negative impact of shaming versus dismissal on reconciliation are apparent in Figure 12. Figure 13 also shows that apology has consistently had the greatest impact on the reconciliation scale. At the same time none of the reparatory measures show any significant impact on the reconciliation scale. Neither did punishment and condemnation of perpetrators significantly affect reconciliation.

Membership in the Communist Party, which was used as a proxy for historical divisions, was a significant predictor of reconciliation. It means that the former communists were more likely to be reconciliatory than noncommunists. How can we explain this finding in view of the defiance of former Communist Party members illustrated in the previous chapter? Rather than a paradox, this finding can be explained by the qualitative evidence presented above as well as by evidence in Chapter 4. They suggest a belief by the Communist Party members that justice and reconciliation have been adequately achieved. As was quoted in Chapter 4, the chairman of the Communist Party stated that the Party had already apologized and any further demands for apologies ought to be refused. Victims and most Czechs would not agree with this position and saw it as a continuing act of defiance by the Communist Party.[63]

Discussion

This section discusses the findings of my experiment. First, it compares the results concerning the perception of justice with results concerning the perception of reconciliation. Second, it compares the results of this "transitional justice experiment" with my "lustration experiment." To effectively compare the experimental effects of transitional justice measures on the perceptions of justice and reconciliation, I decided to plot the mean scores of my experimental variables on a two-dimensional graph with justice and reconciliation as its two axes. Figure 14 presents the results.

We can observe a greater variation in the impact of justice measures on the justice scale than on the reconciliation scale. The mean justice score of shame, which scored the lowest on the justice scale, was 10.22, while the mean justice score for compensation was 12.00, which was the highest. In contrast,

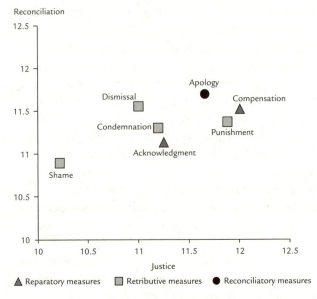

Figure 14. Impact of justice measures on the perceptions of justice and reconciliation.

the lowest score in the reconciliation scale was 10.89 for shame and the greatest score was 11.65 for apology. Hence, all justice measures can be squeezed into a less than 1-point band on the reconciliation scale. The band on the justice scale is almost twice as wide. This signals that all justice measures have a better bearing on the perception of justice than on reconciliation.

Figure 14 also shows variations within the three clusters of justice measures. First, there is a great variation among retributive justice measures in the perception of justice. The difference between punishment and shaming in respect of the perceived justice is 1.66 points. Dismissal and condemnation represent a middle-of-the-road approach to justice, whereby they are seen as considerably more effective than shame but considerably less effective than punishment. Among the family of reparatory measures of justice, it is a little surprising to observe that compensation has a greater effect on the perceptions of justice and reconciliation than social acknowledgment. It means that the impact of tangible measures—punishment and financial compensation—is more pronounced than that of intangible measures. Notwithstanding, the impact of apology on both justice and reconciliation scales comes as a surprise. It shows that reconciliatory measures are capable of acting as an efficient mechanism for achieving justice.

The results of this experiment are in accordance with the results of my previous survey experiment on lustration systems in the Czech Republic, Hungary, and Poland.[64] As I mentioned earlier in this chapter, the lustration experiment examined the effects of dismissal, which can be seen as a proxy for retributive measures of transitional justice; exposure, which could be seen as a retributive measure (shaming) or a revelatory measure (disclosure of truth); and confession, which could be seen as a reconciliatory measure. In my previous study, dismissal was the significant predictor of the perception of justice in the merged dataset from the three countries. Confession, contrasted with denial, was also a highly significant predictor of justice in the merged dataset, which is similar to the effect of apology in the transitional justice experiment. Hence, there is growing evidence that reconciliatory measures can indeed increase the positive perception of justice.[65]

The exposure, or shaming, of secret agents was the lowest-performing variable in both experiments. In contrast to no exposure, exposure had no significant effect on justice in the lustration experiment. But it had a significant negative effect in contrast to all other retributive measures. Thus, I can conclude that in the Czech Republic truth fails to act as a proxy for justice, as hypothesized in the transitional justice literature. One of the possible explanations is that exposure fails to convey the message of condemnation. Members of the public may not have enough empathy to realize that such exposure creates a great deal of embarrassment for the secret agent.[66]

Both experiments also showed that reconciliatory measures are strong predictors of the perception of reconciliation. In the lustration experiment, only confession was able to produce a significant effect on the perception of reconciliation.[67] In the transitional justice experiment, the effect of apology was the only significant predictor of the perception of reconciliation. Apology and confessions thus truly deserve their labels as reconciliatory measures. They have formidable potential to contribute to reconciliation in the Czech Republic. It is therefore a pity that reconciliatory measures have been so rare in the country.[68]

Did Justice Measures Transform the Divided Society? Class and Ideological Divides

> Without condemnation, lustration, and restitution, there can be no transformation.
>
> —Vojtěch Cepl

> *Transform* verb: 1, to change the form of something; 2, to completely change the appearance or character of something, especially so that it is better.
>
> —*Oxford Advanced American Dictionary*

The previous chapter investigated the "potential" effects of justice measures on people's perceptions of justice and reconciliation by means of an experimental design. In contrast, this chapter examines the effects of justice measures on society "in reality" by means of a nationwide survey conducted in 2015. It focuses on the impact of justice measures on social transformation. Because justice measures, as they were implemented in the Czech Lands, could produce tangible as well as intangible effects, social transformation is conceptualized for the purpose of this chapter as a two-dimensional process, which encompasses material as well as ideological transformation of the three communist-era classes: those who bore the brunt of discrimination, former Party members, and the rest of society.

This chapter consists of three sections. The first section conceptualizes social transformation and its objectives.. The second section examines whether the position in the three major communist-era classes predicted income in the current society and whether justice measures played any role in that process. The third section examines the degree of transformation of the ideological divides. It starts with the qualitative data to gauge views about the communist regime. It then uses quantitative data to describe the perceptions of the communist regime, justice, and reconciliation and to explore the perception of justice measures by the three classes. It then turns to a path analysis to determine whether justice measures were able to forge shared perceptions of justice and reconciliation and whether they discouraged people from supporting a return to the communist regime.

Two Dimensions of Social Transformation

Transitional justice measures have been theorized to be capable of transforming an entire society.[1] They not only have a direct impact on groups of victims and perpetrators but also affect the rest of society. They delegitimize the previous regime and its power structures; they send an ideological message about those who held sway; and, in so doing, solidify the loyalty of bystanders to the new regime.[2] The utility of justice measures can thus be assessed against their ability to transform the divisions of the past. Because they generate both tangible and intangible effects, the utility of justice measures can be gauged from their material impact in facilitating socioeconomic redistribution and the strength of the citizens' ideological adherence to the current system in conjunction with their rejection of the old regime.

First, the measures of justice are expected to affect socioeconomic divisions inherited from the previous regime. A regime change is often accompanied by a change in people's statuses and positions in society. Measures of justice have the potential to play a critical role in this socioeconomic redistribution. In the Czech Lands, they may have affected the inherited class structure directly by a massive process of property restitution; widespread dismissals due to lustrations;[3] and social rehabilitation, reinstatement in the previous profession, and financial compensation of victims. Moreover, they may have affected the inherited class structure indirectly. For instance, condemnation of the communist regime may have led to the demotion of the discredited officials or deprivation of their promotion opportunities without them having been directly affected by the lustration law.[4]

Second, the measures of justice carry symbolic meanings that delegitimize the past regime. Reparatory, revelatory, and retributive justice each point to a particular dimension of illegitimate relations in the past. Lustration signals, among others, that positions in the state were not distributed on the basis of merit but on an affiliation to the Communist Party and the degree to which individuals collaborated with the regime. Restitution shows that private property was essentially stolen, illegitimately held, and carelessly managed. Expropriation of the assets of the Communist Party signifies its illegitimate position as the state party and decries the illegitimate use of public resources. The Act on the Illegitimacy of the Communist Regime essentially condemned the communist regime as criminal (see Chapter 2).

In addition to delegitimization, other social mechanisms that transmit the intangible effects of transitional justice measures are deterrent effect and socialization. Retributive measures in particular are argued to have a deterrent effect[5] (making people afraid of eventual norms' violations in future) although unequivocal empirical evidence of the effect is still lacking.[6] Socialization as a factor of transmission operates via people's learning experiences, such as the internalization of a human rights culture, that may result from revelatory, retributive, and other justice measures.[7]

Social transformation may thus be affected by the tangible and intangible effects of justice measures. Hence, there are several outcome categories against which the effects of justice measures could be examined. Since I am interested in studying their impact on the entire society, I measure the tangible effects by the personal incomes of different classes of people: those who were privileged as pre-1989 members of the Communist Party; those who had been discriminated against by the communist regime; and those who did not belong to either of these groups. The intangible effects will be captured by three variables: the effect of the justice measures on the perception of justice by society as a whole; the effect of the justice measures on the perception of reconciliation by society as a whole; and popular attitudes toward a rejection of the communist regime.

I consider class positions as transformed in *material* terms if (1) the class position that an individual held during the communist regime no longer affected his or her income in the current system. I consider class position transformed in *ideological* terms if (2) the perceptions of justice and reconciliation[8] and (3) support for a return to the communist regime were no longer determined by the class position that an individual held in the past. If there were no transformation, then the communists who mostly benefited from the regime and victims who *experienced* wrongdoing, persecution, and discrimination would hold opposite views about justice, reconciliation, and a return to the regime.[9] This is merely an assumption, which will be investigated in this chapter.

Before I commence my analysis of the two dimensions of social transformation, I need to illustrate how these outcomes were viewed by the three groups of the divided society. Second, I also need to describe how the measures of justice were viewed by the divided society.

Did Justice Measures Transform Class Positions?

In *Making Capitalism Without Capitalists*, Gil Eyal, Iván Szelényi, and Elizabeth Townsley examined, among other things, a link between lustration measures and postcommunist class structure.[10] Although seemingly obvious, the link between "justice" and "class" has been rather overlooked in many studies of transitional justice, social transformation, and democratization. Lustration may affect the position of members of the old elite directly via dismissals and indirectly via limiting their labor-market participation, suggesting that some people are unfit to participate in the new system.[11]

The visibility of former Communist Party members in the political and business elite suggests that the pre-1989 Party membership brings benefits years after the regime change. Indeed, research from Poland conducted in the 1990s before lustration law had been adopted suggested that the membership in the pre-1989 communist elite was the best predictor of membership in the post-1989 business elite.[12] If true, how were former communist elites able to maintain their privileged positions? Maria Łoś and Andrzej Zybertowicz asserted that former communist elites in Poland exchanged political power for economic capital and then converted the economic capital to regain power. The massive "capital conversion process" was possible because the communist elites were rich in social capital and were able to use their networks, including the expertise of former secret police members, in acting at the margins of law and behind it.[13]

This poses a question about whether injustices of the past persist in material terms in the Czech Republic.[14] The communist regime split the society into three major classes: pre-1989 members of the Communist Party; those who were, or whose families were, discriminated against in the past; and the rest of society, who did not belong to either of the two classes. The nationwide survey of 1,043 respondents conducted in 2015, which is used in this analysis, included 118 former communists (11.3 percent), 199 persons who reported discrimination in their families (19.1 percent), and 743 people who did not belong to either of the two classes (71.2 percent). Seventeen people indicated both membership in the Party and discrimination during the communist regime. This is perfectly plausible because communists turned against each other in the 1950s and after 1968; some former communists may have come from families in which a parent had been discriminated against (see Chapter 4).

Did justice measures change the class positions of former adversaries? Did those who benefited from the communist era and their children continue to benefit in the current system? Vice versa, were families of those who had been discriminated against by the communist regime disadvantaged after twenty-five years of transition? Indeed, justice measures in the scale in which they were adopted in the Czech Lands had enormous potential for redistributing rights, benefits, and opportunities and hence the status of all people. Justice measures also carried symbolic meanings, which may have affected class positions of people indirectly. For instance, owing to lustration law, people who were beneficiaries of the communist regime were not seen as trustworthy enough to occupy public positions, regardless of whether they fell within the scope of the lustration law or not.[15]

Class position usually predicts personal income.[16] Hence, for the purposes of this analysis, I considered communist-era stratification as transformed if there was no significant income difference among the communist-era classes, namely former members of the Party and their offspring no longer benefit from their privileged positions in the past; and those whose families had been discriminated against in the past are no longer disadvantaged. In order to empirically investigate the question, I examined the impact of justice measures on the income of the pre-1989 party members, the discriminated, and the bystanders.

Table 9 indicates that the mean net income in society was CZK 13,884, the discriminated earned on average CZK 15,584, and the average income of a pre-1989 Party member was CZK 13,019. As mentioned earlier, the finding indicates that the material injustice expressed in terms of personal income may have been remedied. However, the descriptive data cannot tell whether the levels of incomes were consequences of justice measures or other factors. The income may have been affected by the age of the respondents; most of the ex-communists in the sample may have already retired, while those who were discriminated against were still productively employed. At this

Table 9. Assessment of Justice Outcomes and Historical Divisions in Society

Mean Income (CZK)	Discriminated 15,584 ± 9,159		Pre-1989 Party Members 13,019 ± 5,703		Rest of Society 13,575 ± 8,414		Total Sample 13,884 ± 8,388	
	N	%	N	%	N	%	N	%
Justice	55	27.6	54	45.8	278	37.6	379	36.4
Trust 1	24	12.1	18	15.2	95	12.9	131	12.6
Trust 2	21	10.5	30	25.4	119	16.1	166	16
Return to the past	23	11.6	36	30.5	61	8.3	114	11
N	199		118		743		1,043	

Source: Roman David, "Twenty-Five Years of Dealing with the Past," machine-readable data file, 2015 (on file with the author).
Notes: The table displays positive attitudes to the following statements:
—The greatest injustices of the past have been rectified.
—There is trust between former political prisoners and the members of KSČM today.
—There is trust between society and the members of KSČM today.
—We should return to the political system we had before 1989.
Reconciliation was conceptualized as a measure that encompasses the two dimensions of trust and was measured on a scale ranging from 0 to 8. The row percentage may differ marginally from the total number in the column due to missing data.

stage, it is also impossible to say whether the measures of justice played any role in the process of class transformation.

I therefore used a statistical analysis to disentangle the predictors of personal income.[17] In addition to the variables of interest, I also controlled for a number of variables that may be predictors of personal income, such as gender, age, marital status (divorced), employment status (retired), religious belief, and urban residency. Table 10 shows the results of the statistical analyses.

The results reveal that the respondents' relation with the previous regime did not affect their current income. All else being equal, former members of the Communist Party and their children did not benefit from their relation with the past regime; and the families of those who were discriminated against in the past were no longer disadvantaged. Thus, the results confirm that the class structure of the communist regime has been transformed. Persisting historical divides were not based on incomes.[18] Transitional justice appeared successful in redressing the material aspect. The nature of historical divides may have been purely ideological.

Table 10. Predictors of Income

Predictor	B	SE	β
Sex (female)	−3292	487	−.20***
Age	232	21	.50***
Education	3192	262	.37***
Retired	−8694	855	−.45***
Divorced	−116	777	−.004
Catholic	−1202	580	−.06*
Urban	1044	567	.05^
Pre-CP member	−1044	904	−.04
CP parent	−633	529	−.04
CP voter	13	898	.00
Discriminated	−851	805	−.04
Rehabilitated	3018	1135	.10**
Restituee	1096	631	.05^
Evicted	−68	1293	−.002
Lustrator	1042	710	.04
Constant	2408		
R^2		.372	
N		792	

Source: Roman David, "Twenty-Five Years of Dealing with the Past," machine-readable data file, 2015 (on file with the author).
$^\wedge p < .10$; $^* p < .05$; $^{**} p < .01$; $^{***} p < .001$.

The critical finding that justice measures facilitated this transformation in socioeconomic position came from the positive impact made by rehabilitation and restitution processes. First, those who had been rehabilitated earned a significantly higher income than the others. It means that those who had been discriminated against in the communist regime were either compensated for their imprisonment or reinstated to their posts after 1989 or both; and the pensions of all of the discriminated increased. Likewise, those whose property had been nationalized in the past and returned after 1989 also earned larger incomes. Although the latter is marginally significant, it adds another piece of evidence to the broader picture that justice measures did help to rectify historical injustices. Indeed, Table 9 shows that those who were discriminated against were beneficiaries of restitution and rehabilitation policies, which carried significant material benefits.[19]

In line with this statistical analysis, I did not find any qualitative evidence concerning a drop in living standards among the pre-1989 Party members. Interviews with them did not indicate that they had experienced downward mobility, although some of them complained that daily necessities were expensive after the liberalization of prices in the early 1990s. Although many of them changed employment, they did not indicate that it was because they had been discriminated against. Chapter 3 provided qualitative evidence about the financial situation of former political prisoners. Although their situation appeared dire during the first decade of democracy, financial compensation has increased since then.

To be sure, there may be endogeneous reasons why an eventual positive effect of Party membership and an eventual negative effect of discrimination have been neutralized. For instance, the discriminated class was discriminated against because of their property ownership in the past; hence they may have possessed qualities such as an entrepreneurial spirit, work ethic, and willingness to take risks, which may be transmitted via the family to the next generation. Conversely, the pre-1989 communist class may have included those who were incapable of pursuing their careers without the help of their Communist Party membership. As a result, the discriminated may be thriving in the market economy, while the ex-communists may experience unemployment and downward mobility due to the diminishing influence of the Party.

Did Justice Measures Stultify a Return to the Communist Regime?

I shall now turn to the ideological outcomes of transitional justice. The previous chapter assessed *the potential* of justice measures to facilitate perceptions of justice and reconciliation. This section investigates the impact of justice measures on perceptions about justice and reconciliation *in reality*, and it adds another attribute: averting a return to the previous regime.

Justice after transition, according to Ruti Teitel, is both prospective and retrospective.[20] It serves as a means for strengthening democracy[21] and non-repetition of the past.[22] The prospective assessment is, however, rather elusive. Transitional situations suffer from many deficiencies that contaminate the perception of the new system. For instance, transitions typically bring economic downturns, social reforms, changes in the media landscape, and political infighting among former allies in the antiregime coalitions: All of these problems can unsettle the perception of the new system. For this reason, I used the notion of averting a return to the previous regime as the ideological criterion for assessing the utility of justice measures. Thus, two backward-looking variables (justice and averting a return to the past) and two forward-looking variables (equality and reconciliation) were used in the analyses in this chapter.

Views of the Communist Regime

To illustrate the data, I now provide narratives of former communists and former political prisoners who represent two poles of the divided society. Since, in the previous chapter, I examined perceptions of justice and reconciliation, I limit my illustration to the new outcome variable: a return to the communist regime. Before I start, I need to clarify that the "communist system" was used in the interviews with former Communist Party members, while the "communist regime" was used with former political prisoners. Although they espouse the same meanings—both refer to the pre-1989 communist era—"regime" underscores its regimented character, whereas "system" sounds more neutral. The different use was motivated by research conducted in the divided society.

Former political prisoners, obviously, did not wish to return to the communist regime. Their adverse assessment of the past was unequivocal and understandable. For them it was a terrorist regime, which brought misery to hundreds of thousands of people. A parallel with Nazism emerged frequently. Some political prisoners were anti-Nazi resisters and experienced both communist and Nazi jails; others had been in communist jails together with anti-Nazi resisters. Nazism also emerged as a reference category that served to mobilize the public for the political prisoners' cause. Almost everyone was able to condemn Nazism but not everyone was willing to condemn the communist regime.

> [We should] realize how draconically we punished the representatives of Nazism and how lenient we were toward the representatives of communism.[23]

> Fascism and Nazism were condemned at an international tribunal. Communism has not been condemned [in the same way] so far![24]

As Chapter 3 has already shown, former political prisoners held an unyielding view of the communist regime. The communists and former communists, on the other hand, held an ambiguous view of the regime. They highlighted the benefits of communism but at the same time claimed that the communist system had essentially the same problems as the current system. I was surprised to find a number of parallels between the present and the past regime that emerged in the interviews conducted with pre-1989 Party members.

> I did not vote for ODS [a major center-right political party]. Because the biggest rascality comes from there. . . . It is obvious that because they were [members of] ODS they reached [political] positions as people reached [political positions] via their [Communist] Party membership cards before.
>
> That Office for the Study of Totalitarian Regimes and so on, so what they are working on, how they are working on. Well again they just quarrel for positions, when you look at the political events and the background, they just go after their jugulars, and even in worse way than before [1989]. Before it at least had rules . . . now it is nepotism, envy, hatred and money. . . . Before money was not that important.[25]

> Today, take when you watch television, even the respectable [speaking ironically], our Czech Television, a public broadcaster, it is also such a massaging of brains sometimes and that's not pretty. . . . First we pulled to the East, now to the West, before massaging the brain . . . against the West, today it is reversed, so . . . it's fifty-fifty.[26]

> [The petition like] There Should Be No Talk with Communists [S komunisty se nemluví], it is nice [sarcastic], but again it gets to the same situation as the communists [did write petitions] back then.[27]

> If we were to ban the KSČM, we would need to ban all organizations and parties, which we have. . . . just let's take a look how many members of these organizations—ODS-ers and TOP-ers and don't know what else—were in the KSČM? Plenty, plenty.[28]

The similarities between the past and the present proliferate, in the eyes of communists, into social issues such as gender. A female respondent stated, "It will still take time to make [the position of women] a little more even, and then what bothers me is the ones who want [quotas], and that seems like as they said during totalism [sic], when they [now] scream that there should be quotas for women in politics, yeah. And it reminds me something like before [when they said] there will be that many workers, so many of those, so many women in positions."[29]

Parallels between the present and the past turned into the contest between democracy and the communist regime; they transpired in the eyes of former communists into international politics and played out in the form of the East versus the West.[30] On the other hand, the similarities in the international arena in the past and the present did not always carry negative implications. An interviewee actually resented that Czech society had not learned from past mistakes:

[We should not completely return to the past. We should avoid mistakes of the past, including the damaging connection with the Soviet Union]. So we are dependent on the European Union, they pretty much dictate what to do, what not to do. . . . Overall they constantly restrict us, it still goes on and on.[31]

Although most of the similarities in domestic and international politics were used with the intention to discredit the present system, they all carried a positive aspect. The mention of these similarities showed that their authors realized that these had been problems in the past; therefore they mentioned them. On the other hand, if the present regime had the same problems as the past one, they may ask why not return to the past, which gave them job security and social benefits that the new system did not provide. It is therefore unsurprising that the problems of the current system increase the desire for a return to the past regime.

Others maintained that the systems were different. A former Party member who did not know about Václav Havel before 1989 and considered a former chairperson of the KSČM, Miroslav Grebeníček, insane, said, "Back then it was impossible to talk about democracy. That someone went into the street and shouted that the KSČ were cretins, it was a no-go. Today I can walk on the street and say that the ODS are morons. I can say it easily."[32]

An individual's ambiguous attitude to the past was not only related to his or her memory of the past as a political system but also to his or her memory of the economic system. Both political transition and economic transition occurred simultaneously, rapidly, and dramatically. Older generations remembered the exact prices of milk, bread, beer, and daily necessities, which dramatically increased over the years. Those who had bought property before 1989 celebrated their gains, while those who sold before 1989 resented.[33]

Another type of positive attitude toward the communist regime stemmed from the mundane experience of simply surviving under the communist regime. Although it is difficult to establish how typical the case was, the Little Czech was, to my surprise, alive and well twenty-five years after the fall of communism. It even helped me to fathom the reception of justice measures among former Party members. In an interview conducted in 2015, the Little Czech, though not explicitly mentioned, even appeared as a normative ideal:

> The system [*pause*] I would say, for a normal person who does not desire a career, wants to live a normal life, sometimes sally out to the [holiday] cottage, or go fishing, or like that, just to live that ordinary life to satisfy his needs, and is not interested in too much around, no extra interests and desires of wandering perhaps around the world, or so, so for that person it was quieter, because he had his job, everybody had to work . . . [*later in the interview*] *So, what do you think about the demands for apology of KSČ for the past regime?* [*pause*] Ts, it seems to me quite, quite strange, weird question raised . . . who demanded an apology? For the system? How can they apologize for something that was kind of dictated and implemented. . . . We are again going back to history.[34]

In the eyes of the interviewee, the socialist regime provided for the Little Czechs. As long as they remained private citizens and did not make demands that transcended their expected roles in the areas of career, public interests, and travel, they could peacefully coexist with the regime. The interviewee did not find anything problematic with this view. Hence, in his eyes, there was nothing to apologize for when it came to the previous regime.

The interviews thus indicate that justice measures have important implications for the meaning of communism as far as former political prisoners are concerned. In their eyes, communism is synonymous with crime. A failure to fully implement justice measures undermines the legitimacy of the current system (see Chapter 3). For the former communists, however, the preference for a return to the communist regime resulted from a variety of considerations, including social security, unemployment, affordability of basic necessities, and their specific conception of meritocracy. Numerous examples showed that many of them used the apparent problems of the past to criticize the present. Justice measures may delegitimize the past regime in the eyes of political ex-prisoners; but the problems of the current system—as well as the problem of justice measures (see also Chapter 4)—may relegitimize the past regime. Thus, for both groups, justice measures could play a role in their views about averting a return to the past.

Perceptions of Justice Outcomes in a Divided Society

Figure 15 indicates that the pre-1989 Party members showed by far the greatest approval for all the outcomes of social transformation. Table 9 specified that almost 46 percent of former communists thought that historical injustices had been rectified, 15 percent thought that trust had developed between former political prisoners and members of KSČM (Trust 1), and more than 25 percent of respondents agreed that there was trust between the society and members of KSČM (Trust 2). Views about a return to the past regime revealed by far the largest discrepancy between former communists and other groups. More than 30 percent of former communists wished to return to the past. But the glass can be seen as half empty: Almost 60 percent of them did not wish to return to the communist regime.

Conversely, those whose families had been discriminated against held the bleakest view of the justice and reconciliation outcomes. Less than 28 percent of them considered that major injustices had been rectified; a mere 12 percent thought that trust had developed between ex-prisoners and ex-communists; and only 10.5 percent agreed that trust had developed between former communists and the rest of society. More than 11 percent of those who had been discriminated against indicated that they would like to return to the past. Ironically, this figure is more than the 8.5 percent indicated by the rest of society. It again indicates that discrimination in the past also affected former communists and their families.

For the purposes of this analysis, reconciliation was conceived as a forward-looking concept (see Chapter 5). It was conceptualized as a measure that encompasses two dimensions of trust:[35] trust between former political prisoners and members of KSČM, and trust between the society and members of KSČM. The scale did not include trust between former political prisoners and the rest of society because, as we shall see throughout this section, the opinions of the discriminated against and the rest of society converged. The questions about trust did not concern trust per se but the assessment of trust. The reason was that many respondents in my survey

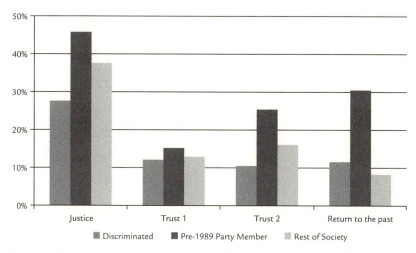

Figure 15. Assessment of justice outcomes and historical divisions in society. David, "Twenty-Five Years of Dealing with the Past." Reconciliation was conceptualized as a measure that encompasses (1) trust between former Party members and former political prisoners and (2) trust between former Party members and the rest of society.

indicated that they had not personally encountered a former communist or a former political prisoner during the past five years.

Perceptions of Justice Measures in a Divided Society

Measures of justice have frequently been mandated to rectify historical injustices[36] or to achieve reconciliation,[37] both of which are based on the assumption that justice will help overcome the past. However, optimism about the transformative impact of justice measures faces a tough reality check. Justice after transition is among the most divisive policies in new democracies. Surveys conducted by the team led by Gábor Tóka in several post-communist countries in the early 1990s showed that the dismissal of former Communist Party members was one of the most controversial policies.[38]

Nevertheless, this observation may not apply to all justice measures. Although punishment, amnesty, revelation, apology, and compensation may be viewed differently by different groups in a divided society, the degree of difference in their perceptions may vary. Some measures may be more divisive than others. Hence, different justice measures may carry different sociopolitical costs. If both measures A and B facilitate the same social transformation

Table 11. Experience of Justice and Historical Divisions in Society

	Discriminated		Pre-1989 Party Members		Rest of Society		Total Sample	
	N	%	N	%	N	%	N	%
Rehabilitated	80	40.2	5	4.2	0	0	80	7.7
Restituee	77	38.7	23	19.5	106	14.3	201	19.3
Evicted	19	9.5	6	5.1	18	2.4	42	4.0
Lustrator	50	25.1	29	24.6	83	11.2	159	15.2
N	199		118		743		1,043	

Source: Roman David, "Twenty-Five Years of Dealing with the Past," machine-readable data file, 2015 (on file with the author).
Notes: The ex-communist group and the discriminated group overlap in seventeen cases. The table cross-tabulates positive answers to the following questions:
—Were you ever a member of KSČ before the year 1989?
—Were you or any of your parents or grandparents disadvantaged due to political reasons in the pursuit of studies or in the workplace?
—Could you or any of your parents or grandparents return to their studies or their original profession [after 1989]? (rehabilitation)
—Did you or any of your parents or grandparents receive any property during the restitution [process]? (restitution)
—Did you or any of your parents or grandparents have to move out from a house or flat that was returned during restitution? (eviction)
—Did you look for information (e.g., on the Internet, in a library) concerning the collaboration with StB of anyone from your circle (e.g., neighbors, coworkers, acquaintances, business partners)? (lustration)
The row percentages may differ marginally from the total numbers in the column due to missing data.

outcomes, and A is perceived as more divisive than B, then B better serves the interests of transitional society.[39] These considerations prompt a question of how the measures of justice were viewed among the three historical classes. Table 11 and Figure 16 disaggregate the differences in the perception of justice measures.

I captured justice measures by behavioral and attitudinal variables. The former inquired about respondents' experiences with justice measures, while the latter asked about respondents' assessment of the justice measures. Questions about individual experiences could address only those justice measures that were broad in their reach in order to have a realistic chance of anticipating that the nationwide survey would return a sufficient number of answers. The broad measures included provisions of the Rehabilitation Act, the Restitution Act, and the Lustration Law (see Chapter 2). Due to ethical

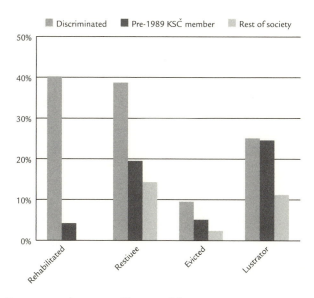

Figure 16. Experience of justice and historical divisions in society. Source: David, "Twenty-Five Years of Dealing with the Past."

considerations, my survey questions did not ask respondents whether they were demoted or dismissed as a consequence of lustration. A positive answer would implicate the respondent as a secret police collaborator or a member of another branch of the former state's repressive apparatus. It was unlikely that a negative answer would always be correct as respondents were likely to try to conceal such affiliations in the past. Instead, I inquired whether the respondents had searched secret police archives for information concerning someone they knew, such as a colleague, business partner, acquaintance, or neighbor. Hence, the survey question about lustration was conceived in the original meaning of lustration as a revelatory rather than as a retributive measure.[40]

Table 11 shows that 159 respondents (15.2 percent) had searched a list of secret police collaborators for any known name; they performed "lustration." Both former communists and those discriminated against checked the background of others more frequently than the rest of society did. Those who were discriminated against in the past were the major beneficiaries of reparatory measures. Among them, 80 had been rehabilitated (40.2 percent) and 77 had property returned to them through a restitution program (38.7 percent). The restitution of property concerned all citizens,

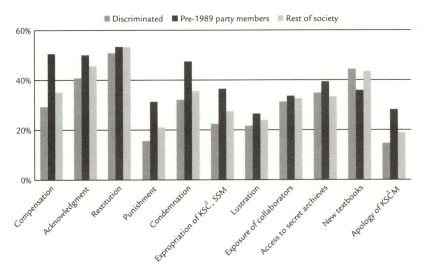

Discriminated   ■ Pre-1989 party members   ■ Rest of society

Figure 17. Assessment of justice measures and historical divisions in society.
Source: David, "Twenty-Five Years of Dealing with the Past."

including former communists. Twenty-three of them had family property returned to them, which represented 19.5 percent and was more than the rest of society, with 14.3 percent.

Because justice measures can create new injustices, I asked respondents whether they were evicted from a house or flat that was returned during the restitution process. Unexpectedly, the discriminated group experienced the largest proportion of the evictions (9.5 percent). One would have expected the largest proportion to have been among former Party members. Before 1989 they would have prioritized the procurement of "state flats" in buildings, which would then subsequently have been returned to the original owners. Nonetheless, 5 percent of former Party members were evicted, which was still a larger proportion than the 2.4 percent in the rest of society.

In total, eleven different justice measures were assessed by inquiring about their success. The word "successful" was chosen because it captures both a normative and a positive assessment of justice in a divided society. In contrast, "agreement" or "approval" of a measure may point to misleading answers. A former communist and a former political prisoner both may "disagree" or "disapprove" a measure of justice, albeit for different reasons: the former may find it excessive, while the latter may find it insufficient. "Success" thus better

Table 12. Assessment of Justice Measures and Historical Divisions in Society (Percentage of positive answers)

Were the following measures successful or unsuccessful?	Discriminated	Pre-1989 Party Members	Others
Financial compensation of former political prisoners	29.3	50.5	35.0
Social acknowledgment of former political prisoners	40.8	50.0	45.6
Restitution of nationalized property to original owners or their heirs	50.8	53.3	53.2
Punishment for crimes of the communist regime	15.6	31.3	21.0
Moral condemnation of the crimes of the communist regime	32.1	47.4	35.6
Expropriation of the property of KSČ	22.4	36.5	27.5
The departure of people connected to the pre-1989 system from leading positions in the state administration and the police	21.6	26.5	23.9
Official publication of the names of secret collaborators with StB	31.3	33.6	32.6
Accession of materials of StB to the public	34.8	39.3	33.3
Publication of new history textbooks	44.4	35.9	43.4
Apology of the leadership of KSČM for its role in the pre-1989 system	14.6	28.2	18.8
N	199	118	743

Source: Roman David, "Twenty-Five Years of Dealing with the Past," machine-readable data file, 2015 (on file with the author).
Note: The response categories were captured on the five-point Likert scale. The table displays positive answers.

captures the degree to which justice is approximated. Table 12 and Figure 17 capture the assessment of eleven justice measures by the three groups in society. As expected, former Party members considered the measures relatively successful, perhaps expressing their wish to stop them, while those who had been discriminated against tended to view the justice measures as less successful. An exception to this prevalence was the positive view of history textbooks by those who were discriminated against in the past. With regard to most justice items, the responses of the rest of society fell largely between those of the ex-communists and those who had suffered discrimination. However, the views of the rest of society were closer to those of the group who had been discriminated against than to the ex-communists. It means that although the society remained divided, it converged toward the perspective of the victims rather than towad the perspective of the ex-communists.

The experiences and views expressed by former communists and by those who suffered discrimination diverged in most areas. Compensation of political prisoners, punishment of communist crimes, expropriation of the property of the KSČ and the SSM, and an apology by the KSČ (see Figure 17; see also Chapter 2) seemed the most divisive justice measures in terms of divergent views and experiences. On the other hand, some of the measures may have had the propensity to foster consensus about the past. The restitution of property and the exposure of secret collaborators were viewed in the same light by ex-communists and those discriminated against; both groups also made similar use of secret archives, as shown in Table 11. This may suggest that former communists and those formerly discriminated against found a common scapegoat for the past: the secret police collaborators.

A comparison of the perception of different justice measures by the same historical class also yielded some revealing findings. The ex-communists assessed an apology by the KSČ as less successful (28.2 percent) than the expropriation of its property (36.5 percent) and the condemnation of the crimes of the communist regime (47.4 percent). This means that even the ex-communists themselves, despite their ideological opposition, took reality into account in assessing different justice measures, including the defiance of the KSČM over its apology.

Did Justice Measures Contribute to Ideological Transformation?

The question of whether justice measures played a role in transforming ideological divisions stemming from the past is a task of the following analysis.[41] When can we say that justice measures transformed society in ideological terms? If justice measures were able to transform ideological divisions in society, then the current views of justice, reconciliation, and the desire to return to the past regime would not be directly affected by those divisions.[42] Instead, justice measures are likely to act as mediating factors between the historical divisions (i.e., whether the person was a member of

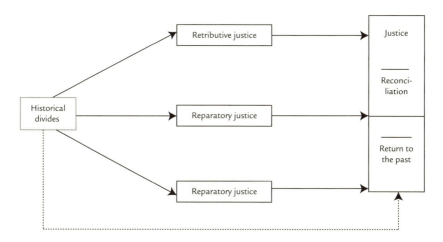

Figure 18. Hypothesized path model. The model is built on the following assumptions: (1) views of retributive, reparatory, and revelatory justice depend on the position of the individual vis-à-vis historical divisions (i.e., whether the person was a member of the Communist Party in the past, whether she or he was discriminated against); and (2) the assessment of justice, the assessment of reconciliation, and the view of whether a society should return to the past depend on the historical divisions and the three categories of justice measures that dealt with those divisions. If the historical divides were transformed and injustices rectified, they would no longer directly affect justice, reconciliation, and the desire to return to the past.

the Communist Party in the past, whether she or he was discriminated against) and the three outcomes of ideological transformation. In other words, the current assessment of justice, reconciliation, and the desire to return to the past would be indirectly linked to historical divisions via transitional justice measures, if ideological transformation had occurred. Based on these considerations, a path model emerges, in which justice measures play a mediating role in achieving justice and reconciliation and in averting a return to the past.[43] Figure 18 maps the hypothesized relations.

Obviously, the path model is a logical construct that needs to be empirically examined and cross-examined vis-à-vis the effect of other variables. Nevertheless, it provides us with an ideational map that captures the process of social transformation, sheds light on the utility of justice and reconciliation as the purported objectives of justice measures, and, more important, elucidates the effects of the three types of justice measure. If the former Party members still wished to return to the previous regime, and if society held an

Table 13. Significant Results of the Path Analysis

Predictor		Justice Measure		Objective	Estimate*
Age	→	Revelatory			−.110
Age	→			Justice	−.067
Education	→			Reconciliation	−.058
Education	→			The past	−.105
Divorced	→			Justice	−.065
Urban	→	Retributive			−.090
Pre-1989 KSČ member	→	Retributive			.073
Pre-1989 KSČ member	→			The past	.077
KSČ parent	→	Reparatory			.060
KSČ parent	→			Justice	.072
KSČM voter	→	Retributive			.111
KSČM voter	→	Reparatory			.096
KSČM voter	→			Reconciliation	.074
KSČM voter	→			The past	.258
Discriminated	→	Retributive			−.108
Discriminated	→			Justice	−.061
Restituee	→	Revelatory			.094
Restituee	→			Justice	−.057
Restituee	→			The past	−.073
Evicted	→			The past	.068
		Retributive	→	Justice	.374
		Retributive	→	Reconciliation	.427
		Retributive	→	The past	.354
		Reparatory	→	Justice	.296
		Reparatory	→	The past	−.073
		Revelatory	→	Reconciliation	−.160

Source: Roman David, "Twenty-Five Years of Dealing with the Past," machine-readable data file, 2015 (on file with the author).
* Standardized regression weights.

ambiguous view about justice and reconciliation, and only those who were discriminated against in the past opposed a return to the previous regime, then justice measures inspired little, if any, ideological transformation. Graphically speaking, if the transformation occurred, I would expect that the dotted lines in the hypothesized path model (Figure 18) would disappear in reality.

In order to examine the model, I used the data from my nationwide survey, which I conducted in 2015 and which was administered by the CVVM.

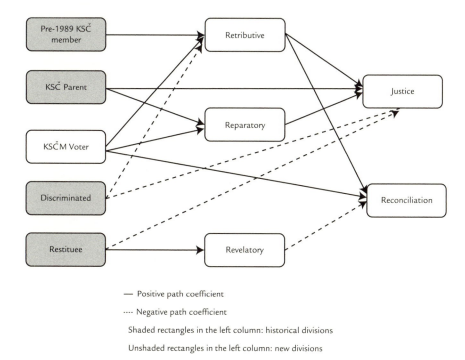

Figure 19A. Historical divides, justice measures, and the perceptions of justice and reconciliation.

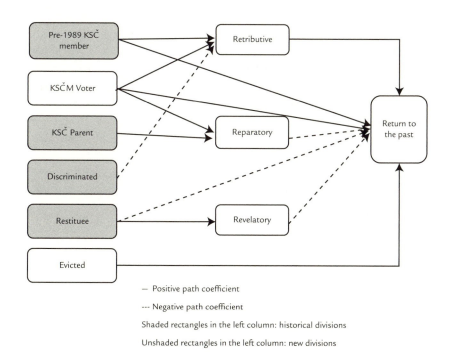

Figure 19B. Historical divides, justice measures, and a return to the past.

The results of the path model are summarized in Table 13 and Figures 19A and 19B. The question of whether justice measures mattered requires an exploration of whether any direct path from the historical divisions leads to the three outcomes: justice, reconciliation, and a return to the past.[44] The direct path would suggest that justice either did not matter at all, or that it mattered a little when both direct and indirect paths existed. The results would help us reach tentative conclusions about (1) the transformation of historical divisions; (2) the emergence of new divisions in society; (3) the utility of justice measures vis-à-vis a return to the past; (4) the utility of justice measures vis-à-vis the perceptions about justice and reconciliation; (5) other sociodemographic characteristics that were immune from the implementation of justice measures but affected at least one of the three outcomes; and (6) items that did not have any significant effect in the path model.

Were Justice Measures Relevant for Overcoming Historical Divisions?

Looking from one angle, it is possible to say that historical divisions persist in one form or another. Starting with justice as an outcome category, those who were discriminated against in the past and those whose property was returned through restitution were more likely to see that the injustices of the past have not been rectified. Hence, those who had a direct experience of injustice did not see that justice had been done. Indeed, this may appear counter-intuitive at first glance but it actually makes sense. There are inherent limitations to what justice measures can remedy. Nothing can bring back the deceased; nothing would make up for the loss of a victim's most productive years spent in jails or in professions that were well below the person's education. Such limitations may then cloud the assessment of all processes of dealing with the past from the victims' perspectives.

On the other hand, those who grew up in families with communist parents were more likely to see that injustices of the past have been rectified. For them, the rectification of injustices may have been seen as an excessive process. This finding corresponds with other research in divided societies, in which each part retains its own group-based interpretation of justice.[45] It signifies a lack of ideological transformation.

Likewise, turning to the issue of a return to the past, historical divisions were not resolved: Pre-1989 Party members were more likely to seek a return to the past regime than other respondents, while those who received their property through restitution were more likely to oppose a return to the communist regime.[46] Hence, regardless of the justice measures, historical divisions still largely predict people's opinions about justice and the wish for a return to the past regime.

As every glass can be seen as half full or half empty, by looking from another angle one may be tempted to say that historical divisions may have been transformed in other respects. Pre-1989 party membership does not have a direct effect on views about justice and reconciliation; growing up in a communist family does not affect a respondent's views of reconciliation and a return to the past regime. Conversely, an opinion about reconciliation and a return to the past by those who were discriminated against may have changed for the better; this is demonstrated in the opinion about reconciliation by the restituees. The problem is that I do not have evidence for these transformations. My model allows me to determine when transformation did not occur by *finding the direct link*.[47] Alas, I can only observe that the glass is half full.

New Divisions Emerged in Society

New divisions in society appeared in two forms: new political divisions and new injustices. First, the desire to return to the communist rule of yore continued in cases of not only former Party members but also communist voters. Thus, the KSČM was successful in attracting the new electorate for their orthodox ideas. Because my analysis controlled for pre-1989 Party membership and parents' Party affiliation, these voters did not have anything to do with the KSČ: They were not members of the Party in the past, and neither were their parents.

Second, those who were evicted from the houses or flats, which were returned in the restitution process, were also more likely to prefer a return to the communist regime. Their number in the sample of more than a thousand respondents was relatively small: Forty-two people were evicted and eight of them preferred to return to the past regime. The statistical analysis nevertheless suggests the effect was significant and that the evicted were not the voters of the KSČM, its former members, or their offspring. The evicted were victims of the justice process. They were simply people who lost faith in the new system, which deprived them of what the previous system had awarded them: housing. As Chapter 2 already showed, many households who faced eviction could not afford to purchase new property and the replacement properties offered by landlords may have been of substandard quality or in remote locations. They lived for years in uncertainty, being harassed by land-lords; landlords, on the other hand, had to take responsibility for the main-tenance of the houses but were not allowed to increase the rent beyond the regulated limit. Apart from regulating rents, the state washed its hands of the consequences of the restitution process. It returned rental houses with the tenants still in them, shedding its responsibility for previously having granted them the tenancy. For the laudable purpose of achieving justice, the state created new injustices and a new set of victims.

Justice Measures and Their Effect on the Preference for a Return to the Past

Earlier analysis in Chapter 4 showed that the justice measures were divisive, whereby pre-1989 KSČ members considered them too extensive, while the dis-criminated saw them as insufficient. The path analysis showed that retributive measures not only failed to transform those divisions (Figure 19B), but also augmented them. It means that any eventual trial, high-profile dismissal, or introduction of a new retributive measure would most likely backfire and in-crease the pre-1989 Communist Party members' desire to return to the past.[48]

In any case, the divisive role of retributive measures was not dramatic. These measures merely played a mediating role in the increase of the desire to return to the past; former Party members wished to return to the past, re-gardless of retribution. The increase in the desire to return to the past due to retributive justice was marginal. It would be fair to say that retributive mea-sures largely perpetuated and marginally increased historical divisions.

The role of reparatory justice is, in contrast, marginally positive in trans-forming divisions. Reparatory justice is positively linked with historical divisions (respondents with KSČ parents) and with new divisions (KSČM voters) and negatively linked with a return to the past. Reparatory measures thus reduce the desire of the communist voters to return to the past and transform their communist offspring.

Finally, the revelatory justice measures produced a significantly negative effect on the desire for a return to the past. It means that truth dissuaded people from returning to the past. In the particular case of restituees, the revelation magnified their opposition to a return to the past.

My model did not capture the utility of reconciliatory justice measures. Apology as the only reconciliatory measure operated on the same dimension and in the same direction as retributive measures. Further analysis showed that apology had more or less the same effects as retributive measures.[49]

Justice Measures and Their Effect on Justice and Reconciliation

Retributive and reparatory measures have a positive effect on justice. It means that more prosecutions, lustration, and condemnation are likely to result in a more positive perception of justice having been done. However, this would result—as suggested above—in an increase in the preferences for a return to the previous regime. How can we explain this paradox?

A closer look at another outcome—reconciliation—provides us with some answers to this paradox. The findings suggest that reconciliation is promoted by retributive justice and inhibited by revelatory justice. The reason for this apparent discrepancy is that my understanding of reconciliation has perhaps been too normative, rather than purely descriptive. I envisaged transformative reconciliation, which would encompass reshaping interpersonal relations and transforming them. Such reconciliation would mean the acknowledgment of historical injustices and the forging of consensus about human rights abuses committed in the past. In contrast, reconciliation that emerged was an untransformative concept. It was a strategic preference of the formerly privileged class of communists. In their view, reconciliation was synonymous with forgetting and not dealing with the past. For others, such reconciliation signified that others wanted to get away with crime. This explains why the view of reconciliation was negatively linked to revelatory justice and positively linked to a return to the communist regime.

Age and Education Mattered

Older people were more likely to prefer a return to the past. They may have been motivated by sentiments and desires for social security rather than political preferences (which I controlled for). Their position was actually quite moderate: On the one hand, they were more likely to oppose revelatory measures;[50] on the other, they did not agree that the greatest injustices had been remedied. Their negative attitude to revelatory justice measures could have been not because of their reluctance to learn new facts but because of their opposition to the revelation that did not correspond with their life experiences. Their experience also placed them in a better position to observe whether injustices had been rectified or not. The gradually increasing retirement age may also have been a motive for their affinity with the past; people wanted to retire earlier to get their state pensions. Conversely, younger people, closer to their school years, may have considered the information about the past sufficient. They had learned that some justice had been done, which was sufficient for them to refuse a return to the communist regime, although they had had no practical experience with it.

Education was a negative predictor of both the perception of society as reconciled and a return to the communist past. Since education entails increasing knowledge, a more qualified judgment, and higher opportunity costs of a return to the egalitarian communist regime, it made sense that the more educated were less likely to prefer a return to the past than the less educated members of the populace.

The outcomes could also be affected by marital status. I expected that divorcees would be more likely to wish for a return to the communist past due to, first, the factors of downward mobility, economic uncertainty, and the lack of social contact typically associated with the consequences of divorce; and, second, the causes resulting from a changing socioeconomic environment, in which some partners were not able to adapt to living in the market economy and their relationships consequently broke down. I also expected that divorcees would be likely to assess reconciliation differently because they had been unable to overcome conflict and maintain their marital relationships. However, the only variable significantly associated with the divorcees was their view of the justice measures as unsuccessful. It is hard to speculate about the cause of this unexpected result. For instance, dissatisfaction with a divorce settlement may have been reflected in dissatisfaction with justice after transition. The effect may also have been transmitted via mistrust for the courts as institutions that administer justice.

Among other factors, urban residents did not see retributive justice as successful. Historical changes have taken effect more prominently in cities and towns than in villages. The unfulfilled expectations of political change, which did not bring justice, may have been more perceived among those who actively participated in the political changes of 1989, which took place in larger towns and cities.

Irrelevance of Experience with Justice Measures

Searching in the lists of secret police collaborators and being rehabilitated did not have any effect on ideological transformation in any way. The absence of the effect of searching for collaborators, an activity that is called "lustrating," may have signified that the activity was performed, regardless of the position in historical divides. Indeed, my data and the interviews with Communist Party members revealed that many of them also searched for collaborators among their acquaintances.[51]

The absence of the effect of rehabilitation on any of the justice measures and their outcomes was surprising but similarly explicable. It was surprising because those who had been rehabilitated after 1989 had a significantly larger income than the nonrehabilitated interviewees (Tables 8 and 12). The effect of rehabilitation may have disappeared due to controlling for discrimination. All the rehabilitated interviewees had suffered discrimination in the past and the number of rehabilitated was half the number of the discriminated (Table 11). Hence, rehabilitation appeared to have no effect.

Discussion

This chapter has drawn a mixed picture about the outcomes of social transformation. On the one hand, the net incomes of those who were discriminated against in the past have exceeded the net incomes of those who benefited from the previous regime; the class structure of the former communist regime no longer presaged personal income in the Czech society twenty-five years after the end of communism. Moreover, only 11 percent of respondents wished to return to the communist regime. All this suggests that material and ideological transformation has occurred. However, many ideological divisions persist: Only 36.4 percent of the respondents considered that the greatest injustices have been rectified; 16 percent agreed that there is trust between society and members of KSČM; and 11 percent agreed that there is trust between former political prisoners and members of KSČM.

The question dealt with in this chapter is did justice measures contribute to these outcomes of transformation in the Czech Lands? Could justice measures alone, rather than other factors in the complex process of political, social and economic transformation, account for the outcomes? The answer to the question depends on which of two dimensions relating to social transformation is being considered. First, justice measures contributed to the overcoming of historical divisions in material terms. Disparities in incomes caused by political discrimination were remedied by reparatory measures, which included the rehabilitation of victims (encompassing the reinstatement in the previous profession, increase in pensions, and compensation for imprisonment, if applicable) and the restitution of their property.

Second, justice measures failed to rectify ideological divides. Pre-1989 KSČ members were more likely than others to wish to return to the past. The results of the path analyses also showed that retributive measures marginally contributed to the desire to return to the communist past. The reconciliatory measures, though in a separate analysis, produced the same marginally negative result as the retributive measures. Only the reparatory measures were able to transform the divides and were likely to dissuade those whose parents were KSČ members from wanting to return to the past. The revelatory measures inhibited views about reconciliation; any reconciliation that emerged was tantamount to forgetting and was not a true reflection of dealing with the past. The assessment of individual measures of justice (Figure 17) also largely depended on the position of the respondent, or his or her family, in the communist regime. Historical differences affect the views of retributive measures (punishment, condemnation of the communist regime, expropriation of the assets of KSČ and SSM), financial compensation, and apology. On the other hand, restitution and the revelatory measures, especially the exposure of secret collaborators, were the least controversial measures of justice.

Finally, two new kinds of social division emerged. First, the KSČM was able to attract new voters who supported a return to the communist regime. They indicated that they would not be dissuaded from this position by the implementation of any kind of justice measure. A measure of justice was nevertheless linked to creating the second new kind of social division. The restitution process created a class of persons who were evicted from the properties they occupied up until 1989 when the properties were returned to their original owners or the heirs of the original owners. Although small in numbers, people in this evicted class were more likely to support a return to the communist regime, although the statistical analysis shows they had nothing in common with the regime. Their support for the return was significant even despite controlling for the pre-1989 membership in the Communist Party, parents in the Party, and voting for KSČM.

Conclusion:
From Observations to the Transformative
Theory of Justice

It is mankind's fate that human beings are placed into power
relations, and this situation gives rise to their responsibility to
champion the forces which will make human rights a reality.
—Vladimír Čermák, Decision of the Constitutional Court of the
Czech Republic, Pl. ÚS 14/94 (1995)

To say that dealing with the past in the Czech Republic either succeeded or
failed would oversimplify the conclusion. The book examined eight major
outcomes of dealing with the past: two from the perspective of former political prisoners, two from the perspective of former Communist Party members, and four from the perspective of society as a whole.[1] The results cannot
be mechanically compared to a football score because the different outcomes
have different weighting. At the same time, however, assigning such weighting does not betoken an objective conclusion because any weighting would
be normatively loaded. It is impossible to rate justice higher than reconciliation, or victims' integration as more important than the transformation of
communist offspring. Arguments for and against the import of each goal
will subsist. It would be fair to say that dealing with the past succeeded in
some aspects and failed in others and that justice measures played sometimes positive and sometimes negative role in the process.

Table 14. Outcomes of Dealing with the Past in the Czech Republic

Outcome	Affirmative Percentage	Negative Percentage
Victims' healing	47.0	45.1
Victims' redress	41.0	50.4
Personal transformation of former communists	42.4	57.6
Intergenerational transformation of offspring	66.2	33.7
No return to the past	63.4	11.0
Equality (income)*	56.1	46.9
Reconciliation	15.3	61.9
Justice	36.4	30.7

Note: Positive values above 50 percent represent an absolute success, while a positive value above negative values represents relative success.
* Equality was measured by personal income. The average national income was set at 50 percent. It means that the average income of those who had been discriminated against were about 6 percent better off than the rest of society as a whole and the ex-communists had incomes that were on average 3 percent lower than society as a whole.

Outcomes of Dealing with the Communist Past: Successes and Failures

The findings, summarized in Table 14 and illustrated in Figure 20, provide a complex picture of the outcomes of dealing with the past in the Czech Republic. Starting from the perspective of the victims, the healing of former political prisoners, conceptualized as overcoming the physical and psychological consequences of their imprisonment, was marginally assessed positively. On the other hand, the sociopolitical redress, conceptualized as their social integration, was assessed rather negatively. In view of the moral high ground that former political prisoners occupy as a result of their victimhood, and in view of corresponding victim-centered approaches to transitional justice, both results are rather unsatisfactory. But in view of the immeasurable losses they suffered, these results may be seen as positive. Particularly promising is the effect of reparatory measures, which convey deep symbolic meaning that acknowledges their suffering and produces material effects that elevate those who were considered second-class citizens.[2]

The outcomes were also mixed from the perspective of former communists. Personal transformation of former communists, conceptualized as the internalization of human rights, occurred in about two out of five of them. Most former communists remained in denial about the systematic violation

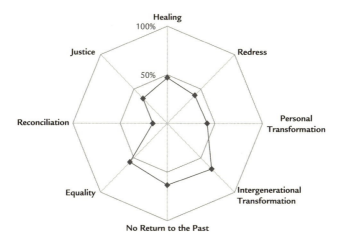

Figure 20. Outcomes of dealing with the past in the Czech Republic. Equality was measured by net income. The average national income is set at 50 percent.

of human rights committed during the communist regime. On the other hand, the intergenerational transformation appeared to be relatively successful. The denial was not reproduced in most communist families, where about two-thirds of offspring agreed that the regime systematically violated human rights. The denial of human rights violations does not seem to be passed from one generation to the next.

From the perspective of society as a whole, dealing with the past has been positively appraised in several aspects. The class structure of the communist regime no longer affects personal incomes. Contrary to research conducted in the 1990s, being a member of the Communist Party before 1989 did not result in a higher income twenty-five years after the fall of communism. The average income of former communists was 94 percent of the total national average even after taking into account other factors, such as gender, education, and employment status (retirement). More important, those who suffered discrimination in the past earned income that was higher than the national average, more precisely 112 percent. It is thus possible to conclude that material injustices have been largely overcome.

A promising result also stems from overcoming one aspect of ideological divides: Society no longer wished to return to the past regime. Merely 11 percent of the whole sample wished to return to the past. The number among former Communist Party members stood at 30 percent. Both are not high numbers, which suggests that Russia—even with the help of its state-controlled media propaganda—will have difficulty persuading the Czechs back into its fold via sentimental ideological arguments. Even many former Czech communists were critical of the communist regime.[3] However, the unwillingness to return to the communist regime did not signify their support for democracy: My qualitative evidence suggests that they used the failures of the communist regime as a rationale for discrediting the democratic system.

The perception of whether justice in society had been achieved was less satisfactory. More than one-third of respondents considered that the greatest injustices had been rectified, while less than a third disagreed. Although relatively positive, this is not an impressive result in view of the large arsenal of measures adopted to deal with the past. Worse still, perceptions about reconciliation scored the lowest result among all outcomes. Being conceptualized as trust among former political prisoners, the former Communist Party members, and the rest of society, reconciliation was positively assessed by a mere 15 percent of respondents.[4] Almost two-thirds of respondents considered that there had been no reconciliation in society.

Indeed, the concave shape of the octagonal radar chart (Figure 20) clearly reveals the magnitude of the apparent deficit: The reconciliation score is the lowest among all other objectives of postconflict justice. The lack of reconciliation corresponds with the finding that many former political prisoners did not feel integrated into society and that the attitudes of the former communists remained unchanged with regard to the atrocities and injustices committed under communist rule. These links form a pattern that revolves around the lack of reconciliation. I thus consider the *lack of reconciliation* as the first major deficit of dealing with the past in the Czech Republic.

Measures of Dealing with the Past: Roads to Successes and Failures

In the second step, I address the question of whether the measures of justice affected the outcomes of dealing with the past, and whether their effect was positive or negative. In order to assess the measures of justice, I compare their impact on eight objectives from the perspective of victims, former communists, and the society as a whole. What was the utility of retributive, reparatory, revelatory, and reconciliatory measures of justice? My findings are summarized in Table 15.

The retributive measures played a role that ranged from indifference (they were irrelevant for the healing and redress of former political prisoners, as

Table 15. Summary of Major Findings

Focus	Outcome	Measure of Justice			
		Retributive	Reparatory	Revelatory	Reconciliatory
Victims	Healing	N.S.	+Financial compensation[R] +Return to previous profession	+Private truth-telling	−Suspected by neighbors
	Sociopolitical redress	N.S.	+Financial compensation[R] +Return to previous profession	−Public truth-telling	−Suspected by neighbors −Wrongdoers arrogant
Communists	Personal transformation	−Scale of retributive measures[R]	+Scale of reparatory measures[R]	+Scale of revelatory measures[R]	−Apology[R]
	Intergenerational transformation	−Scale of retributive measures[R]	N.S.	+Scale of revelatory measures[R]	−Apology[R]
Society (survey experiment)	Justice	+Punishment +Probation +Dismissal	+Financial compensation +Social acknowledgment	−Shaming	+Apology
	Reconciliation	+Dismissal	N.S.	−Shaming	+Apology
Society (survey)	Justice	+Scale of retributive measures[R]	+Scale of reparatory measures[R]	N.S.	N.A.
	Reconciliation	+Scale of retributive measures[R]	N.S.	−Scale of revelatory measures[R]	+Apology[R]
	Income (class transformation)	N.A.	+Rehabilitation +Restitution	N.S.	N.A.
	Return to the communist regime (lack of ideological transformation)	+Scale of retributive measures[R]	+Eviction	−Scale of revelatory measures[R]	+Apology[R]

Notes: +positive predictor; −negative predictor; [R] possibility of reverse causality; N.S. measure not significant; N.A. measure not tested in the model.

shown in Chapter 3) to counterproductivity (they were negatively associated with personal and intergenerational transformation of former communists, as shown in Chapter 4).[5] To be sure, many communists were defiant before the justice measures were adopted. Hence, I can only conclude that retributive measures were not able to overcome the defiance. This interpretation is in line with my previous research, on lustration in the Czech Republic.[6]

But should the retributive measures help to challenge that defiance in the first place? Is the expectation about the effect of retributive measures realistic? Many believe that it is. For instance, the International Criminal Tribunal for Former Yugoslavia (ICTY) was expected to combat denial by providing judicially corroborated evidence of mass atrocities,[7] although empirical evidence about the results of "this combat" remains mixed. Some suggested "shrinking the space for denial" in Serbia,[8] while others questioned the ability of criminal trials to challenge the one-sided version of events attached to the group's ethnic identity.[9] The findings from the Czech Republic thus add to the body of empirical literature, which has not found any positive evidence for the alleged transformative effect of retributive justice.

The potential impact of retributive measures on the perception of justice and reconciliation in society attained from experimental evidence (Chapter 5) appears to be in accord with the positive impact on justice and reconciliation attained from a survey (Chapter 6). However, these findings contrast with the positive impact of retributive justice on the people's preference for a return to the communist regime in Chapter 6. Qualitative and quantitative evidence point to a trivial explanation of this paradox: Retributive measures were seen as excessive by the communists and insufficient by victims and the rest of society. Many communists did not perceive the violation of human rights during the communist regime as a systematic aspect of communist repression. They were ready to admit a few unfortunate aberrations. Hence, any lustration, condemnation, and punishment was unnecessary or excessive justice in their eyes. Retribution degraded the results of their work in the past, inhibited their transformation, and strengthened their desire for a return to the communist regime.

Reconciliatory measures conformed to the same pattern as retributive measures (Chapters 4 and 6). Retributive measures bolstered the defiance of communists who felt that their achievements had been denigrated. In a similar vein, communists did not want to further dishonor the Party and themselves by apologizing. This explains why the appraisal of apologies was negatively associated with the personal and intergenerational transformation of former communists and why the untransformed communists viewed the Party's apology as excessive. The lack of reconciliatory measures inhibited victims' healing and redress. Apology, however, not only may have helped victims but also could have potentially inspired transformation in the entire society: The survey experiment showed that an individual apology led to perceptions of both justice and reconciliation.[10] The positive perception of an apology is in accordance with my previous experiments about the role of apologies in South Korea, and confession in the Czech Republic, Hungary, and Poland. In all these instances, reconciliatory measures were strongly associated with successful outcomes of justice measures.[11]

Reparatory measures fared well in all aspects. They facilitated victims' healing and sociopolitical redress, and they were associated with the personal transformation of former communists. Although reparatory measures did not affect reconciliation, they positively affected the perception of justice. Not only financial compensation but also social acknowledgment affected perceptions of justice significantly. Other strong evidence of their effects came from their transformative impact on the class system. Thanks to the reparatory measures, historical divisions no longer perpetuated inequality in society twenty-five years after the fall of communism. On the other hand, the downside of reparatory measures was exposed during the restitution process. Although their overall percentage was small, those who had to move out of properties that were returned through the restitution process were likely to support a return to the previous regime. By dispossessing occupants in the restituted properties, restitution created new injustices: It created a class of victims of transitional justice whose families sought a return to the past.

Revelatory measures were positively associated with the transformation of former communists (Chapter 4). Any revelation seemed to have a positive effect on the intergenerational transformation in communistic families. Many children—equipped with new history textbooks—continue to resist the opinions of their parents. For the same reasons, revelatory measures led to society as a whole not advocating a return to the past (Chapter 6).

Revelatory measures played an ambiguous role in assisting victims. Private truth-sharing made a positive impact on victims' healing, while public truth-sharing made a negative impact on sociopolitical redress. The dual effect did not undermine but accentuated its potential to assist victims. Sharing painful experiences may, under certain conditions, lead to healing. Whether such conditions can be created in a public forum is another question. Such forums can at least minimize the negative effect of public truth-sharing via the media or sharing at schools. For example, the experience of the daughter of a political prisoner who shared her life experience with students was psychologically draining (see Chapter 3).

Revelatory measures were negatively associated with the prospect for reconciliation (Chapter 6). Nevertheless, this does not necessarily invalidate James Gibson's study that truth—at least for some social groups—leads to reconciliation.[12] As mentioned earlier, reconciliation in the Czech Republic was not transformative reconciliation that had been spurred by personal changes such as remorse or regret. The more that members of society knew about the past, the less sympathetic they became toward those associated with the human rights violations of the past. Knowledge of truth about the past in the Czech Republic did not lead to an understanding of the motives of the perpetrators, nor to empathy for, and the "rehumanizing" of, the adversaries.[13] Instead they were stereotyped, condemned, and dehumanized. Consequently, the reconciliation score in society remained very low.

Overall, reparatory measures were the most successful in dealing with the past, while retributive measures were largely irrelevant or counterproductive. Retributive measures were irrelevant in the healing and redress of victims, and they inhibited the transformation of communists and their offspring. They were positively associated with the "pseudoreconciliation" and with a wish to return to the communist regime. Their desire for a return to the past was because they considered that there had been very little wrong with the past. I identify the convoluted effects of *retributive measures* as the second major deficit of dealing with the past in the Czech Republic.

Justice Without Reconciliation, Collectives Without Individuals

The previous sections identified two deficits in dealing with the past in the Czech Republic: lack of reconciliation, and the contradictory effects of retributive justice. Why was the perception of reconciliation so low? Why have retributive justice measures largely failed to contribute to social transformation? The two problems may be interrelated. This section offers two plausible explanations for these issues.

Collectives Without Individuals

I suggest that a first plausible reason for the low reconciliatory score and the malfunctioning of retributive measures was the preference for collective justice measures: *Justice was sought for groups, not for individual members.*

Justice measures adopted to deal with the past in the Czech Republic were inadequate to address the nuances of individual responsibility. The predominantly collective character of the measures suppressed the complexity of each individual's life story under the weight of the totalitarian regime. Reparatory measures defined victims as a class; revelatory measures exposed the collaborators with the regime as a list; and reconciliatory measures were limited to a collective apology. The most prominent indiscriminate measures of justice were retributive measures: Lustration condemned all secret police members, its informants, the People's Militia, and other groups as a whole; the laws on the expropriation of the assets condemned the entire Communist Party; and the Act on the Illegitimacy of the Communist Regime condemned the whole communist regime, suggesting, "You, the regime, are responsible."

However, gross violations of human rights and other injustices were not committed by an anonymous communist regime but by identifiable individuals, whether political leaders, accomplices in crime, secret informants, or cadre secretaries. Some people were willingly involved in the regime, while others could not withstand its pressure; others dodged it and a few resisted.

The leaders of the Velvet Revolution were mostly vague about the individual dimension of dealing with the past.[14] However, according to Antonín Huvar, a priest and former political prisoner, dealing with the past is dealing with one's past and with one's role in that past.[15] Almost everybody in society was responsible for injustices of one kind or another. In dealing with the past, according to Huvar, teachers should reach out to those talented children who were for political reasons sent to apprentice schools, essentially forgoing the opportunity to study and never being able to use their intellectual abilities for the benefit of society. A multitude of individuals in a range of professions, schools, and churches all can "deal with the injustices" they committed by reaching out to those who suffered various degrees of harm at their hands.

My findings show that the victims appreciated the state's condemnation of the communist regime but I have not found any evidence that they benefited from that condemnation. They benefited from the collective rehabilitation and restitution laws, which were rapidly implemented, but even these laws overwrote their individual stories by a single collective narrative. The collective condemnation made wrongdoers defiant, while the reparatory laws deprived people of the opportunity to learn about the individual experiences of victims. The arrogance of wrongdoers and the ignorance of neighbors negatively affected victims. Victims strove to share their stories publicly but, in the absence of any public forum for truth-sharing, the channels for sharing their stories were not suitable and inhibited their redress.

With regard to the effect of the justice measures on perpetrators, collective retributive measures put communists on the defensive and inhibited their transformation. Those communists who were not responsible for any wrongdoing sought to have their individual contributions recognized and felt unfairly treated by collective retributive measures. Ordinary Party members did not understand why they should be held responsible for crimes that were committed by others, in some cases before they were born. Although revelatory measures contributed to the transformation of some pre-1989 Party members, the defiance spurred by retributive measures led to the filtering out of inconvenient information about the past, and it halted the prospect for apology. The fundamental problem was that the so-often-demanded and so-controversial apology was a collective one: an apology of all Communist Party members for all injustices against all people, not an apology of an individual cadre secretary for discrimination against a churchgoer in employment. On the other hand, none of the measures adopted denied former Party members their agency. Each of them, starting with public figures, could have issued an individual apology. The absence of individual apologies from ordinary members contributed to the collectivist thinking and demands for collective retributive justice.

The collective nature of legal measures was fortified by public demands and petitions, which emerged as a response to the defiance of many former communists. They again aimed at collectivities: "The government," "the communists," or the "others" should do something about the past. The government had to compile a list, the Parliament had to pass a law, the courts had to ban the Party, politicians were "not to talk to the communists," and "the Party" had to apologize—for communism and to everyone, of course.

Public demands for the expansion of justice measures was thus shaped by the collectivist nature of justice measures approved earlier on; by the absence of individual apologies; and by collectivist thinking of the communist era, which these measures were unable to dispel. Indeed, some ordinary Party members may have even identified themselves as "we" in the elusive communist-era dichotomy of "we" and "they" (see Chapter 1). However, collective measures of justice erased individual biographies and created a monolith of former Party members as "they." It created enemies among those who may not have been enemies in the first place.

It would be incongruous to criticize all justice measures adopted in the Czech Republic. The collective measures of justice were rather a double-edged sword. On the one hand, they allowed a swift resolution of major injustices committed by the communist regime. The cancelation of wrongful convictions, reinstatement into previous positions, financial compensation, and the restitution of property undoubtedly benefited large classes of previously discriminated citizens. On the other hand, the collective nature of the justice process was unable to challenge, and perpetuated, the collectivist thinking of the communist regime. The implementation of justice after the regime change merely signified a reversal of previous positions and roles: The victims were collectively honored, and perpetrators collectively damned. The collective nature of these measures suggested—both implicitly and explicitly—that the communist regime was a criminal regime devoid of criminals. As a result, the communist regime has been eargely discredited but the collectivist ideology persists.

Justice Without Reconciliation

The second possible explanation of the results could be called justice without reconciliation. Chapter 2 showed that retributive and reparatory measures were the focal measures chosen by the postcommunist Czech administrations for dealing with the past, followed by revelatory measures. Although an apology for the gross violations of human rights and other injustices was demanded from the Communist Party, reconciliatory measures were never seriously considered to be necessary for dealing with the communist past in the Czech Republic. Chapter 2 therefore characterized the strategy that the country adopted as the policy of *justice without reconciliation*, whereby an emphasis on settling scores was accentuated without even considering the possibility of political and social reconciliation.

At first glance, any further explanation seems redundant. If a country did not adopt a policy that was designed to arrive at outcome R, why would it be necessary to explain why the country failed to achieve R?[16] Allied to this problem is another: Why did a country that vigorously pursued a policy designed to arrive at J score poorly on J? In spite of the vast amount of sources and attention devoted to achieving justice, the outcomes for both justice and reconciliation were unimpressive (Figure 20). As if justice and reconciliation, though conceptually operating on different dimensions, were connected: Retributive justice not only failed to bring reconciliation but also paradoxically inhibited the perception of justice.

I suggest that a society's perception of whether both justice and reconciliation have been achieved depends on the transformative status of the addressees of justice measures: the victims and the perpetrators. Are former political prisoners healed, integrated, and satisfied? Are former communists transformed? Did justice measures produce a change? Did they transform? Untransformed communists and frustrated victims signify that no real change has occurred and would produce low scores for both justice and reconciliation. The less reformed the communists are and the less satisfied the victims, the less justice and reconciliation there will be.

This transformative perspective explains why the perception of justice scored low even after so many measures of retributive justice were adopted in the Czech Republic. The expropriation of Communist Party property, lustration law, and the condemnation of communist wrongdoing were far-reaching measures of retributive justice. Although the number of criminal trials with perpetrators was not commensurate with the scale of victimization, the number of trials was comparable with the number of trials held during transition in many other countries and on par with the general efficiency of law enforcement agencies in the Czech Republic (see Chapter 2). The experimental evidence (see Chapter 5) suggested that all justice measures had a significant effect on the perception of justice as an outcome category. This means that society should have been satisfied with retributive measures that took place, but it was not.

A vicious cycle emerges in which retributive justice measures play a lead role (Figure 21). Retributive measures made many former communists defiant and inhibited their transformation. Many communists did not see themselves as having done anything wrong in the past and now they were all being condemned. Others took pride in what they saw as their contribution to "the achievements of socialism" in the country. These former communists were then perceived as defiant and recalcitrant by the rest of society. To teach them a lesson, society demanded more retributive measures against them.

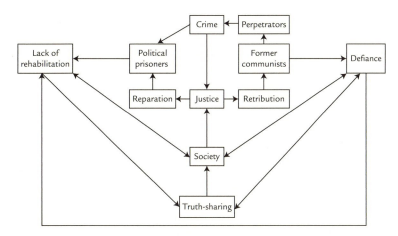

Figure 21. Vicious cycles of justice without reconciliation. This figure captures some of the interrelations that affected the process of dealing with the past. It highlights the problematic side of the process, whereby retributive justice leads to the defiance of former communists, which in turn inhibits the rehabilitation of former political prisoners and frustrates society. As a result, ex-prisoners are compelled to share their stories, which strengthens the defiance of communists, increases anticommunist sentiment in society, and prompts implementation of secondary reparatory and retributive measures. Obviously, there is a positive side of the process, whereby some ex-prisoners are rehabilitated and some communists are transformed.

Hence these *secondary demands* for transitional justice were a response not only to the human rights violations but also to the perceptions about the communists. This may explain why the policy of dealing with the past was so extensive and so many times amended, especially in the area of reparatory and retributive justice. Mounting retributive justice, however, in turn made some of these former communists even more defiant. In the end, instead of transforming them, the retributive justice measures probably fueled desires of some communists to return to the past regime, which would shelter them from retribution and honor their work for society.

In parallel, this defiance of the communists inhibited the healing of victims. Chapter 4 illustrated that the lack of reconciliation, manifested in the arrogance of wrongdoers, inhibited the sociopolitical redress of victims. The negative interpersonal experiences then led former political prisoners to demand further measures to deal with the past. They demanded more retribution against the former communists and, in particular, the banning of the Communist Party, which they—as democrats—had not initially demanded in 1989. As a recompense for their frustration stemming from the defiance of some former communists, many victims also demanded more reparatory measures, which were positive factors in their healing and redress. Moreover, to combat the defiance of former communists, they felt obliged to share their life experiences, although many of them found public sharing problematic. They were keen to reveal the truth, not necessarily as their personal legacy but as public mementos of the past, as a warning to society about the crimes of the communist regime. The conception of public truth-sharing as a duty of victims may explain its negative effect on victims' redress. The society then listens to the story of victims, observes their dissatisfaction, and concludes that justice has not been done.

In sum, justice and reconciliation are entwined in the sense that the assessment of both justice and reconciliation is a function of whether the former adversaries have been transformed. It means that justice, in order to be effective, requires a degree of reconciliation. The social dynamic of the effect of reconciliation on justice is dual: First, reconciliatory measures are likely to reduce the need for secondary retributive and reparatory measures, which were adopted not as a response to injustices per se but as a response to the defiance of former communists and the dissatisfaction of victims, which the defiance caused. Second, as shown in Chapter 5, apology as an instance of reconciliatory measures can increase both the perception of justice and the perception of reconciliation. In accordance with the proposed explanation, apology demonstrates that the wrongdoer has been transformed.

It may be too late for any of these reconciliatory alternatives to complement dealing with the past in the Czech Republic.[17] But other countries can learn from its experience in dealing with the past and thereby avoid its mistakes. Despite all the efforts to prosecute the wrongdoers, marked by establishing two governmental centers and lifting the statute of limitations, individual trials resulted in a small number of convictions in the Czech Republic. The pursuit of collective justice may be a beneficial alternative in terms of speed and efficiency. Nonetheless, the cost that the lack of individual reconciliation carries in terms of stereotypical thinking may be too high to sustain a steady commitment to individual rights.

Toward the Transformative Theory of Justice

The interpretation of my findings can be distilled into the transformative theory of justice. This is what social scientists since Robert Merton have called "a middle range theory."[18] Middle range theories are more abstract than hypotheses; in fact, they allow drawing a number of hypotheses, but they are less complex than macro-structural theories, such as the modernization theory, conflict theory, functionalism, and others. Unlike such macro- or grand theories, which aspire to explain almost all social relations, middle range theories are quite modest in their ambitions, which are limited to particular themes. Generalization of an empirical phenomenon provides us with another defining feature of the middle range theories and distinguish it from the macro theories.

According to the transformative theory, the perception of justice is a function of the transformative status of former adversaries, which is created by a particular justice measure.[19] The assessment of justice thus depends on the transformative status of both recipients of justice: the perpetrator and the victim. If a justice measure were able to facilitate that transformation, it would be assessed positively. A justice measure that makes, or shows, perpetrators reformed and victims rehabilitated would likely be perceived as just. The perpetrator may be seen as less dangerous, victims as no longer victimized, and justice measures as effective. Conversely, if a justice measure were to inhibit, perpetuate, or signal through its implementation that the perpetrator was unreformed, intractable, and recalcitrant it would be assessed negatively as inadequate, insufficient, and ultimately unjust. Likewise, if a victim still bore all consequences and ramifications of the crime, the justice measure would be seen in the same way as unjust.

I expect that retributive justice measures have a low transformative value. They are likely to keep, or instigate, the defiance of perpetrators. I also expect that reconciliatory measures that allow disassociation of the wrongdoer from the wrongdoing and validate the victims are more likely to be seen as transformative measures. The effect of revelatory measures that lead to shaming is likely to stimulate, or uphold, the defiance of perpetrator. Truth-sharing may nevertheless inspire victims' transformation. Such victims' transformation may also be advanced by reparatory measures, which may affect victims directly by providing them with material remedies or indirectly via the symbolic meanings these remedies convey.

The proposed transformative theory of justice is different from extant retributive, restorative, and procedural justice approaches. In the case of *retributive* justice, perceptions about the achievement of justice depend on the (commensurable) suffering imposed on the offender and the "repayment of debt" to the victim.[20] In the main strand of this theory, the greater the punishment, or the compensation, the higher the perception of justice. *Restorative justice* theory is rather a normative set of postulates than a descriptive theory. In the victim-offender-mediator programs,[21] justice is assessed against its ability to restore relations between the victim and the offender, or reintegrating the offender within the community. The degree of such restoration and reintegration is expected to affect justice scores. In the *procedural justice* perspective, the perception of whether justice has been achieved is a function of the administration of justice. Fairness, transparency and impartial procedures; trust and confidence in the motives of authorities who make decisions; the treatment of all protagonists with dignity and respect; and participation in justice procedures are more likely to result in higher justice scores.[22]

In the *transformative justice theory*, justice is a function of the degree of transformation of the addressees of justice. The transformation itself and its perceptions are critical factors rather than the restoration of relationships per se.[23] The more defiant the perpetrator and the more unsatisfied the victim, the lower the justice score. Justice measures that perpetuate, or create, inimical relations between the major protagonists of the previous regime indicate a low perception of justice. Even harsh retributive justice measures, which would be expected to produce a high justice score according to the retributive justice theory, would result in a low justice score because they are likely to result in the defiance of perpetrators. Even a fair and impartial trial that should produce a high justice score according to the theory of procedural justice would result in low justice scores if the perpetrator remains defiant. In transitional situations, whereby both sides may adhere to partisan interpretations of history, the offender—in line with Hannah Arendt's thesis on the banality of evil—may not see himself or herself as doing anything wrong and hence is likely seen as unreformed and justice as inadequate in spite of severe punishment and rigorous procedures. Moreover, the proposed theorization can explain situations in nontransitional settings as well. The transformative theory can comprehend the effect of remorse expressed by a perpetrator in the courtroom, which is something that existing theories of justice cannot fully account for.

The transformative theory can also contribute to the explanation of the origins of transitional justice.[24] In situations where perpetrators are seen as untransformed, the demand for their punishment and dismissals would be greater than in situations when transformation occurred. Evidence of such transformation may emanate from the cessation of hostilities, cease-fires, negotiated settlements, and transitional pacts, through which the protagonists of the ancien régime are able to portray themselves as rational actors who are reasonable in making a political deal. Political liberalization that precedes transition, the mode of exit of the authoritarian regime, and the reform of the regime's party also demonstrate the degree of transformation.

By extension, the transformative theory can explain the secondary demands for justice, or the virtual cycles of justice (see Figure 21). Demands for additional justice measures may not be as much a response to the crime of the past but rather to the dearth of transformative outcomes of existing measures. If existing measures of justice did not transform the perpetrator and rehabilitate the victim, a new demand for justice may appear. The retributive measures of justice on their own bring less transformation, which in turn brings demands for new justice measures. Such secondary demands may also shape social relations in nontransitional settings, for instance, before the expected release of a convicted offender from jail.

Finally, the transformative theory entwines justice and reconciliation in a dynamic relationship. The perception of justice and the perception of reconciliation as conceptually distinct outcome categories share a common origin in the degree of transformation of former adversaries. I have illustrated that—besides the perception of justice depending on the perception of the transformation of both protagonists under particular constellation of justice measures—the degree of the transformation of communists affected the rehabilitation of victims and vice versa (Figure 21). I also presented experimental evidence that the transformative status can be enhanced by reconciliatory measures, which are capable of increasing both justice and reconciliation. I showed that the neglect of reconciliatory measures generates secondary demands for retributive and reparatory justice measures and also undermines the effort to deal with the past.

The proposed theory originates in the empirical observations and conversely could allow researchers drawing testable hypotheses about the origin and the effect of justice measures. By extension, it could also explain the recurrent justice demands in transitional societies, which make transition an endless endeavor; and it links justice with reconciliation, potentially stipulating the conditionality between the two. A transformative theory of justice applies to the area of transitional justice but can also lead to hypotheses concerning ordinary justice.

Notes

Introduction

The epigraphs for this chapter are from the following three sources, in the order of their appearance: ÚV KSČ, "Poučení z krizového vývoje ve straně a společnosti po XIII. sjezdu KSČ" (December 11, 1970), http://www.totalita.cz/txt/txt_pouceni.php (accessed September 1, 2015); Václav Havel, "Projev prezidenta ČSFR Václava Havla k výročí okupace Československa vojsky pěti zemí Varšavského paktu" (August 21, 1990), http://old.hrad.cz/president/Havel /speeches/index.html (accessed September 1, 2015); "Варшавский договор: Рассекреченные страницы" [The Warsaw Pact: Declassified pages], TV Rossiya 1 (May 23, 2015).

1. The role of writers in the communist regimes was to engineer human souls. *The Engineer of Human Souls* was a novel by a Czech exiled writer, Josef Škvorecký. In fact, the communist regime could be seen as an attempt at engineering human souls, values, and needs.

2. See Neil J. Kritz ed., *Transitional Justice: How Emerging Democracies Reckon with Former Regimes* (Washington, D.C.: United States Institute of Peace Press, 1995); Ruti G. Teitel, *Transitional Justice* (Oxford: Oxford University Press, 2000); Lavinia Stan and Nadya Nedelsky, *Encyclopedia of Transitional Justice*, 3 vols. (New York: Cambridge University Press, 2013); Roman David, "What We Know About Transitional Justice: Survey and Experimental Evidence," *Political Psychology* 38 (S1): 151–77.

3. For criticism, see Laurel E. Fletcher and Harvey M. Weinstein, "Violence and Social Repair: Rethinking the Contribution of Justice to Reconciliation," *Human Rights Quarterly* 24 (2002): 573–639; David Mendeloff, "Truth-seeking, Truth-telling, and Postconflict Peacebuilding: Curb the Enthusiasm?" *International Studies Review* 6, no. 3 (2004): 355–80; Leslie Vinjamuri and Jack Snyder, "Advocacy and Scholarship in the Study of International War Crime Tribunals and Transitional Justice," *Annual Review of Political Science* 7 (2004): 345–62.

4. Hugo van der Merwe, "Editorial Note," *International Journal of Transitional Justice* 7 (2013): 1–7.

5. Dean Makau Mutua, ed., "Transitional Justice: Does It Have a Future? A Special Issue," *International Journal of Transitional Justice* 9, no. 1 (2015).

6. See, e.g., *Adler v. Board of Education*, 342 U.S. 485 (1952); *Glasenapp v. Germany*, 9 E.H.R.R. 25 (1986). Security reasons were used to justify torture and the violation of the right to live.

7. See Lavinia Stan and Nadya Nedelsky, eds., *Post-Communist Transitional Justice: Lessons from Twenty-Five Years of Experience* (New York: Cambridge University Press, 2014). Unfortunately, the volume appeared a few weeks before the Russian annexation of Crimea. Its authors thus could not take into account essentially a new political situation.

8. With the exception of Senator John McCain in the United States, Western politicians paid little attention to Russia's occupation of territories belonging to Moldova and Georgia. Radio Free Europe/Radio Liberty, "McCain Backs Demand for Russian Troop Withdrawal from Transdniester" (June 13, 2011), http://www.rferl.org/content/mccain_backs_demand _for_russian_troop_withdrawal_from_transdniester/24233530.html (accessed September 1, 2015).

9. In 2005, Putin described the collapse of the USSR as the greatest geopolitical catastrophe of the twentieth century. In 2014, Putin stated that he could "take Kiev in two weeks." In 2015, Russia's Prosecutor General started to examine the legality of the recognition of Baltic states. See "Putin Deplores Collapse of USSR," *BBC News*, April 25, 2005; Jessica Elgot, "Vladimir Putin: 'I Can Take Kiev in Two Weeks If I Want,'" *Huffington Post UK*, September 1, 2014; "Russia Examines 1991 Recognition of Baltic Independence," *BBC News*, June 30, 2015.

10. Bridget Kendall, "Russian Propaganda Machine 'Worse Than Soviet Union,'" *BBC News* (June 6, 2014), http://www.bbc.com/news/magazine-27713847 (accessed June 7, 2016); Neil MacFarquhar, "A Powerful Russian Weapon: The Spread of False Stories," *New York Times* (August 29, 2016), http://www.nytimes.com/2016/08/29/world/europe/russia-sweden -disinformation.html?smprod=nytcore-iphone&smid=nytcore-iphone-share&_r=0 (accessed September 6, 2016).

11. See, e.g., Henry Foy and Christian Oliver, "Czech President Milos Zeman in War of Words over Russia Stance," *Financial Times*, February 9, 2015.

12. "Russian TV Doc on 1968 Invasion Angers Czechs and Slovaks," *BBC News* (June 1, 2015), http://www.bbc.com/news/world-europe-32959054 (accessed September 1, 2015).

13. K231 was in fact an association of former political prisoners in 1968.

14. ÚV KSČ, "Poučení z krizového vývoje."

15. Ibid.

16. "Healthy core" was an official term that denoted the hard-line communists who were members of the purge committees in the aftermath of the invasion.

17. Some district cells of the KSČM in the Czech Republic have been spreading the Rossiya 1 propaganda video and other fake news via their websites. See, e.g., District Committee in Frýdek-Místek, http://www.ovkscmfm.estranky.cz/ (accessed September 1, 2015).

18. Paloma Aguilar, Laia Balcells, and Hector Cebolla-Boado, "Determinants of Attitudes Toward Transitional Justice: An Empirical Analysis of the Spanish Case," *Comparative Political Studies* 44, no. 10 (2011): 1397–430.

19. *Lidové noviny*, "Mladí komunisté: Pro nás české zákony neplatí, my chceme jen socialismus" (May 23, 2015), http://www.lidovky.cz/mladi-komuniste-pro-nas-ceske-zakony -neplati-chceme-jen-socialismus-116-/zpravy-domov.aspx?c=A150522_141101_ln_domov_ele (accessed September 1, 2015).

20. Roman David, "Ukrainian Lustration and European Standards: Building Democracy Capable of Defending Itself," *USAID's FAIR Justice Project Ukraine*, February 24, 2015.

21. In stipulating the accession criteria, the EU did not require countries that applied for membership to deal with the communist past as a condition for EU membership. See Milada

A. Vachudová, *Europe Undivided: Democracy, Leverage, and Integration After Communism* (Oxford: Oxford University Press, 2005).

22. Roman David, *Lustration and Transitional Justice* (Philadelphia: University of Pennsylvania Press, 2011); Roman David and Susanne Y. P. Choi, "Getting Even or Getting Equal? Retributive Desires and Transitional Justice," *Political Psychology* 30 (2009): 161–92.

23. Laurel E. Fletcher, Harvey M. Weinstein, and Jamie Rowen, "Context, Timing and the Dynamics of Transitional Justice: A Historical Perspective," *Human Rights Quarterly* 31 (2009): 163–220.

24. Ibid., 170.

25. Since I consider liberal democracy as a preferred, or creditable, form of government, I align myself with the vast majority of scholars who directly or indirectly adopt this normative perspective as a background for assessment. See Teitel, *Transitional Justice*; Tricia D. Olsen, Leigh A. Payne, and Andrew G. Reiter, "The Justice Balance: When Transitional Justice Improves Human Rights and Democracy," *Human Rights Quarterly* 32 (2010): 980–1007; and Natalia Letki, "Lustration and Consolidation of Democracy," *Europe-Asia Studies* 54 (2002): 529–52.

26. James L. Gibson, "Truth, Reconciliation, and the Creation of Human Rights Culture in South Africa," *Law and Society Review* 38, no. 1 (2004): 5–40; James L. Gibson, "Does Truth Lead to Reconciliation? Testing the Causal Assumptions of the South African Truth and Reconciliation Process," *American Journal of Political Science* 48, no. 2 (2004): 201–17; David and Choi, "Getting Even or Getting Equal?"; Cynthia M. Horne, "Lustration, Transitional Justice, and Social Trust in Post-Communist Countries: Repairing or Wrestling the Ties That Bind?" *Europe-Asia Studies* 66, no. 2 (2014): 225–54.

27. In this book, I examine transitional justice in the context of dealing with the undemocratic regime, not in the context of a civil war or armed conflict.

28. The classic literature in democratization speaks of transition to "something else," which may or may not be a democratic regime. Guillermo O'Donnell, Phillipe Schmitter, and Laurence Whitehead, eds., *Transitions from Authoritarian Rule* (Baltimore: Johns Hopkins University Press, 1986).

29. Fareed Zakaria, *The Future of Freedom: Illiberal Democracy at Home and Abroad* (New York: W. W. Norton, 2003); Steven Levitsky and Lucan A. Way, *Competitive Authoritarianism: Hybrid Regimes After the Cold War* (Cambridge: Cambridge University Press, 2010).

30. Arend Lijphart and Carlos H. Waisman, eds., *Institutional Design in New Democracies: Eastern Europe and Latin America* (Boulder, Colo.: Westview, 1996).

31. James L. Gibson, "Social Networks, Civil Society, and the Prospects for Consolidating Russia's Democratic Transition," *American Journal of Political Science* 45, no. 1 (2001): 51–68.

32. Bronwyn A. Leebaw, "The Irreconcilable Goals of Transitional Justice," *Human Rights Quarterly* 30, no. 1 (2008): 95–118.

33. Eric Stover and Harvey M. Weinstein, eds., *My Neighbor, My Enemy: Justice and Community in the Aftermath of Mass Atrocity* (Cambridge: Cambridge University Press, 2004), 3.

34. Teitel, *Transitional Justice*.

35. Richard A. Wilson, *The Politics of Truth and Reconciliation in South Africa: Legitimizing the Post-Apartheid State* (Cambridge: Cambridge University Press, 2001).

36. Based on a review of the psychological literature, Sarah Cullinan argues that the absence of sanctions against perpetrators can function as "a second injury," causing additional anxiety, creating "a life of repetition of the trauma," and prolonging psychopathological

consequences of repression. See Cullinan, *Torture Survivors' Perceptions of Reparation* (London: Redress, 2001), 27.

37. Iris Chang speaks of the absence of justice in the case of the rape of Nanking as a "second rape." See Iris Chang, *Rape of Nanking* (New York: Penguin, 1997), 199.

38. See also James W. Booth, "'From This Far Place': On Justice and Absence," *American Political Science Review* 105 (2001): 750–64, quote on 757.

39. Dismissals are vigorously demanded in transitional countries owing to their strong and expressive power. Dismissals represent a means of personnel discontinuity. Maria Łoś, "Lustration and Truth Claims: Unfinished Revolutions in Central Europe," *Law and Social Inquiry* 20, no. 1 (1995): 117–61; Roman David, "Lustration Laws in Action: The Motives and Evaluation of Lustration Policy in the Czech Republic and Poland (1989–2001)," *Law and Social Inquiry* 28, no. 2 (2003): 387–439. See generally David, *Lustration and Transitional Justice*, chap. 2.

40. Weinstein and Stover, *My Neighbor, My Enemy.*

41. Cynthia M. Horne, *Building Trust and Democracy: Transitional Justice in Post-Communist Countries* (Oxford: Oxford University Press, 2017).

42. James L. Gibson and Amanda Gouws, *Overcoming Political Intolerance in South Africa: Experiments in Democratic Persuasion* (Cambridge: Cambridge University Press, 2003).

43. Gibson, "Truth, Reconciliation, and the Creation of Human Rights Culture."

44. In my previous work, I defined social reconciliation as a multifaceted concept encompassing interpersonal trust, tolerance, and decreasing social distance. David, *Lustration and Transitional Justice*, chap. 7.

45. See, e.g., Richard J. Goldstone, "Peace Versus Justice," *Nevada Law Journal* 6 (2005–6): 421–24. The moral dilemma inevitably causes certain unease among activists and deontologists. For many, it is inconceivable that such moral imperatives as peace and justice can be achieved at another's expense. See, e.g., International Center for Transitional Justice, "Peace Versus Justice: A False Dilemma," https://www.ictj.org/news/peace-versus-justice -false-dilemma (accessed July 22, 2016).

46. David, "Lustration Laws in Action."

47. This citation is attributed to the former East German dissident Barbel Bohley. Since then, it has been cited by the *New York Times*, the *Economist*, and by Pippa Norris, Dieter Fuchs, Wojciech Sadurski, and others.

48. Obviously, there has been an overlap among these categories. Being a communist does not inevitably mean that one cannot also be a victim or a bystander in another era.

49. Chile could stand out as another country with far-reaching measures. See volume 2 of Stan and Nedelsky, *Encyclopedia of Transitional Justice.*

Chapter 1

1. This chapter does not aspire to provide readers with a comprehensive overview of the communist regime in Czechoslovakia. Although the topic of injustices is known to area specialists, this chapter's review of that topic provides requisite contextual information for the book.

2. After its independence from the Austro-Hungarian monarchy in 1918, Czechoslovakia established an independent democratic state. Led by Tomáš G. Masaryk, a sociology professor, the country held free elections based on proportional representation, and it promulgated

a constitution based on the separation of powers with constitutionally protected human rights. It established the first-ever Constitutional Court and was admired for being a democratic enclave against Nazism until the 1938 Munich Accords led to the annexation of border regions by Hitler. For sources on the Czechoslovak history in English, see, e.g., S. Harrison Thompson, *Czechoslovakia in European History*, 2nd ed. (London: Frank Cass, 1965); Archie Brown, *The Rise and Fall of Communism* (New York: HarperCollins, 2009); Jaroslav Krejčí and Pavel Machonin, *Czechoslovakia 1918–92* (London: Macmillan, 1996); and other sources cited below. For the Czechoslovak struggle to resist pro-Nazi groups before World War II, see Karl Loewenstein, "Militant Democracy and Fundamental Rights," part I, *American Political Science Review* 31, no. 3 (1937): 417–32.

3. For the election results, see Český statistický úřad, "Výsledky voleb do Poslanecké sněmovny—1920–2006," https://www.czso.cz/csu/czso/vysledky-voleb-do-poslanecke-snemovny-v-letech-1920-2006-n-tgdmpl7urw (accessed August 11, 2017). The victory was spurred by several factors. First, Czechoslovakia was not spared by the general inclination of the electorate to the left, which occurred after the war in all European countries. Second, the expulsion of about three million Czechoslovak Germans from the Sudetenland shifted the balance of voting preferences toward the communists. Third, the KSČ was oriented to the Soviet Union, which liberated most of the territory and which was seen as more reliable than Britain and France, the two signatories of the Munich Accords. Fourth, the communists had a record of being able to operate within the constitutional and political framework of Czechoslovak democracy.

4. Brown, *The Rise and Fall of Communism*. On Soviet pressure on Gottwald to execute his deputy Rudolf Slánský, Brown stated: "if Gottwald had been a Tito, he could have refused to give way."

5. Jiří Bílek and Vladimír Pilát, "Závodní, Dělnické a Lidové milice v Československu," *Historie a vojenství* 44, no. 3 (1995): 79–106.

6. For the concept of totalitarianism, see Zbigniew Brzezinski and Carl J. Friedrich, *Totalitarian Dictatorship and Autocracy* (Cambridge, Mass.: Harvard University Press, 1956).

7. The same people thus debated the same agenda three times as members of the party, government, and a parliament. Jiří Kabele et al., "Rekonstrukce komunistického vládnuti na konci osmdesátých let: Dědictví komunistické vlady V.," *Sociological Papers* SP03, no. 10 (2003): 51.

8. *Nomenklatura* was "a secret list of these important positions at all levels of the economic and state administrations, and all other areas of institutional life, which are formally reserved for loyal party members." Maria Łoś, *Communist Ideology, Law, and Crime* (New York: St. Martin's, 1988), 147.

9. Lenka Kalinová et al., eds., *K proměnám sociální struktury v Československu 1918–1968* (Prague: UPSV, 1993); Krejčí and Machonin, *Czechoslovakia*, 159.

10. Pavel Tigrid, *Dnešek je váš, zítřek je náš: Dělnické revolty v komunistických zemích* (Prague: Vokno, 1990); Krejčí and Machonin, *Czechoslovakia*, 45.

11. Krejčí and Machonin, *Czechoslovakia*, 41–48, 154.

12. See Petr Pithart, *Osmašedesátý*, 3rd ed. (Prague: Rozmluvy, 1990).

13. Kabele et al., "Rekonstrukce," 15n13.

14. See, e.g., Robert Bideleux and Ian Jeffries, *A History of Eastern Europe: Crisis and Change*, 2nd ed. (New York: Routledge, 2007).

15. See, e.g., Condoleezza Rice, *The Soviet Union and the Czechoslovak Army, 1948–1983: Uncertain Allegiance* (Princeton, N.J.: Princeton University Press, 1984).

16. Czechoslovakia was a producer and exporter of weapons, ammunition, and explosives, including the infamous Semtex. This side of Czechoslovak history has not been fully mapped. Craig R. Whitney, "Evolution in Europe: East's Archives Reveal Ties to Terrorists," *New York Times,* July 15, 1990.

17. Tony Judt, *The Postwar: The History of Europe Since 1945* (New York: Penguin, 2006), 446.

18. See, e.g., Josef Korbel, *Twentieth Century Czechoslovakia* (New York: Columbia University Press, 1977); Ivan Gadourek, *The Political Control of Czechoslovakia*, 2nd ed. (Leiden: Greenwood, 1974).

19. Constitutional Court of the Czech Republic, Decision Pl. ÚS 19/93 (1993), http:// www.usoud.cz/en/decisions/?tx_ttnews%5Btt_news%5D=613&cHash=4b0aefbdd1833ddb38 627d8bb12ea1fa (accessed September 1, 2015).

20. Ladislav Holý, *The Little Czech and the Great Czech Nation* (Cambridge: Cambridge University Press, 1996).

21. "Palach claimed he chose such an extreme form of protest in order to arouse his fellow citizens from their apathy and to shock them into taking action against what was happening in their country." Coilin O'Connor, "Jan Palach—the Student Whose Self-immolation Still Haunts Czechs Today," *Radio Prague* (January 21, 2009), http://www.radio.cz/en/section /czechs/jan-palach-the-student-whose-self-immolation-still-haunts-czechs-today (accessed June 7, 2016).

22. Jonathan Bolton, *Worlds of Dissent: Charter 77, the Plastic People of the Universe, and Czech Culture Under Communism* (Cambridge, Mass.: Harvard University Press, 2010).

23. Vladimir Lenin, *The State and Revolution*, chap. 5, pt. 2, https://www.marxists.org /archive/lenin/works/1917/staterev/ (accessed September 1, 2015).

24. Krejčí and Machonin, *Czechoslovakia*, 41–48. In addition to the literature cited below, a lot of new material is published by ÚDV, http://www.policie.cz/clanek/urad-dokumentace-a -vysetrovani-zlocinu-komunismu-679905.aspx (accessed November 11, 2014); ÚSTR, http:// www.ustrcr.cz (accessed November 11, 2014), and the Institute for Contemporary History, http://www.usd.cas.cz (accessed November 11, 2014).

25. Focus group with members of KPV, Olomouc, November 4, 2014.

26. There were more than 3,000 officially recognized cases of disappearance and/or extrajudicial executions in Chile underPinochet's rule. Cath Collins and Claudio Fuentes Saavedra, "Chile," in Stan and Nedelsky, *Encyclopedia*, vol. 2, p. 99.

27. There are minor discrepancies about the exact number, which ranges from 248 (Liška) to 262 (ÚDV). ÚDV, "Oběti komunistického režimu," http://www.policie.cz/clanek /obeti-komunistickeho-rezimu.aspx?q=Y2hudW09Mg%3d%3d; Otakar Liška et al., *Vykonané tresty smrti: Československo 1918–1989* (Prague: ÚDV, 2000); Prokop Tomek, *Počty obětí komunistického režimu v Československu v letech 1948–1989* (Prague: ÚDV, n.d.), http://www .policie.cz/clanek/obeti-komunistickeho-rezimu.aspx?q=cHJuPTE%3d (accessed November 11, 2014).

28. Liška et al., *Vykonané tresty smrti*, 161.

29. Krejčí and Machonin, *Czechoslovakia*, 161.

30. In total about 4,500 prisoners died in jail; the estimate of 4,000 political prisoners was provided by the head of the KPV archives, Otto Stehlík in Prague on January 18, 2000.

31. Martin Pulec, *Organizace a činnost ozbrojených pohraničních složek. Seznamy osob usmrcených na státních hranicích 1945–1989* (Prague: Úřad dokumentace a vyšetřování zločinů komunismu, 2006), 173.

32. See ibid.

33. At least 140 people were killed or died at the Berlin Wall between 1961 and 1989. See Fatalities at the Berlin Wall, Berlin War Memorial, http://www.berliner-mauer-gedenkstaette.de/en/todesopfer-240.html (accessed on August 12, 2017).

34. Between 1973 and 1985, Uruguayan dictatorship imprisoned more than 55,000 people out of around three million. Michael Humphrey and Estela Valverde, "Uruguay," in Stan and Nedelsky, *Encyclopedia*, vol. 2, p. 498.

35. František Gebauer, Karel Kaplan, František Koudelka, and Rudolf Vyhnálek, eds., *Soudní perzekuce politické povahy v Československu 1948–1989: Statistický přehled* (Prague: ÚSD, 1993). See also Karel Pacner, "Stovky zmařených lidských životů, statisíce rozbitých rodin," *MF Dnes*, February 25, 2000. The population of Czechoslovakia was around 12.3 million in 1950 and 15.6 million before its breakup in 1992–93.

36. See Karel Kaplan, *Political Persecution in Czechoslovakia 1948–1972* (Cologne: Index, 1983), 11–31; Jiří Bílek and Karel Kaplan, *Pomocné Technické Prapory 1950–1954. Tábory nucené práce v Československu 1948–1954* (Prague: ÚSD, 1992); Karel Bartošek, *Český vězeň: Svědectví politických vězeňkyň a vězňů let padesátých, šedesátých a sedmdesátých* (Prague: Paseka, 2001).

37. Státní ústřední archiv, Archiv ÚV KSČ, fond 02/1 sign. P 66/88 č.j.: P4570, www.ustrcr.cz (accessed September 2, 2015).

38. Kalinová et al., *K proměnám sociální struktury.*

39. The status inconsistency is based on the distinctions between class, status, and power. Status inconsistency occurs when an individual occupies a higher level in at least one of the three aspects and a low level in the remaining aspect(s). The concept comes from Max Weber and was poignantly applied by Eastern European sociologists to the study of communist regimes. See Krejčí and Machonin, *Czechoslovakia*, 162.

40. Adam Hradilek, "Milan Kundera's Denunciation," *Respekt*, October 13, 2008; Kateřina Šafaříková, "Milan Kundera's Denunciation, Part II," *Respekt*, October 22, 2009; *Lidové Noviny*, "Zemřel Miroslav Dvořáček. Muž, kterého prý udal Milan Kundera," March 13, 2012.

41. Hradilek, "Milan Kundera's Denunciation"; Šafaříková, "Milan Kundera's Denunciation, Part II"; *Lidové Noviny*, "Zemřel Miroslav Dvořáček."

42. See Kieran Williams and Dennis Deletant, *Security Intelligence Services in New Democracies: The Czech Republic, Slovakia and Romania* (New York: Palgrave, 2001); Maria Łoś and Andrzej Zybertowicz, *Privatizing the Police-State: The Case of Poland* (New York: Palgrave, 2001).

43. See Helmut Gebhardt, "The Police Reforms of Joseph II in the Province Capitals of Austria," http://irhis.recherche.univ-lille3.fr/dossierPDF/CIRSAP-Textes/Gebhardt.pdf (accessed November 24, 2014); Robert J. Goldstein, *Political Repression in 19th Century Europe* (London: Routledge, 1983).

44. Jaroslav Hašek, *The Good Soldier Svejk and His Fortunes in the World War* (London: Penguin Classics, 2000). In one episode, Švejk was arrested by the secret policeman Bretschneider.

45. Ústav pro studium totalitních režimů, "Německé bezpečnostní a represivní složky," http://www.ustrcr.cz/cs/nemecke-bezpecnostni-a-represivni-slozky (accessed November 24, 2014).

46. Karel Kaplan, *Nebezpečná bezpečnost: Státní bezpečnost 1948–1956* (Brno: Doplnek, 1999).

47. Policie ČR, "STB—vznik, struktura a normy," http://www.policie-cr.cz/stb-seznamy .php (accessed November 24, 2014); Pavel Žáček, *Přísně tajné! Státní bezpečnost za normalizace* (Prague: Votobia, 2001).

48. Williams and Deletant, *Security Intelligence Services*; David, *Lustration and Transitional Justice*.

49. Marián Gula, "Vývoj typů spolupracovníků kontrarozvědky StB ve směrnicích pro agenturní práci," *Securitas imperii: Sborník k problematice bezpečnostních služeb* 1 (1994): 6–17; Pavel Žáček, "Ostrá zbraň Státní bezpečnosti: Spolupracovníci StB ve směrnicích pro agenturně operativní práci 1947–89," ÚSTR, http://www.ustrcr.cz/data/pdf/clanky/ostra-zbran-stb.pdf (accessed September 1, 2015).

50. Gula, "Vývoj typů"; Žáček, "Ostrá zbraň."

51. Žáček, "Ostrá zbraň," 7–8.

52. Williams and Deletant, *Security Intelligence Services*.

53. Rozkaz Ministra vnitra ČSSR, no. 3, Směrnice pro práci se spolupracovníky kontrarozvědky (January 25, 1978), available at Archiv bezpecnostních slozek, ÚSTR, www.ustrcr.cz (accessed September 1, 2015).

54. Gula, "Vývoj typů spolupracovníků"; Žáček, *Přísně tajné*.

55. Rozkaz Ministra vnitra, no. 3.

56. Ibid., art. 3.

57. The list was later transferred into an online searchable database at ÚSTR, www.ustrcr.cz.

58. The number of individuals who judicially challenged the inclusion of their names in the list was relatively minor in comparison with the robustness of the database.

59. I examined the list of collaborators in the registration protocols that captured the opening of the files of secret collaborators. Before the analyses, all duplicate cases were deleted.

60. In contrast, the liberalization era in Poland in the 1980s was associated with an increase in the number of secret informers. Łoś and Zybertowicz, *Privatizing the Police-State*.

61. *Dead Souls* is the title of a novel written by Nikolai Gogol in 1842. Its main protagonist buys the names of deceased servants in order to raise loans against them. Secret police collaborators were said to be recruited in a similar way in order to impress the bosses. For the analysis, see Łoś, "Lustration and Truth Claims."

62. Digitální knihovna, Poslanecká Sněmovna Parlamentu ČR, http://www.psp.cz/sqw /fsnem.sqw?org=265&zvo=1 (accessed May 15, 2015)

63. Zdena Salivarová-Škvorecká, *Osočení: Pravdivé příběhy lidí z "Cibulkova seznamu"* (Brno: Host, 2000).

64. Cibulka's lists were unofficial lists of alleged secret informers, which were compiled based on the leaked documents from the Ministry of the Interior. *Czechoslovak TV*, "Vyprávěj: Byly zveřejněny tzv. Cibulkovy seznamy tajných spolupracovníků Státní bezpečnosti, Česká Televize" (June 4, 1992), http://www.ceskatelevize.cz/ivysilani/10195164142-vypravej/bonus /7345-byly-zverejneny-tzv-cibulkovy-seznamy-tajnych-spolupracovniku-statni-bezpecnosti (accessed June 7, 2016).

65. Škvorecká, *Osočení*, 209.

66. Ústav pro studium totalitních režimů "Vyhledávání v archivních pomůckách," http://www.abscr.cz/cs/vyhledavani-archivni-pomucky (accessed May 15, 2015).

67. Škvorecká, *Osočení*, 59.

68. Ústav pro studium totalitních režimů, "Vyhledávání v archivních pomůckách."

69. Holý, *Little Czech*.

70. Owen Jones, *Chavs: The Demonization of the Working Class* (London: Verso, 2012).

71. Holý, *Little Czech*, 62.

72. Václav Havel, *Living in Truth*, ed. Jan Vladislav, trans. Paul Wilson (London: Faber and Faber, 1986), 41.

73. An "informal curriculum" is essentially the same concept as a "hidden curriculum," which is used in gender studies. I avoid the latter for its misleading connotation with hidden repression, described earlier.

74. While cheating during exams is normally disapproved of in most countries, it was common in many communist states, where it represented a "collective problem-solving in the face of authority." Anthony Giddens, *Sociology* (Cambridge: Polity Press, 2003), 22.

75. Direct empirical evidence about the degree of the ideological support for the communist regime is difficult, if not impossible, to obtain. An indirect indication of the ideological support for the regime can be demonstrated by the Communist Party's losses in the first democratic elections in 1990: The Party won 13.48 percent of the seats in the House of the People and had not been able to make any improvements. Further evidence is provided by the dramatic drop in Party membership in December 1989 (see Chapter 4).

76. Milan Šimečka, *Obnovení pořádku* (London: Edice Rozmluvy, 1984), cited in Holý, *Little Czech*, 23.

77. Holý, *Little Czech*, 16–33.

78. It means that people often performed formal "work rituals" in their workplaces rather than working productively.

79. Šimečka, *Obnovení pořádku*.

80. Ibid., 24. For the role of networks under the communist regime, see also Olga Šmídová, "Co vyprávějí naše byty," in *Otevřená minulost: Autobiografická sociologie státního socialism*, ed. Zdeněk Konopásek et al. (Prague: Karolinum, 1999), 178–80.

81. Milan Kundera, *The Joke: Definitive Version* (New York: HarperCollins, 1993).

82. Vladimír Škutina was a Czech humorist who was imprisoned twice. Vladimír Škutina, *Presidentův vězeň*, 2nd ed. (Prague: Středočeské nakladatelství a knihkupectví, 1990).

83. Konopásek et al., *Otevřená minulost*, 159. Some children blamed their parents for their class background, which prevented many from continuing their studies or getting into a profession of their choice. Ibid., 160.

84. Jiří Kabele, "Ďábelský koktejl sametové revoluce," in Konopásek et al., *Otevřená minulost*, 205–16, 208.

85. This news originated from the independent East European Information Agency and was transmitted by the Associated Press. The RFE cautioned that it had not been verified by a second source. Although other agencies were broadcasting it as well, the RFE had probably the widest reach. Lída Rakušanová, Už tehdy jsem si říkala, že nechci vidět tu kocovinu, http://www.denik.cz/z_domova/lida-rakusanova-uz-tehdy-jsem-si-rikala-ze-nechci-videt -tu-kocovinu-20141115.html?hc_location=ufi (accessed August 12, 2017).

86. According to Thomas Schelling, "People are responding to an environment that consists of other people responding to their environment, which consists of people responding to an environment of people's responses." Schelling, *Micromotives and Macrobehavior* (New York: W. W. Norton, 1978), 14.

87. The issue of "choices" is also addressed in social psychology literature. It appeared in the research that examined the question of why people obey authorities. The question was asked in the context of trials of Nazi leaders who defended themselves by claiming that they merely followed orders. To address this issue, the Yale psychologist Stanley Milgram conducted one of the most controversial studies in psychology. In what has become known as a Milgram experiment, participants were recruited to assist with an educational experiment that would examine people's memories. A volunteer acted as a teacher who imposed electric shocks on a learner when he provided incorrect answers. The teacher was in fact deceived and was himself a subject of the experiment, in which he was required to follow orders by the experimenter. The teacher received gradated orders to increase the voltage of electric shocks even though the learner in the fictional experiment apparently suffered more and more pain. Acting as the experimenter, Milgram wanted to know whether the "teachers" would be able to follow his orders. He concluded that many people obeyed his orders, although many participants questioned the value of the experiment and wished to end it. The experiment, though ethically controversial, is featured in many textbooks. See, e.g., Jeffrey H. Goldstein, *Social Psychology* (New York: Academic Press, 2013); John J. Macionis, *Sociology*, 14th ed. (Boston: Pearson, 2012). The regimented nature of the communist regime provided a context in which the exercise of choices was vastly different. Naturally, whether the oppressive context meant that people were more likely to understand that the consequences of their choice would contravene human rights, or whether it would make them less likely to anticipate these consequences, is an empirical question that needs to be addressed by further studies.

Chapter 2

1. Susanne Y. P. Choi and Roman David, "Lustration Systems and Trust: Evidence from Survey Experiments in the Czech Republic, Hungary, and Poland." *American Journal of Sociology* 117, no. 4 (2012): 1172–201.

2. For studies on the process of justice after transition in the Czech Republic and Slovakia, see Nadya Nedelsky, "Divergent Responses to a Common Past: Transitional Justice in the Czech Republic and Slovakia," *Theory and Society* 33 (2004): 65–115; Nadya Nedelsky, "Slovak Republic," in *Encyclopedia*, ed. Stan and Nedelsky, vol. 2, 433–39; Roman David, "Czech Republic," in *Encyclopedia*, ed. Stan and Nedelsky, vol. 2, 131–38; and other studies cited below.

3. Václav Žák, "Lustrace nebo spravedlnost?" *Český rozhlas* 6 (December 10, 2005), http://www.rozhlas.cz/cro6/komentare/_zprava/210146 (accessed October 16, 2009).

4. For population changes in the context of World War II and its aftermath, see Judt, *Postwar*, 22–32.

5. Czechoslovakia became significantly *more* homogeneous during the twentieth century, but it was not entirely homogeneous. During the communist regime, the major groups were Czechs, Slovaks, Hungarians, and Roma.

6. An alternative explanation is that the winners from 1948 were the losers in 1968. Tigrid, *Dnešek je váš*.

7. Prezidenti v minulosti: Gustáv Husák, https://www.hrad.cz/cs/prezident-cr/prezidenti-v-minulosti/gustav-husak.shtml (accessed September 8, 2015). Husák also imprisoned a historian, Milan Hubl, who played a critical role in Husák's political rehabilitation.

8. Prezidenti v minulosti: Václav Havel, https://www.hrad.cz/cs/prezident-cr/prezidenti-v-minulosti/vaclav-havel.shtml (accessed September 8, 2015).

9. Magdaléna Bartková, "Historical Names of Streets and Places in Opava" (B.A. diss., Palacky University, 2009).

10. Michal Folta, "Orloj mohl vypadat jinak, je to škoda, říká sochař Olbram Zoubek," Statutarní město Olomouc, https://www.olomouc.eu/aktualni-informace/aktuality/18320 (accessed September 8, 2015).

11. As we shall see later in this chapter, and in Chapters 4 and 6, transitional justice redistributes the social statuses of people. During the communist regime being a district party secretary, for instance, carried a high position in society. After the approval of the lustration law, the district secretaries were disqualified from holding certain state positions; their social prestige plummeted as the lustration law and the law on the illegitimacy of the communist regime symbolically condemned them. Conversely, many of those who went to jail were socially and politically rehabilitated; and the property of those dispossessed by the communist regime was returned and, in so doing, elevated them to a higher strata.

12. Samuel P. Huntington, *The Third Wave: Democratization in the Late Twentieth Century* (Norman: University of Oklahoma Press, 1991). Huntington misclassifies the Czechoslovak transition. See Roman David and Susanne Y. P. Choi, "Victims on Transitional Justice: Reparations of Victims of Human Rights Abuses in the Czech Republic," *Human Rights Quarterly* 27, no. 2 (2005): 392–435, quote on 397n11.

13. Constitutional Act No. 135/1989.

14. Although the transitional government of Marián Čalfa was nominally conceived in negotiations, it included communists handpicked by the opposition.

15. It received 13.48 percent of votes in the Assembly of the People, and 13.80 percent in the Assembly of the Nations, the two chambers of the Federal Assembly. ČSÚ, "Výsledky voleb a referend," volby.cz (accessed on July 28, 2015).

16. Jakub Charvát, "Bohumínské usnesení—co to je, k čemu bylo a je," *Listy*, no. 6 (2013), http://www.listy.cz/archiv.php?cislo=136&clanek=061308 (accessed September 8, 2015).

17. ČSÚ, "Výsledky voleb a referend."

18. Although Havel criticized lustration law, he signed it in 1991. He vetoed the law in 1995 and 2000 but allegedly not due to the law itself but to speed up the approval of a civil service act. See Roman David, "Lustration Laws in Action: The Motives and Evaluation of Lustration Policy in the Czech Republic and Poland (1989–2001)," *Law and Social Inquiry* 28, no. 2 (2003): 387–439; David, *Lustration and Transitional Justice.*

19. David, *Lustration and Transitional Justice.*

20. Act No. 119/1990.

21. Petr Cibulka, "Kompletní seznamy spolupracovníků StB I–III," *Rudé krávo: Necenzurované noviny*, nos. 13–15 (1992).

22. ÚSTR, "Chronologie vzniku Ústavu pro studium totalitních režimů a Archivu bezpečnostních složek," http://www.ustrcr.cz/cs/chronologie-vzniku (accessed September 8, 2015).

23. Roman David, "Transitional Justice Effects in the Czech Republic," in Stan and Nedelsky, *Postcommunist Transitional Justice*, 97–121.

24. Josef Kopecký, "Rektoři nepřesvědčili Zemana, tři nové profesory jmenovat odmítá," *iDnes* (May 28, 2015), http://zpravy.idnes.cz/rektori-nepresvedcili-zemana-tri-nove-profesory-jmenovat-odmita-py7-/domaci.aspx?c=A150528_133358_domaci_kop (accessed September 8, 2015).

25. Reporters Without Borders, 2015 World Press Freedom Index, https://rsf.org/en/ranking/2015 (accessed August 22, 2017).

26. Transparency International, Corruption Perception Index 2014, http://www.transparency.org/cpi2014/results (accessed September 8, 2015).

27. Constitutional Act 496/1990; Constitutional Act 497/1990.

28. Roman David, "Twenty Years of Transitional Justice in the Czech Lands," *Europe-Asia Studies* 64, no. 4 (2012): 761–84, 765.

29. Petr Jarolímek, "Zákony o navrácení majetku KSČ a SSM lidu," *Časopis soudobé dějiny* 9, no. 1 (2002): 65–81.

30. David, "Twenty Years."

31. Postcommunist mentality is characterized by political submissiveness and an inability to make independent decisions. See, e.g., Vojtěch Cepl and Mark Gillis, "Making Amends After Communism," *Journal of Democracy* 7 (1996): 118–24.

32. Act No. 198/1993, §5.

33. "Přehled případů vyšetřovaných na ÚDV" (January 31, 2014), http://www.policie.cz/clanek/prcehled-pripadu-vysetrovany-udv.aspx (accessed February 28, 2014).

34. Ministry of Justice, "Statistika a výkaznictví," http://cslav.justice.cz/InfoData/statisticke-rocenky.html (accessed September 8, 2015).

35. For an insightful commentary on the Czech judiciary and the process of dealing with the past, see Karel Hvížďala, "Oběť je projevem nejvyššího sociálního výkonu: S Vladimírem Čermákem o soudcích za totality, Ústavním soudu a Václavu Klausovi," in *Vladimír Čermák: Člověk—filozof—soudce*, ed. Jiří Baroš (Brno: Masaryk University Press, 2009), 201–10.

36. Legal positivism is a stream of legal thought that emphasizes written law codes. Undemocratic regimes are fortified by legal positivism because it enables power to be translated into law without restraint. The legal training that students received at law schools during the communist era was predominantly aligned to legal positivism. For a criticism of the persisting trend, see Aviezer Tucker, "Reproducing Incompetence: The Constitution of Czech Higher Education," *East European Constitutional Review* 9, no. 3 (2000): 94–99.

37. See Chapter 1.

38. Jakub Pokorný, "Policie kvůli hranicím prověřuje už i Štrougala," *MFDnes*, November 3, 2014, A1–A2.

39. For the origin of the term, see David, *Lustration and Transitional Justice*.

40. For other studies concerning the historical-political and legal context of lustration in the Czech Republic, see Nadya Nedelsky, "Czechoslovakia, and the Czech and Slovak Republics," in *Transitional Justice in Eastern Europe and the Former Soviet Union: Reckoning with the Communist Past*, ed. Lavinia Stan (New York: Routledge, 2009); Cynthia M. Horne, "International Legal Rulings on Lustration Policies in Central and Eastern Europe: Rule of Law in Historical Context," *Law and Social Inquiry* 34, no. 3 (2009): 713–44.

41. The database lists birthdates but does not indicate whether the person is deceased. The expected age of a person in 1989 means the age of the person in 1989, if he did not die prematurely before that.

42. Jiří Maňák, "Čistky v Komunistické straně Československa 1969–1970," *Sešity Ústavu pro soudobé dějiny*, AV ČR 28/1997, 45.

43. Bílek and Pilát, "Závodní, Dělnické a Lidové milice."

44. CVVM, "Postoje veřejnosti k lustracím," 2014, http://cvvm.soc.cas.cz/media/com_form2content/documents/c1/a7289/f3/po141111.pdf (accessed September 8, 2015).

45. David, "Lustration Laws in Action."

46. The Constitutional Court abrogated the indefinite category (c). Decision Pl. ÚS 1/92.

47. Roman David, "Transitional Justice and Changing Memories of the Past in Central Europe," *Government & Opposition* 50, no. 1 (2015): 24-44.

48. ČSÚ, "Výsledky voleb a referend," 2015.

49. Jakub Pokorný, "Babiš a Němcová byli mými zkouškami ohněm, přiznal Zeman," *iDnes*, August 13, 2014, http://zpravy.idnes.cz/milos-zeman-popsal-dve-nejtezsi-chvile-v -urade-fqi-/domaci.aspx?c=A140813_191908_domaci_jp (accessed September 8, 2015).

50. Reuters, "Czech Billionaire Politician Babis Cleared in Communist Secret Police Case" (June 30, 2015), http://www.reuters.com/article/2015/06/30/us-czech-slovakia-babis -idUSKCN0PA27S20150630 (accessed September 8, 2015).

51. Speech by Deputy Miroslav Kalousek (Chamber of Deputies, 2013–), 17th session, pt. 336, September 26, 2014.

52. Speech by Deputy Miroslav Grebeníček (Chamber of Deputies, 2013–), 5th session, pt. 49, January 22, 2014.

53. See *iDnes*, "Grebeníčka u soudu omluvil fax," May 12, 2003.

54. In 2005, the UN General Assembly adopted "Basic Principles and Guidelines on the Right to a Remedy and Reparation" (see below), which were drafted by Professor Theo van Boven and Professor Cherif Bassiouni.

55. See Theo van Boven, "The United Nations Basic Principles and Guidelines on the Right to a Remedy and Reparation" (2010), http://legal.un.org/avl/pdf/ha/ga_60-147/ga_60 -147_e.pdf (accessed September 8, 2015).

56. Stan and Nedelsky, *Encyclopedia*.

57. Priscilla B. Hayner, *Unspeakable Truths: Confronting State Terror and Atrocity* (New York: Routledge, 2001).

58. Act No. 119/1990.

59. Ibid.

60. Focus-group session with KPV members, Olomouc, November 4, 2014.

61. Act No. 198/1993, §§3–4.

62. Act No. 262/2011.

63. See Michael L. Bazyler, "The Holocaust Restitution Movement in Comparative Perspective," *Berkeley Journal of International Law* 20 (2002): 11–34; John Torpey, "'Making Whole What Has Been Smashed': Reflections on Reparations," *Journal of Modern History* 73 (2001): 333–58.

64. See, e.g., Jaime E. Malamud-Goti, *Game Without End: State Terror and the Politics of Justice* (Norman: University of Oklahoma Press, 1996), 13; David and Choi, "Victims on Transitional Justice."

65. Martha Minow, *Between Vengeance and Forgiveness* (Boston: Beacon, 1998), 103.

66. Act No. 119/1990.

67. For example in 1994 the organization received a subsidy of CZK 1.75 million that contributed 85 percent of such expenses for about six hundred of its members. *Zpravodaj KPV* 4 (1994): 5.

68. Act 261/2001 compensated persons imprisoned in military labor camps. Government directive 102/2002 compensated persons in military forced labor camps, including the infamous Auxiliary Technical Battalions. Act 172/2002 compensated persons who were abducted to the USSR or detained in camps run by the USSR in other states. Government

directive 122/2009 compensated university students who had not been permitted to complete their education for political reasons.

69. Act No. 403/1990; Act No. 87/1992.

70. Gerald Gaus, Shane D. Courtland, and David Schmidtz, "Liberalism," in *Stanford Encyclopedia of Philosophy* (Spring 2015 ed.), ed. Edward N. Zalta, http://plato.stanford.edu /archives/spr2015/entries/liberalism/ (accessed June 8, 2016).

71. Václav Havel, *Prosím Stručně* (Prague: Gallery, 2006), 187–88.

72. Konopásek et al., *Otevřená minulost*, 201.

73. Case of Čapský and Jeschkeová v. The Czech Republic (Application Nos. 25784/ 09 and 36002/09), European Court of Human Rights, Strasbourg, 9 February 2017 (Final 03/07/2017).

74. ČSÚ, "Sčítání lidu, domů a bytů 2011," https://www.czso.cz/csu/sldb (accessed September 9, 2015).

75. CVVM, "Názor veřejnosti na roli církví ve společnosti a na navrácení církevního majetku" (2012), https://cvvm.soc.cas.cz/cz/tiskove-zpravy/politicke/instituce-a-politici /1525-nazor-verejnosti-na-roli-cirkvi-ve-spolecnosti-a-na-navraceni-cirkevniho-majetku (accessed August 22, 2017).

76. Top 09 received 11.99 percent of the votes in 2013, down from 16.70 percent in 2010. ODS received 7.72 percent, down from 20.22 percent in 2010. See ČSÚ, "Výsledky voleb a referend."

77. Act 428/2012.

78. Act 87/1991.

79. Some countries do not allow dual citizenships, or they did not allow dual citizenship in the past.

80. Decision of the Constitutional Court, Pl. ÚS 3/94.

81. ČTK, "Ústavní soud odmítl prodloužit restituce pro emigranty," *iDnes.cz* (September 20, 2010), http://zpravy.idnes.cz/ustavni-soud-odmitl-prodlouzit-restituce-pro-emigranty -pe4-/domaci.aspx?c=A100920_095903_domaci_js (accessed September 9, 2015).

82. The Czech National Awakening, or the Czech National Revival of the eighteenth and the nineteenth centuries, aspired to revive the Czech language, tradition, culture, and identity. It was a cultural and political opposition to the Habsburg Empire and was shaped by historical claims about the Czech statehood. The historical "injustice" that Czechs suffered became a foundational feature of the Czech culture. For a detailed historical examination of the era, see Mikuláš Teich, ed., *Bohemia in History* (Cambridge: Cambridge University Press, 1998); Zdeněk V. David, *Realism, Tolerance, and Liberalism in the Czech National Awakening: Legacies of the Bohemian Reformation* (Washington, D.C.: Woodrow Wilson Center Press with Johns Hopkins University Press, 2010).

83. Hayner, *Unspeakable Truths*.

84. See, e.g., Mendeloff, "Truth-seeking, Truth-telling, and Postconflict Peacebuilding"; Vinjamuri and Snyder, "Advocacy and Scholarship."

85. Audrey R. Chapman and Patrick Ball, "The Truth of Truth Commissions: Comparative Lessons from Haiti, South Africa, and Guatemala," *Human Rights Quarterly* 23, no. 1 (2001): 1–43.

86. David, "Lustration Law in Action."

87. Ibid.

88. The Bartončík affair was the first major lustration scandal before the elections. The then leader of the Christian Democratic Party, Josef Bartončík, was exposed as a secret police informant by a deputy federal minister of the interior, Jan Ruml, two days before the first elections in 1990. For a comprehensive overview of the affair, see CT24, "Osobitý svéráz českých voleb—předvolební aféry (1)," *Česká Televize* (February 24, 2010), http://www.ces katelevize.cz/ct24/blogy/1353217-osobity-sveraz-ceskych-voleb-predvolebni-afery-1 (accessed June 8, 2016).

89. Petr Cibulka, *Cibulkovy seznamy spolupracovniku StB* (Olomouc: Votobia, 1999).

90. Act No. 140/1996.

91. Act No. 107/2002.

92. Act No. 181/2007.

93. Salivarová-Škvorecká, *Osočení*.

94. Ibid., 67.

95. Ibid., 70.

96. Ibid.

97. Ibid., 70–71.

98. Arthur Stinchcombe, "Lustration as a Problem of the Social Basis of Constitutionalism," *Law and Social Inquiry* 20, no. 1 (1995): 245–73.

99. See David, "Twenty Years," 773.

100. See Základy společenských věd, "Osnovy pro 1.–4. ročník čtyřletého a 5.–8. víceletého gymnázia," http://www.eucebnice.cz/zaklady_spolecenskych_ved/osnovy2.htm (accessed June 9, 2016); Roman David, *Politologie: Základy společenských věd*, 6th ed. (Olomouc: Nakladatelství Olomouc, 2005).

101. Huntington, *Third Wave*; John P. Moran, "The Communist Torturers of Eastern Europe: Prosecute and Punish or Forgive and Forget?," *Communist and Post-Communist Studies* 27, no. 1 (1994): 95–109..

102. See, e.g., Robert I. Rotberg and Dennis Thompson, eds., *Truth v. Justice: The Morality of Truth Commissions* (Princeton, N.J.: Princeton University Press, 2000); Minow, *Between Vengeance and Forgiveness*.

103. The slogan was invoked by Havel and other political elites to dispel desires for retribution against the perpetrators of crimes committed under the communist regime and its main protagonists. The elites were aware of the strong retributive wave in Czechoslovakia in the aftermath of World War II. See Judt, *Postwar*, 50.

104. Havel explained: " 'We are not like them,' I said once on Wenceslas Square, but if we do not want to be like 'them,' we must not be blinded by fanaticism, hatred and the desire for bloodthirsty revenge. This does not mean, however, that we can tolerate whatever 'they' do, or that we should not prosecute those who committed criminal offenses." Václav Havel, "New Year's Address to the Nation," Prague, January 1, 1992.

105. KSČ, "Prohlášení k občanům ČSSR," Extraordinary Congress of KSČ, December 20–21, 1989.

106. In spite of this fact, some former political prisoners expressed a willingness to forgive. Roman David and Susanne Y. P. Choi, "Forgiveness and Transitional Justice," *Journal of Conflict Resolution* 50, no. 3 (2006): 339–67.

107. Radmila Zemanová-Kopecká, "Nelžete pořád, za minulost KSČ jsme se omluvili, rozčílil se Filip," *Parlamentní Listy*, October 20, 2012.

108. KSČM, "Stanovisko VV ÚV KSČM k 25. výročí 17. listopadu 1989" (November 14, 2014), https://www.kscm.cz/politika-kscm/stanoviska-kscm (accessed September 9, 2015).

109. David, *Lustration and Transitional Justice*, chap. 5.

110. Justice has not only an objective but also a subjective dimension. Justice needs to be done and be seen as being done. The assessment of justice measures by means of opinion surveys is a legitimate tool not only from the sociological perspective but also from the legal perspective.

111. Three scales were computed by adding their components for the purpose of further analyses in Chapters 4 and 6: the Retributive Justice scale, consisting of lustration, punishment, moral condemnation, and expropriation of property, and ranging from 0 to 16 (alpha = 0.827); the Reparatory Justice scale, consisting of financial compensation, social acknowledgment of political prisoners, and restitution of property, and ranging from 0 to 12 (alpha = 0.765); and the Revelatory Justice scale, consisting of official publication of the names of secret collaborators, accession of secret police archives, and publication of new history textbooks, and ranging from 0 to 12 (alpha = 0.778).

112. Transitional justice measures affect what we remember about the past. See Inga Markovits, "Selective Memory: How the Law Affects What We Remember and Forget About the Past: The Case of East Germany," *Law and Society Review* 35, no. 3 (2001): 513–63; David, "Transitional Justice and Changing Memories of the Past".

Chapter 3

1. Theo van Boven, "Study Concerning the Right to Restitution, Compensation and Rehabilitation for Victims of Gross Violations of Human Rights and Fundamental Freedoms," excerpted in *Transitional Justice: How Emerging Democracies Reckon with Former Regimes*, vol. 1, ed. Neil J. Kritz (Washington, D.C.: United States Institute of Peace, 1995). This chapter uses the term "victims," which, in the sources quoted, is more common than "survivors."

2. See David Becker, Elizabeth Lira, María Isabel Castillo, Elena Gómez, and Juana Kovalskys, "Therapy with Victims of Political Repression in Chile: The Challenge of Social Reparation," *Journal of Social Issues* 46 (1990): 133–49; Cullinan, *Torture Survivors' Perceptions of Reparation*, 24 ("The end, or aimed-for situation has been variously described as 'healing,' 'closure,' 'rehabilitation,' or 'mastery' [terms connected with a therapy ideal], and as '[re]integration' or restoration to the original state [which are connected with a more political approach]"); Pablo De Greiff, ed., *The Handbook of Reparations* (Oxford: Oxford University Press, 2006).

3. "Redress" is one of the English synonyms for "reparation"; its meaning in very early usage underlines this sociopolitical sense. "The stripping of the Egyptians and the 'redressing' of the Israelites signifies more than a material settlement, it is a setting straight, a ceremonial re-dressing, a rehabilitation in the public eye." See Teitel, *Transitional Justice*, 120.

4. For a discussion of the concept of healing, see Wendy Orr, "Reparation Delayed Is Healing Retarded," in *Looking Back, Reaching Forward: Reflections on the Truth and Reconciliation Commission of South Africa*, ed. Charles Villa-Vicencio and Wilhelm Verwoerd (London: Zed, 2000), 240–41.

5. "Basic Principles and Guidelines on the Right to a Remedy and Reparation for Victims of Gross Violations of International Human Rights Law and Serious Violations of International Humanitarian Law," UN General Assembly resolution 60/147, of December 16, 2005.

6. Ibid. This approach is informed by social research conducted by van Boven and Bassiouni and is widely accepted by other scholars. Hayner adopted the same definition: Hayner, *Unspeakable Truths*. See also Orr, "Reparation Delayed Is Healing Retarded," 241. According to Teitel, "The vocabulary of 'reparatory justice' illustrates its multiple dimensions, comprehending numerous diverse forms: reparations, damages, remedies, redress, restitution, compensation, rehabilitation, tribute." Teitel, *Transitional Justice*, 119.

7. Minow, *Between Vengeance and Forgiveness*, 103.

8. Ibid. However, she also warns against the danger of retraumatization at the truth commission's hearings. The architect of the TRC, Desmond Tutu, said that he "had not been expecting that those who approached the Commission would often find healing and a closure in the process of recounting their often devastating stories." Desmond M. Tutu, *No Future Without Forgiveness* (New York: Doubleday, 1999).

9. Nkosinathi Biko, "Amnesty and Denial," in Villa-Vicencio and Verwoerd, *Looking Back, Reaching Forward*, 197.

10. Elizabeth Kiss, "Moral Ambitions Within and Beyond Political Constraints," in Rotberg and Thompson, *Truth v. Justice*, 68–98; Jodi Halpern and Harvey M. Weinstein, "Rehumanizing the Other: Empathy and Reconciliation," *Human Rights Quarterly* 26, no. 3 (2004): 561–83.

11. See International Center for Transitional Justice, ictj.org (accessed November 14, 2014).

12. Fletcher and Weinstein, "Violence and Social Repair."

13. For a review, see ibid. See also David and Choi, "Victims on Transitional Justice."

14. For a review of both perspectives, see David and Choi, "Getting Even or Getting Equal?"

15. Fletcher and Weinstein, "Violence and Social Repair," 603.

16. See David Backer, "Watching the Bargain Unravel? A Panel Study of Victims' Attitudes About Transitional Justice in Cape Town, South Africa," *International Journal of Transitional Justice* 4, no. 3 (2010): 443–56. Others also link PTSD with transitional justice: Phuong N. Pham, Harvey M. Weinstein, and Timothy Longman, "Trauma and PTSD Symptoms in Rwanda: Implications for Attitudes Toward Justice and Reconciliation," *Journal of the American Medical Association* 292, no. 5 (2004): 602–12; Patrick Vinck, Phuong N. Pham, Eric Stover, and Harvey M. Weinstein, "Exposure to War Crimes and Implications for Peace Building in Northern Uganda," *Journal of the American Medical Association* 298, no. 5 (2007): 543–54; Jeffrey Sonis, James L. Gibson, Joop T. V. M. de Jong, Nigel P. Field, Sokhom Hean, and Ivan Komproe, "Probable Posttraumatic Stress Disorder and Disability in Cambodia: Associations with Perceived Justice, Desire for Revenge, and Attitudes Toward the Khmer Rouge Trials," *Journal of the American Medical Association* 302, no. 5 (2009): 527–36.

17. Mendeloff, "Truth-seeking, Truth-telling, and Postconflict Peacebuilding."

18. Ivan Gaďourek and Jiří Nehněvajsa, *Žalářovaní, pronásledovaní a zneuznaní: Svědectví ještě žijících obětí stalinismu v českých zemích* (Brno: Masaryk University Press, 1997).

19. Roman David, "Situace bývalých politických vězňů," machine-readable data file, 2000 (on file with the author).

20. I was unable to verify this statement as those who had experienced both types of concentration camps had already passed away. I am inclined to accept it, given the frequency with which it arose during my interviews, but there are two reasons for exercising caution. First, given the contested nature of the communist regime and uncontested nature of Nazism, former political prisoners may be motivated to make this comparison to gain the same social acknowledgment as victims of Nazism received. Second, it is possible that the second period

of incarceration was more difficult simply because the prisoner was older and bore the consequences of the first one.

21. Interview with František Zahrádka, director of the Museum of the Third Resistance, Příbram (January 2000).

22. Ibid. See also Gaďourek and Nehněvajsa, *Žalářovaní, pronásledovaní a zneuznaní.*

23. Šimková, *Byly jsme tam taky.*

24. Kaplan, *Political Persecution in Czechoslovakia.*

25. Jiří Kocian, ed., *Slovníková příručka k Československým dějinám 1948–1989* (Prague: ÚSD, 2006).

26. Ibid.

27. Correspondence interview with respondent no. 129 (February 11, 2000).

28. Correspondence interview with respondent no. 56 (February 2000).

29. See, e.g., Dcery, http://www.dcery.cz (accessed November 11, 2014).

30. Letter from J. R. to Roman David (February 15, 2000).

31. Focus-group session with former political prisoners, Olomouc (June 2006).

32. Yael Danieli, "Preliminary Reflections from a Psychological Perspective," in *The Right to Restitution, Compensation and Rehabilitation for Victims of Gross Violations of Human Rights and Fundamental Freedoms*, Netherlands Institute of Human Rights, special issue no. 12, ed. Theo C. van Boven et al. (1992): 196–213; Stan and Nedelsky, *Encyclopedia*, 1.

33. David, "Situace bývalých politických vězňů."

34. Interview with Stanislav Drobný, Brno (January 2000).

35. David, "Situace bývalých politických vězňů."

36. See David, "Lustration Laws in Action," 420n78.

37. Focus-group session with members of KPV, Olomouc (November 4, 2014).

38. This was raised in all the interviews I conducted between 1999 and 2014. See also Gaďourek and Nehněvajsa, *Žalářovaní, pronásledovaní a zneuznaní.*

39. Jaroslav Spurný, "Odškodné pro estébáky," *Respekt*, June 8, 1992, 4; Rebeka Křižanová and Martin Bartůněk, "Dobře zaplacený civil," *Respekt*, November 23, 1992, 5.

40. Government Directives 135/2009 and 165/1997.

41. David, "Situace bývalých politických vězňů."

42. Act 261/2001.

43. Government Directive 135/2009.

44. Act 262/2011.

45. Similarly, in the 2015 U.S. presidential primary campaign, the Republican candidate Donald Trump questioned the credentials of John McCain as a war hero in spite of the fact that McCain had spent four years as a prisoner of war in Vietnam.

46. Interview with M. S., Olomouc (November 4, 2014).

47. Interview with J., Olomouc (November 4, 2014).

48. David, "Situace bývalých politických vězňů."

49. Ibid.

50. Ibid.

51. Ibid.

52. Danieli, "Preliminary Reflections."

53. "All efforts should be made that similar violations will not occur in the future. In this connection it is important to restore confidence in the rule of law and to take measures of structural character." Van Boven, "Study Concerning the the Right to Restitution."

54. David, "Situace bývalých politických vězňů."

55. The variable "healing," however, carries several limitations. "Healing" has been self-reported rather than diagnosed. Many victims may not acknowledge traumatic symptoms and may not relate to traumatic events. The aftereffects of trauma may have a wide range; victims may not show PTSD but may show depression or anxiety. Moreover, symptoms of traumas may appear many years after the traumatic experiences. Another limitation is that "healing" was related to the experience of imprisonment. Many former political prisoners suffered other traumatic experiences during the communist regime that were not necessarily related to their imprisonment. I am indebted to manuscript readers for raising this issue.

56. David, "Situace bývalých politických vězňů."

57. Joop T. V. M. de Jong et al., "Lifetime Events and Posttraumatic Stress Disorder in 4 Postconflict Settings," *Journal of the American Medical Association* 286, no. 5 (2001): 555–60.

58. Correspondence interview with respondent no. 24 (February 2000).

59. Letter from H. R. to Roman David (February 14, 2000).

60. Ibid.

61. Focus-group session, Olomouc (June 2006).

62. Ibid.

63. Correspondence interview with respondent no. 85 (February 14, 2000).

64. Enclosure to the questionnaire, respondent no. 363.

65. Letter from J. K. to Roman David (February 15, 2000).

66. Letter from H. R. to Roman David (February 14, 2000).

67. Correspondence interview with respondent no. 164 (February 2000).

68. Focus-group session, Olomouc (November 4, 2014).

69. Letter from O. T. to Roman David (February 7, 2000).

70. Letter from J. R. to Roman David (February 15, 2000).

71. Correspondence interview with respondent no. 119 (February 2000).

72. Letter from respondent no. 89 to Roman David (December 19, 1999).

73. Interview with M. S., Olomouc (November 4, 2014).

74. Ibid.

75. Focus-group session, Olomouc (November 4, 2014).

76. Comment on the questionnaire, respondent no. 231.

77. Comment on the questionnaire, respondent no. 826.

78. Focus-group session, Olomouc (November 4, 2014).

79. Ibid.

80. Metin Başoğlu, Maria Livanou, Cvetana Crnobarić, Tanja Frančišković, Enra Suljić, Dijana Đurić, and Melin Vranešić, "Psychiatric and Cognitive Effects of War in Former Yugoslavia: Association of Lack of Redress for Trauma and Posttraumatic Stress Reactions," *Journal of the American Medical Association* 294, no. 5 (2005): 580–90. Cf. Pham et al., "Trauma and PTSD Symptoms in Rwanda."

81. Focus-group session, Olomouc (November 4, 2014).

82. Enclosure to the questionnaire from respondent no. 148.

83. Interview with J., Olomouc (November 4, 2014).

84. Interview with M. H., Olomouc (November 4, 2014).

85. Debra Kaminer, Dan J. Stein, Irene Mbanga, and Nompumelelo Zungu-Dirwayi, "The Truth and Reconciliation Commission in South Africa: Relation to Psychiatric Status

and Forgiveness Among Survivors of Human Rights Abuses," *British Journal of Psychiatry* 178 (2001): 373–77.

86. Ibid.

87. Focus-group session, Olomouc (June 2006).

88. Başoğlu et al., "Psychiatric and Cognitive Effects of War in Former Yugoslavia."

89. Kaminer et al., "Truth and Reconciliation Commission in South Africa."

90. Başoğlu et al., "Psychiatric and Cognitive Effects of War in Former Yugoslavia."

91. David, "Situace bývalých politických vězňů."

92. Enclosure with questionnaire no. 84.

93. Correspondence interview with respondent no. 105 (February 2000).

94. See Gaďourek and Nehněvajsa, *Žalářovaní, pronásledovaní a zneuznaní*, 47 (quoting a respondent who blamed the political system for the death of a family member).

95. Letter from respondent no. 89 to Roman David (December 19, 1999).

96. Letter from P. B. to Roman David (on file with author).

97. While adhering to the principle of the universality of human rights, the fact that reparation for human rights violations poses serious challenges in various cultural settings must be recognized. Different societies may have different understandings of the concepts of justice, healing, reconciliation, and forgiveness. Victims of other types of human rights abuses, such as slavery, rape, and genocide, and victims who suffered in other contexts, such as civil war and ethnic conflict, may have different needs from those of prisoners of totalitarian regimes. Opinions may differ among victims themselves and between victims and their immediate families and dependents. This points out to a pressing need for cross-cultural and comparative research in this field.

98. Aguilar, Balcells, and Cebolla-Boado, "Determinants of Attitudes Toward Transitional Justice."

99. David and Choi, "Getting Even or Getting Equal?"

100. David and Choi, "Forgiveness and Transitional Justice."

101. Roman David, "What We Know About Transitional Justice: Survey And Experimental Evidence," *Political Psychology: Advances in Political Psychology* 38, supp. 1 (2017): 151–77.

102. James L. Gibson and Amanda Gouws, "Truth and Reconciliation in South Africa: Attributions of Blame and the Struggle over Apartheid," *American Political Science Review* 93 (1999): 501–17; Gibson, "Does Truth Lead to Reconciliation?"

103. Backer, "Watching the Bargain Unravel?"

Chapter 4

1. I am indebted to CVVM and to Veronika Hřebenářová Lenka Chudomelová, Markéta Těthalová, and Renáta Topinková for carrying out the survey and the interviews, respectively.

2. Since 1990, Václav Klaus started to ideologically redefine the Czech center-right as an opposition to the OH. The "third wayism" of OH was "constructed biographically by identifying them as former reform communists" who posed a threat to political and economic reforms. See Seán Hanley, *The New Right in the New Europe: Czech Transformation and Right-Wing Politics, 1989–2006* (New York: Routledge, 2008), 164–65.

3. Hilary Appel, *A New Capitalist Order: Privatization and Ideology in Russia and Eastern Europe* (Pittsburgh: University of Pittsburgh Press, 2004), 162–65.

4. *Novinky.cz*, "Schwarzenberg: Za návrat komunistů si můžeme sami" (February 25, 2013), http://www.novinky.cz/domaci/294291-schwarzenberg-za-navrat-komunistu-si-muzeme-sami .html (accessed August 16, 2017).

5. For the criticism, see Petr Příhoda, "Někdejší 'politruk' krajským hejtmanem," *Parlamentní listy* (February 3, 2014), http://www.parlamentnilisty.cz/arena/nazory-a-petice/Petr-Prihoda-Nekdejsi-politruk-krajskym-hejtmanem-302399 (accessed September 16, 2015).

6. David, *Lustration and Transitional Justice*.

7. It is a historical paradox that most members of the center-right elite could study in the 1970s and the 1980s, while many children of the "sixty-eighters" were excluded from studies.

8. *Novinky.cz*, "Schwarzenberg."

9. iDnes, "V KSČ byla třetina státních zástupců a pětina soudců, seznamy jsou na webu" (January 7, 2011), http://zpravy.idnes.cz/v-KSČ-byla-tretina-statnich-zastupcu-a-petina-soudcu-seznamy-jsou-na-webu-1l7-/domaci.aspx?c=A110107_140624_domaci_bar (accessed September 16, 2015).

10. Ibid.

11. Hvížďala, "Oběť je projevem nejvyššího sociálního výkonu."

12. Zdeněk Matyáš, "Grebeníčkova soudkyně kvůli chybám opouští justici" (April 11, 2006), http://zpravy.idnes.cz/grebenickova-soudkyne-kvuli-chybam-opousti-justici-f90-/domaci.aspx?c=A060411_161056_domaci_ton (accessed September 16, 2015).

13. Charvát, "Bohumínské usnesení."

14. See KSČM, "Stanovisko ÚV KSČM k situaci na Ukrajině" (September 27, 2014), kscm.cz (accessed September 16, 2015).

15. "Mladí komunisté: Pro nás české zákony neplatí, my chceme jen socialismus," http://www.lidovky.cz/mladi-komuniste-pro-nas-ceske-zakony-neplati-chceme-jen-socialismus-116-/zpravy-domov.aspx?c=A150522_141101_ln_domov_ele (accessed September 16, 2015).

16. Ibid.

17. The original is "Not to be a republican at twenty is proof of want of heart; to be one at thirty is proof of want of head."

18. Alan S. Gerber, Donald P. Green, and Christopher W. Larimer, "Social Pressure and Voter Turnout: Evidence from a Largescale Field Experiment," *American Political Science Review* 102, no. 1 (2008): 33–48.

19. I am thankful to a reader of this manuscript for this comment.

20. Robert M. Bond et al. "A 61-Million-Person Experiment in Social Influence and Social Mobilization," *Nature* 489 (2012): 295–98. The authors found, however, that the effect of online media is facilitated via existing strong-tie networks.

21. Karl Mannheim, "The Problem of Generations," in *Essays on the Sociology of Knowledge by Karl Mannheim*, ed. P. Kecskemeti (New York: Routledge and Kegan Paul, 1952), 276–320.

22. Howard Schuman and Jacqueline Scott, "Generations and Collective Memories," *American Sociological Review* 54, no. 3 (1989): 359–81.

23. Michael Schudson, *Watergate in American Memory: How We Remember, Forget, and Reconstruct the Past* (New York: Basic Books, 1992).

24. Stephan Lewandowsky et al., "Misinformation and Its Correction: Continued Influence and Successful Debiasing," *Psychological Science in the Public Interest* 13, no. 3 (2012): 106–31.

25. Andy Barr, "51% of GOP Voters: Obama Foreign," *Politico* (2011), cited in Lewandowsky, "Misinformation and Its Correction."

26. For an introductory overview, see John J. Macionis, *Sociology*, 14th ed. (Boston: Pearson, 2012), 110–17.

27. Peter Hatemi and Rose McDermott, "The Genetics of Politics: Discovery, Challenges, and Progress," *Trends in Genetics* 28, no. 10 (2012): 525–33.

28. Zoltán Fazekas and Levente Littvay, "The Importance of Context in the Genetic Transmission of U.S. Party Identification," *Political Psychology* 36, no. 4 (2015): 361–77.

29. One of the rare primary sources on both victims and perpetrators was written in French by Jean Hatzfeld. For an English translation of his books, see Jean Hatzfeld, *Machete Season: The Killers in Rwanda Speak* (New York: Farrar, Straus and Giroux, 2005); and Jean Hatzfeld, *Life Laid Bare: The Survivors in Rwanda Speak* (New York: Other Press, 2007).

30. Gibson, "Does Truth Lead to Reconciliation?"

31. Kathryn Sikkink, *The Justice Cascade: How Human Rights Prosecutions Are Changing World Politics* (New York: W. W. Norton, 2011).

32. For its sociological analysis, see Kabele et al., "Rekonstrukce komunistického vládnutí."

33. Interview R1 with a former member of KSČ (May 28, 2015).

34. Interview L2 with a member of KSČ/KSČM (May 26, 2015).

35. Interview M2 with a former member of KSČ (May 28, 2015), 1.

36. Interview R2 with a former member of KSČ (June 2, 2015).

37. Interview L1 with a former member of KSČ (May 21, 2015), 2.

38. Interview R4 with a former member of KSČ (May 18, 2015) (the interviewee could not continue the membership due to the dissolution of her party cell).

39. Leaving the Party may indicate the personal transformation of the members as well as its redundancy (because those who left may not have believed in communism). But it may also indicate the lack of transformation of the hard-line members because the Party failed to pursue the hard-line policies they supported.

40. Daniel Kunštát, *Za rudou oponou: Komunisté a jejich voliči po roce 1989* (Prague: Slon, 2013).

41. Petr Fiala and Miroslav Mareš, "Vývoj systému politických stran v České republice (1992–1996)," *Politologický časopis* 3 (1997): 305–16.

42. Kunštát, *Za rudou oponou*, 235.

43. iDnes, "Stranám prudce ubývají členové, brzy mohou mít existenční potíže" (April 5, 2015), http://zpravy.idnes.cz/pocet-clenu-cxz-/domaci.aspx?c=A150401_183007_domaci_hv (accessed September 16, 2015).

44. Interview R4.

45. Interview R3 with a member of KSČ/KSČM (June 15, 2015).

46. See Fiala and Mareš, "Vývoj systému."

47. Interview R3.

48. Interview L4, with a member of KSČ/KSČM (June 18, 2015), 7.

49. Ibid., 7, 11.

50. Ibid., 6.

51. Interview L3 with a former member of KSČ (May 18, 2015), 7 (the interviewee could not continue her membership due to the dissolution of her party cell).

52. Interview R3, 6.

53. Interview L4, 11 (the interviewee claimed that the Party voluntarily gave up its property).

54. Interview M1 with a member of KSČ/KSČM (May 22, 2015), 5.

55. Interview R3.

56. KSČ, "Prohlášení k občanům ČSSR" (December 20, 1989), kscm.cz (accessed September 16, 2015).

57. Interview L2, 6.

58. Interview R1.

59. Interview L4, 17.

60. Interview L1, 12.

61. Interview R2.

62. Interview R4, 3, 9, 17.

63. Ibid., 7–8.

64. Ibid., 6.

65. Interview M2, 2.

66. Personal transformation was obtained from this questionnaire item: Do you agree or disagree that the previous system systematically violated human rights? Personal and intergenerational transformation was obtained by selecting those respondents who answered the following questions positively: Were you ever a member of the Communist Party before 1989? Were you or any of your parents or grandparents members of KSČ before 1989? Intergenerational transformation included respondents who were eighteen years old or younger when the regime change occurred. It means persons born in 1971 or later.

67. Grandparents were included in the question because parents of the youngest respondents may have been too young to join the Party.

68. The answers were captured on the five-point Likert scale, whereby the most negative answer was coded 0 and the most positive 4.

69. The multivariate analysis used was ordinal logit.

70. As mentioned in Chapter 2, apology, the only reconciliatory measure, operated on the same dimension as retributive measures. It thus had to be excluded from the model in order to prevent multicollinearity. I therefore replaced retributive measures with apology in a separate model; the results for apology were significant in both models and ran in the same (negative) direction as the results for retributive justice. The results of the models with apology did not much differ from the results of the presented models with retributive justice. The only meaningful difference was that the revelatory measures lost significance in the personal transformation model that used apology.

71. Interview L1.

72. Interview L4, 15.

73. Interview M4 with a former member of KSČ (June 14, 2015), 6.

74. Interview M3 with a member of KSČ/KSČM (June 3, 2015).

75. It is difficult to estimate the number of people who thought that the regime committed a few individual wrongs. The mass protest against the regime in 1989 was not evidence of a response to mass human rights violations. As illustrated in Chapter 1, people protested due to a range of political, economic, and social reasons.

76. Interview M3; interview R3.

77. Roman David, "Transitional Injustice? Criteria for Conformity of Lustration to the Right to Political Expression," *Europe-Asia Studies* 56, no. 6 (2004): 789–812.

78. Petr Fiala and Miroslav Mareš, "Konstituování systému politických stran v České republice (1989–1992)," *Politologický časopis*, no. 1 (1997): 104–26.

79. Interview L3, 7, 8, 15.

80. Interview L2, 11–13. He found lustration slightly excessive because it affected the foreign intelligence officers.

81. Interview L4, 10.

82. The social identity theory offers an explanation of the collective effects of criminal punishments. According to this theory, every person has a dual identity: individual identity and social identity, which is related to the group membership. Consequently, members of the same social group tend to judge actions against in-group members differently than the same actions against out-group members. Punishment against an out-group member is seen as insufficient, while punishment against an in-group member was excessive. Survey evidence and survey experimental evidence of this feature are extant. See Rupert Brown, "Social Identity Theory: Past Achievements, Current Problems, and Future Challenges," *European Journal of Social Psychology* 30 (2000): 745–78; Miklos Biro et al., "Attitudes Toward Justice and Social Reconstruction in Bosnia and Herzegovina," in *My Neighbor, My Enemy*, ed. Eric Stover and Harvey M. Weinstein (Cambridge: Cambridge University Press, 2004); Dinka Corkalo et al., "Neighbors Again? Intercommunity Relations After Ethnic Cleansing," in Stover and Weinstein, *My Neighbor, My Enemy*; Roman David, "International Criminal Tribunals and the Perception of Justice: The Effect of the ICTY in Croatia," *International Journal of Transitional Justice* 8, no. 3 (2014): 476–95.

83. Most literature suggests that the likelihood that wrongdoers become self-reflective as a result of trials is low. Hannah Arendt's iconic study of *Eichmann in Jerusalem* is a well-known example. There are also exceptions when the perpetrator becomes self-reflective: Pumla Gobodo-Madikizela, *A Human Being Died That Night: A South African Story of Forgiveness* (New York: Houghton Mifflin, 2003). It is questionable, however, whether such a story could take place outside South Africa, which pursued largely a reconciliatory method of dealing with the past, and to what extent the self-reflection of the apartheid murderer Eugene de Kock was inspired by Gobodo-Madikizela—who interviewed him—rather than his trial and punishment. Nevertheless, there has been a restorative strand in the criminological literature that aspires to transform offenders, especially juvenile offenders. See John Braithwaite, *Crime, Shame and Reintegration* (Cambridge: Cambridge University Press, 1989). The conceptual problem of restorative justice is, however, its reliance on additional interventions, which are pursued either as an alternative or as a complement to criminal trials, rather than relying on criminal trials themselves.

84. Anca M. Miron, Nyla R. Branscombe, and Monica Biernat, "Motivated Shifting of Justice Standards," *Personality and Social Psychology Bulletin* 36 (2010): 768–79; Mark Tarrant, Nyla R. Branscombe, Ruth H. Warner, and Dale Weston, "Social Identity and Perceptions of Torture: It's Moral When We Do It," *Journal of Experimental Social Psychology* 48 (2012): 516; Stanley Cohen, *States of Denial: Knowing About Atrocities and Suffering* (Cambridge: Polity Press, 2001).

85. See, e.g., Payam Akhavan, "Justice in the Hague, Peace in the Former Yugoslavia? A Commentary on the United Nations War Crimes Tribunal," *Human Rights Quarterly* 20, no. 4 (1998): 737–816.

Chapter 5

1. As mentioned in the Introduction, this selection is based on the review of existing literature in transitional justice. See, e.g., Gibson, "Does Truth Lead to Reconciliation?"; Gibson, "Truth, Justice, and Reconciliation."

2. Teitel, *Transitional Justice*.

3. The "torturer's problem" was coined by Samuel Huntington to encompass a dilemma facing the achievement of justice in transitional countries. See Huntington, *Third Wave*.

4. Nigel Biggar, "Making Peace or Doing Justice: Must We Choose?," in *Burying the Past: Making Peace and Doing Justice After Civil Conflict*, ed. Nigel Biggar (Washington, D.C.: Georgetown University Press, 2003).

5. Phuong Pham, Patrick Vinck, Eric Stover, Andrew Moss, Marieke Wierda, and Richard Bailey, "When the War Ends: A Population-Based Survey on Attitudes About Peace, Justice, and Social Reconstruction in Northern Uganda" (Human Rights Center, University of California, Berkeley; Payson Center for International Development, Tulane University; and International Center for Transitional Justice, 2007).

6. William A. Schabas, "Amnesty, the Sierra Leone Truth and Reconciliation Commission and the Special Court for Sierra Leone," *U.C. Davis Journal of International Law and Policy* (2004): 145–69.

7. Cf. Bronwyn Anne Leebaw, "The Irreconcilable Goals of Transitional Justice," *Human Rights Quarterly* 30, no. 1 (2008): 95–118.

8. While the effect of punishment on the perception of justice seems obvious, its effect on forgiveness seemingly defies "common sense." In fact, I have found that punishment is a significant predictor of forgiveness. See David and Choi, "Forgiveness and Transitional Justice," Peter Strelan and Jan-Willem van Prooijen, "Retribution and Forgiveness: The Healing Effects of Punishing for Just Desserts," *European Journal of Social Psychology* 43, no. 6 (2013): 544–553.

9. Retributive theory may come in many shades. See John Cottingham, "Varieties of Retribution," *Philosophical Quarterly* 29 (1978): 238–46. In fact, retribution and just deserts only partially overlap. Retribution may be construed as an imperative to impose punishment, while just deserts may be an imperative to limit disproportional punishment. See William I. Miller, *Eye for an Eye* (Cambridge: Cambridge University Press, 2006). This distinction has been empirically demonstrated. Monica M. Gerber and Jonathan Jackson, "Retribution as Revenge and Retribution as Just Deserts," *Social Justice Research* 26, no. 1 (2013): 61–80.

10. See David and Choi, "Getting Even, or Getting Equal?"

11. Howard Zehr, *Changing Lenses: A New Focus for Crime and Justice*, 3rd ed. (Scottdale, Pa.: Herald Press, 2005).

12. Cottingham, "Varieties of Retribution."

13. Jeffrie Murphy, *Getting Even: Forgiveness and Its Limits* (Oxford: Oxford University Press, 2003).

14. Cf. Biggar, *Burying the Past*.

15. David and Choi, "Getting Even, or Getting Equal?"

16. Teitel, *Transitional Justice*.

17. Gibson, "Does Truth Lead to Reconciliation?"

18. Lily Gardner Feldman, "The Principle and Practice of 'Reconciliation' in German Foreign Policy: Relations with France, Israel, Poland and the Czech Republic," *International Affairs* 75, no. 2 (1999): 333–56.

19. For conceptualizations inspired by religious teaching, see Tutu, *No Future Without Forgiveness*.

20. David, *Lustration and Transitional Justice*, 198.

21. Tutu, *No Future Without Forgiveness*.

22. James L. Gibson and Amanda Gouws, *Overcoming Political Intolerance in South Africa: Experiments in Democratic Persuasion* (Cambridge: Cambridge University Press, 2003).

23. Gibson, "Does Truth Lead to Reconciliation?"

24. David, *Lustration and Transitional Justice*, 199.

25. Pham et al., "Trauma and PTSD Symptoms in Rwanda."

26. Ibid., 604.

27. The questionnaire item concerning the success of "dealing with the past" was strongly correlated with an item concerning "the rectification of major injustices."

28. Interview R4, 14.

29. Letter by a former political prisoner, questionnaire no. 185.

30. Former political prisoner, enclosure to questionnaire no. 361.

31. Interview R3, 11.

32. Interview L4, 20.

33. Czech-German reconciliation relates to the official process of coexistence between the Czech Republic and Germany in view of the expulsion of Czech Germans from the Czechoslovakian border region of Sudetenland in the aftermath of World War II, and in view of the common European future. The preamble to the Czech-German Declaration of 1997 states that the past cannot be undone, injustice may be addressed without creating new injustice, and future should be based on reconciliation. See "Česko-německá deklarace o vzájemných vztazích a jejich budoucím rozvoji," *Ministerstvo Zahranici CR*, http://www.mzv.cz/jnp /cz/o_ministerstvu/historie_a_osobnosti_ceske_diplomacie/druha_svetova_valka_a_jeji _dusledky/cesko_nemecka_deklarace_o_vzajemnych.html (accessed June 10, 2016).

34. Interview R4, 6.

35. Letter by a former political prisoner, questionnaire no. 148.

36. David and Choi, "Forgiveness and Transitional Justice," 350.

37. Focus group with former political prisoners, Gallery Caesar, Olomouc (June 2006).

38. Interview R4, 15.

39. The following type of lament was quite common: "After 1989, thieves gained and honest fools lost. . . . All state property that existed was stolen" (R4, 4).

40. The interplay between the political sphere, problems of transition, and the views of former political prisoners is illustrated in Chapter 3.

41. James N. Druckman, Donald P. Green, James H. Kuklinski, and Arthur Lupia, "The Growth and Development of Experimental Research in Political Science," *American Political Science Review* 100, no. 4 (2006): 627–36.

42. Paul M. Sniderman and Douglas Grob, "Innovations in Experimental Design in General Population Attitude Surveys," *Annual Review of Sociology* 22 (1996): 377–99.

43. Lawrence W. Neuman, *Social Research Methods: Qualitative and Quantitative Approaches* (Boston: Allyn and Bacon, 2000).

44. Cheryl S. Alexander and Henry J. Becker, "The Use of Vignettes in Survey Research," *Public Opinion Quarterly* 42, no. 1 (1978): 93–104, quote on 94.

45. Gibson and Gouws, *Overcoming Intolerance in South Africa*.

46. Ibid.

47. Martin Fishbein and Icek Ajzen, *Belief, Attitude, Intention, and Behavior: An Introduction to Theory and Research* (Reading, Mass.: Addison-Wesley, 1975).

48. Gibson and Gouws, "Truth and Reconciliation in South Africa"; see also Gibson and Gouws, *Overcoming Intolerance in South Africa*.

49. James L. Gibson, "Truth, Justice, and Reconciliation: Judging the Fairness of Amnesty in South Africa," *American Journal of Political Science* 46, no. 3 (2002): 540–56.

50. David Backer, "*Overcoming Apartheid: Can Truth Reconcile a Divided Nation?* by James Gibson," *Comparative Political Studies* 39 no. 8 (2006): 1157–61.

51. David, *Lustration and Transitional Justice*, pt. 3. See also Susanne Y. P. Choi and Roman David, "Lustration Systems and Trust: Evidence from Survey Experiments in the Czech Republic, Hungary, and Poland," *American Journal of Sociology* 117, no. 4 (2012): 1172–201.

52. David, "International Criminal Tribunals and the Perception of Justice."

53. Roman David, "The Past or the Politics of the Present? Dealing with the Japanese Occupation of South Korea," *Contemporary Politics* 22, no. 1 (2016): 57–76.

54. David and Choi, "Getting Equal, or Getting Even?"

55. The original version of the experiment was based on a 3x4x3 factorial design. The reconciliatory factor was also on three levels: manipulating apology, regret, and no apology. I abandoned this design because it offered limited theoretical gain and could incur large costs stemming from a low number of respondents per cell. A small-scale experiment with a student population has established that apology exercises a significantly larger effect than regret, and regret had a significantly stronger effect than no apology. Roman David, "Symbolic Meaning of Historical Injustices: The Attitudes of South Korean Students to Japan's Policy of Dealing with the Past," in *Proceedings of the Conference "Regional Peace Building: The Korean Peninsula and North-east Asia"* (Hong Kong: Lingnan University, 2010), 7–18. Moreover, unlike in Japan-Korea relations, the issue of regret was not socially and politically relevant in relations of the Communist Party and the rest of Czech society.

56. David and Choi, "Forgiveness and Transitional Justice."

57. Respondents were given five response categories on the Likert scale, ranging from "definitely yes" (coded as 4), "rather yes" (coded 3), "half-half" (coded 2), "rather not" (coded 1), and "definitely not" (coded 0). Because the alpha value of the four questions was 0.78, I composed a realistic vignette scale by adding the values together. The scale ranged from 0 to 16. The mean of the scale was 11.97, which suggested that the vignette was seen as reasonably realistic.

58. The answers to each question were captured on the Likert scale, which ranged from the most positive "definitely agree" (coded 4) to the most negative "definitely disagree" (coded 0), allowing a neutral answer "half-half" (coded 2). The scale was highly reliable (alpha value = 0.86). The individual items were therefore added together to form the justice scale. Its mean was 11.1 and the standard deviation was 4.8.

59. In order to analyze my data, I used the univariate general linear model in the SPSS software. My model included experimental variables as predictors and the justice scale as an outcome variable, controlling for pre-1989 members of the Communist Party.

60. The level of significance was at $p < 0.001$. The F-statistics further revealed that the reconciliatory factor explained the largest part of variation in the justice scale, followed by redress.

61. David and Choi, "Forgiveness and Transitional Justice"; Michael E. McCullough, Kenneth I. Pargament, and Carl E. Thoresen, *Forgiveness: Theory, Research and Practice* (New York: Guilford, 2000).

62. The answers were captured on the five-point Likert scale. They ranged from "definitely agree" (coded 0) to "definitely disagree" (4), and it also allowed a neutral response. In order to match them with the previous questions, the most positive answers to questions concerning retribution were coded from 4 to 0. The alpha value of this scale was 0.672. This value of alpha is not large but is still acceptable. I considered dropping forgetting, which would boost the alpha value to 0.700. However, I was interested in making the results on reconciliation comparable with the results on justice. I therefore retained the whole scale, which ranged from 0 to 20, with the mean of 11.27 and the standard deviation of 3.75.

63. It is routinely assumed that both sides of a divided society are likely to have different views of the past, although the differences may actually appear to be counterintuitive. For instance, when in-group members (noncommunists) are asked whether justice has been achieved as a result of a trial involving a wrongdoer from an out-group (a communist), the in-group members are likely to hold the view that justice was inadequate, while former communists would see it as adequate or excessive. See David, "International Criminal Tribunals and the Perception of Justice."

64. See Roman David, "Lustration and Justice," unpublished manuscript.

65. Intuitively, one would expect that retributive measures would be the most efficient measures of transitional justice in exercising their effects on the perception of justice; and that reconciliatory measures would be the most efficient predictors of the perception of reconciliation. This study shows that apology, as an instance of reconciliatory measures, affects the perceptions of both justice and reconciliation. This begs for a plausible explanation of the social mechanisms of the effects that apologies have. First, apologies are theorized as the perception of justice because an apology may signify an expression of remorse, acceptance of responsibility, admission of wrongdoing, acknowledgment of victims' suffering, forbearance, and promise of repair of damages. See Craig W. Blatz, Karina Schumann, and Michael Ross, "Government Apologies for Historical Injustices," *Political Psychology* 30, no. 2 (2009): 219–41, 221.

66. It does not mean that the experimental evidence suggests that the Czech society was not retributive. We need to see shaming in contrast to other retributive measures, including punishment, which was a very strong predictor of the perception of justice in this experiment.

67. David, *Lustration and Transitional Justice*, 213.

68. The experimental apology was situated at the interpersonal level. It does not allow an extrapolation to the macro-political level, for instance, to predict eventual collective apologies by the KSČM. Moreover, interpersonal apologies cannot be mandated. Any eventual reconciliatory policy would probably need to evolve around a reconciliatory forum, which would resemble the Amnesty Committee of the South African TRC and which would be conducive to apologies. On the other hand, although only interpersonal apologies were tested, the survey results (Chapter 2) suggest that collective apologies by the Communist Party would be welcomed by society.

Chapter 6

The source for the first epigraph for this chapter is Vojtěch Cepl, "Transformation of Hearts and Minds in Eastern Europe," *Cato Journal* 17, no. 2 (1997): 229–34.

1. For instance, Wendy Lambourne argues for departing from a short-term "transition" to a long-term "transformation," which implies "a sustainable process embedded in society and adoption of psychosocial, political and economic, as well as legal, perspectives on justice." Lambourne, "Transitional Justice and Peacebuilding After Mass Violence," *International Journal of Transitional Justice* 3, no. 1 (2009): 28–48. For Paul Gready and Simon Robins, "Transformative justice is understood as transformative change that emphasises local agency and resources; the prioritization of process rather than pre-conceived outcomes; and the challenging of unequal and intersecting power relationships and structures of exclusion at both local and global levels." Gready and Robins, "From Transitional to Transformative Justice: A New Agenda for Practice," University of York, Centre for Applied Human Rights

Briefing Note TFJ-01 (June 2014), http://www.simonrobins.com/Transformative%20Justice%20Briefing%20Paper.pdf (accessed June 11, 2016).

2. The fact that bystanders did not have extreme experiences under communist rule made them more likely to change their negative opinions about communism for several reasons: Some of them may have been negatively affected by hardship that they experienced during economic transformation. The impact of this hardship was accentuated by the Communist Party during the process of political and economic transformation. The changing international context is also likely to have had an effect on the opinions of bystanders. Russia exploited the communist past in Eastern Europe in its international plans (see the Introduction).

3. The widespread dismissals due to lustration were conducted in the pre-lustration stage. They preceded the approval of lustration law. They were conducted as the lustration law was implemented but they were also conducted beyond the scope of the lustration law. See David, *Lustration and Transitional Justice*; David, "Lustration Laws in Action." For a comparative overview, see Lavinia Stan, ed., *Transitional Justice in Eastern Europe and the Former Soviet Union: Reckoning with the Communist Past* (New York: Routledge, 2009); Lavinia Stan and Nadya Nedelsky, eds., *Post-Communist Transitional Justice: Lessons from Twenty-Five Years of Experience* (Cambridge: Cambridge University Press, 2015).

4. We should not conflate tangible and intangible measures with tangible and intangible effects. Tangible measures, for instance, criminal trials, may produce tangible effects, such as punishment of perpetrators and compensation of victims, but also intangible effects, such as condemnation of perpetrators, social acknowledgment of victims, and the revelation of unclear events about the past. Conversely, intangible measures may also produce tangible and intangible effects. For instance, the condemnation of the communist regime may signify the moral condemnation of Communist Party members, which may disadvantage them in the labor market. See Gil Eyal, Iván Szelényi, and Elizabeth Townsley, *Making Capitalism Without Capitalists: The New Ruling Elites in Eastern Europe* (London: Verso, 1998); Gil Eyal, "Antipolitics and the Spirit of Capitalism: Dissidents, Monetarists, and the Czech Transition to Capitalism," *Theory and Society* 29, no. 1 (2000): 49–92.

5. See Rome Statute of the International Criminal Court, United Nations Doc. A/CONF.183/9 (1998); Payam Akhavan, "Beyond Impunity: Can International Criminal Justice Prevent Future Atrocities?" *American Journal of International Law* 95 (2001): 7–31.

6. James Meernik, "Justice and Peace? How the International Criminal Tribunal Affects Societal Peace in Bosnia," *Journal of Peace Research* 42, no. 3 (2005): 271–89; Julian Ku and Jide Nzelibe, "Do International Criminal Tribunals Deter or Exacerbate Humanitarian Atrocities?" *Washington University Law Review* 84 (2006): 777–833; Kate Cronin-Furman, "Managing Expectations: International Criminal Trials and the Prospects for Deterrence of Mass Atrocity," *International Journal of Transitional Justice* 7, no. 3 (2013): 434–54.

7. See Gibson, "Truth, Reconciliation, and Creation of Human Rights Culture"; Sikkink, *Justice Cascade*.

8. As illustrated in Chapter 5, justice and reconciliation may be considered objectives against which the utility of justice measures can be assessed. This assessment will thus enable me to triangulate the experimental finding with the analysis of the survey results.

9. The bystanders' attitudes are likely to be ambivalent and volatile. Some of them may have opposed the communist regime because they did not benefit from the regime as the communists did, but their experience of injustice may not be as intensive as that of victims. This category is therefore more prone to reconsidering political opinions about the past.

10. Eyal, Széléneyi, and Townsley, *Making Capitalism Without Capitalists*.

11. Eyal, "Antipolitics and the Spirit of Capitalism."

12. Jadwiga Staniszkis, "'Political Capitalism' in Poland," *East European Politics and Societies* 5, no. 1 (1990): 127–41; Jadwiga Staniszkis, *Postkomunizm Próba Opisu* (Gdańsk: Wydawnictwo Słowo, 2001); Jacek Wasilewski, *Elita polityczna 1998* (Warsaw: ISP PAN, 1999); Petr Mateju and Blanka Rehakova, "Turning Left or Class Realignment," *East European Politics and Societies* 11 (1997): 507–41.

13. Maria Łoś and Andrzej Zybertowicz, *Privatizing the Police-State: The Case of Poland* (New York: Palgrave, 2000).

14. I ask questions about whether differences inherited from the past persist. It would be useful to examine the evolution (an eventual increase or decrease) of these differences. However, the questions that would have allowed me to determine the position of the respondents in the past were not available in the accessible datasets. The set of surveys conducted by my colleagues in the 1990s that contained the membership of the Communist Party before 1989 omitted questions about income.

15. David, *Lustration and Transitional Justice*, chap. 5.

16. Stephen Edgell, *Class: Key Concept in Sociology* (New York: Routledge, 1993). Here I do not equate class and income. Based on the literature, I suggest that class is a predictor of income. In this chapter, I examine whether social class prior to 1989 affects income in 2015 and whether justice measures played a role in the eventual redistribution.

17. Ordinary least square (OLS) linear regression has been used. Although eighty-five respondents reported no income, OLS is still an appropriate model to analyze the data. The variable "income" is continuous and its distribution is still normal. The sample size is large enough. There are no significant outliers. The observations are independent. The data do not show multicollinearity and the residuals are normally distributed.

18. Material factors may have played a role via property ownership. For instance, it is possible that former communists may have acquired weekend houses and cottages during the era of the communist regime, while the discriminated did not have that opportunity.

19. Among the other significant predictors of income were age, education, gender, employment (whether one was retired or not), and religion: Older and more educated respondents were significantly more likely to earn higher incomes. Women, retirees, and Catholics were more likely to have lower incomes. Many of these predictors of income can be found in other societies. Hence, in parallel with the continuous implementation of the Rehabilitation Act and related legislation, the Czech Republic is as much in need of gender-sensitive social policies as any other Western society.

20. Teitel, *Transitional Justice*.

21. According to Gibson, a series of causal links underpinned the South African truth and reconciliation process: Amnesty leads to the revelation of truth, truth to reconciliation, and reconciliation to democracy. Gibson, "Does Truth Lead to Reconciliation?"

22. See the van Boven-Bassiouni principles in Chapter 4.

23. Correspondence interview with former political prisoner, respondent no. 39.

24. Former political prisoner, respondent no. 706.

25. Interview R1.

26. Interview R4, 4.

27. Interview V1, June 2015, 14.

28. Interview R4, 6.

29. Interview R4, 20.

30. Interview V1, 4.

31. Interview L2, 5.

32. Interview L1, 15.

33. Konopásek, *Otevřená minulost*, 189.

34. Interview R1, 10, 15.

35. The two measures of trust operate on the same dimension and have a high degree of reliability (alpha = 0.740). They have been added into the reconciliation scale, ranging from 0 to 8.

36. Preamble to the Restitution Act, Act 87/1991.

37. Leebaw, "Irreconcilable Goals."

38. Gábor Tóka et al., "The Development of Party Systems and Electoral Alignments in East Central Europe," machine-readable data files (Budapest: Central European University, 1992–96).

39. A question arises about whether it is always beneficial to avoid divisiveness. For instance, swift justice may produce short-term divisions, which may be outweighed by the long-term social benefits of the swift justice. The problem is that divisiveness carries the risk that historical divisions will be accentuated by transitional justice. De-Baathification of Iraq is a case in which a legal process solidified historical divides and fueled ethnic conflict in the post-Saddam era. Dividing society in the name of justice carries significant social risks. See Roman David, "From Prague to Baghdad: Lustration Systems and Their Political Effects," *Government and Opposition* 41, no. 3 (2006): 347–72.

40. For the etymological and historical origin of the word "lustration," see David, *Lustration and Transitional Justice*, 66–70.

41. I shall proceed with quantitative (path) analysis. By and large, quantitative analysis examines *whether* an association between two variables exists; qualitative analysis mostly examines the social mechanism of *how* one variable affects another.

42. As mentioned above, the implementation of justice measures may directly dissuade the rest of society—at least some members of it—from wanting to return to the past. Similarly, the notion of justice indicates that injustices occurred in the past and serves as a yardstick against which measures taken by the new regime to rectify injustices can be gauged. Likewise, reconciliation indicates that the past inimical relations have been overcome.

43. From a social research perspective, the previous analysis of the material transformation may be stronger in establishing causality than the path model. The former used previous class position and income as the critical variables. The latter may be marred by endogeneity because the mediating and outcome variables in the path analysis are both attitudinal. On the other hand, the problem of endogeneity is not so problematic here since the analysis sought to falsify the effect of independent variables, namely, the class position in the past regime, on the wish to return to the past regime. If an eventual direct effect of the class position disappears after adding the mediating variables, then the mediating variables probably played a role in affecting the outcomes. Such models were previously used in social science. For instance, it is common to examine the effect of class position on voting preferences, which may be mediated by self-identification of a voter as conservative or liberal in the United States or as left-leaning or right-leaning in Europe. Here too both the mediator and the outcome are attitudinal variables.

44. It is not in my research interest to study the direct and indirect effects of a predictor variable on the outcome in order to calculate the total effect. My interest is to examine the relevance of the mediating variables.

45. See Fletcher and Weinstein, "Violence and Social Repair"; Biro et al., "Attitudes Toward Justice and Social Reconstruction"; David, "International Criminal Tribunals and the Perception of Justice."

46. Restituees are obviously beneficiaries of justice measures. However, there may be multiple reasons why restituees may not wish to return to the previous regime. Apart from concerns about ownership of their properties, the properties may also have been an important source of their income. Moreover, family identity may be firmly attached to the property, especially in cases of landowners. The experience of dispossession of property can be considered as an attack on the family identity.

47. In statistical terms, the ideological transformation is my null hypothesis. If I were to find significant statistical evidence, I would be able to reject the null hypothesis and say that transformation did not occur. If I do not find significant evidence, I cannot be certain whether this is because ideological transformation occurred or because my sample was not robust enough. Likewise, the fact that a court did not have evidence to convict an accused person does not mean that he or she did not commit the crime.

48. This finding, however, does not allow us to extrapolate about the effects of their absence. It is theoretically possible that these divisions could get deeper in the absence of retributive measures, such as lustration, expropriation of the party, and the condemnation of the communist regime. Communists might have felt closer to the rest of society but the rest of society might have turned on them more strenuously if it felt that justice had not been served. I am indebted to an anonymous reviewer for this remark.

49. The assessment of apology was therefore excluded from the model to prevent multicollinearity. To determine its effect, I replaced the assessment of retributive justice with the assessment of apology. The results were essentially the same as in the original model described in detail in Table 13. Three variables in the model with apology lost significance, although the (negative) direction of their effect remained: The effect of education on the assessment of reconciliation decreased, the effect of urban residency on the assessment of apology decreased, and the size of the effect of revelatory measures on reconciliation largely disappeared.

50. About 44.8 percent of people older than sixty years supported revelatory measures (it means that on the revelatory scale they scored 7 or more). About 55.2 percent of them disapproved of revelatory measures.

51. Further analyses revealed that lustrating was positively associated with political satisfaction.

Conclusion

1. These eight outcomes did not include results from Chapter 5's experimental study, which examined a hypothetical situation. Its findings serve as an important benchmark and will be discussed later.

2. Findings in Chapters 2 and 3 suggest that an expansion of reparatory measures, in particular financial compensation, would likely boost both outcomes.

3. However, this does not mean complacency in facing Russia. The communist regime in Czechoslovakia had been ideologically challenged by the notion of "socialism with a human face" already in the 1960s and discredited through the Soviet-led invasion in 1968. Still, many Czechoslovaks cynically collaborated with the communist regime during the 1970s and 1980s.

4. It means the percentage of respondents who scored above four in the reconciliation scale.

5. Retributive measures showed a marginal positive impact on the perception of reconciliation but this may be due to the negative impact of shaming on reconciliation; shaming was used as a contrast to retribution in Chapter 5.

6. See David, *Lustration and Transitional Justice.*

7. Akhavan, "Justice in the Hague."

8. Diane F. Orentlicher, *Shrinking the Space for Denial: The Impact of the ICTY in Serbia* (New York: Open Society Justice Initiative, 2008).

9. Even local lawyers, attorneys, and judges hold a biased version of history in spite of the ICTY rulings. See Fletcher and Weinstein, "Violence and Social Repair."

10. The survey experiment manipulated an individual apology, not a collective apology. For the classification of apologies, see Nicholas Tavuchis, *Mea Culpa: A Sociology of Apology and Reconciliation* (Stanford, Calif.: Stanford University Press, 1991); Craig W. Blatz, Karina Schumann, and Michael Ross, "Government Apologies for Historical Injustices," *Political Psychology* 30, no. 2 (2009): 219–41. Although a collective apology was demanded from the Communist Party, its eventual effects are a matter for further research. In my personal view, such apologies are likely to be beneficial but would be less effective than individual apologies, which can be given to victims at the community level.

11. David, "What We Know About Transitional Justice."

12. Gibson, *Overcoming Apartheid.* For the criticism, see Backer, "*Overcoming Apartheid.*"

13. Jodi Halpern and Harvey M. Weinstein, "Rehumanizing the Other: Empathy and Reconciliation," *Human Rights Quarterly* 26, no. 3 (2004): 561–83.

14. Havel spoke against collective retribution by coining the slogan "we are not like them," making the Velvet Revolution possible (see Chapter 2). As a president, he also attempted to replace the collective lustration law with an individualized lustration model in late 1991 but was eventually defeated by the Federal Assembly. However, neither Havel nor other intellectual leaders were able to spell out what had to be done to deal with the past effectively.

15. Interview with A. Huvar, Velká Bystřice (January 2000).

16. Scholars routinely evaluate policies against theory-driven outcomes, even though the outcomes are not originally intended. Reconciliation is an outcome that is sometimes explicitly mentioned in the design of some measures of transitional justice and sometimes completely absent; but neither its presence nor its absence can prevent scholars from assessing transitional justice against their ability to arrive at, or undermine, reconciliation, which is a fundamental feature of democratic inclusiveness.

17. Because, in my experiments, reconciliatory measures have consistently produced positive effects on both justice and reconciliation, I would not shy away from recommending reconciliatory measures as a complementary mechanism to retributive measures to increase the effectiveness of dealing with the past. An obvious challenge of reconciliatory policies is that they cannot be mandated by the state. But the state and its political representatives could create conditions where such apologies may take place. Apologies, confessions, and expressions of remorse were not mandated during the transition from apartheid in South Africa; nevertheless, they did take place. But how? Do we need a law for everything?

The first possible step is to establish informal public forums that will encourage dialogue among various protagonists and victims of the previous regime. Such forums can be established in any town or village with the help of a local town hall or nongovernmental organization.

The interpersonal dialogue and interactions among the major players of the past and ordinary citizens are likely to promote understanding of the motives of others. This entails asking people from one side of the historical divide to try to see themselves in the shoes of those on the other side of the divide. Individual forums would require exposing individual stories in the past, a scrutiny of excuses, counternarratives, and triangulation with other testimonies. Learning from the individual failures can make society sensitive to tendencies to repeat the past, confident in the face of propaganda, and resistant to collective thinking. The individualization of one's role in the past as a prerequisite for social transformation is not an empty moralizing but carries practical implications for national security and political stability.

The second possibility would be to formalize the process and emulate one of the existing reconciliatory methods of justice. The Polish lustration law and the South African amnesty processes are significant models that offered incentives for wrongdoers to come forward and reveal the truth that was demanded by their victims. Although they were not ideal institutions, these are the only practical models. At the heart of reconciliatory institutions is the willingness of a tainted individual to come forward and reveal a particular segment of his or her personal truth about the past in exchange for untrammeled participation in the new system. Although reconciliatory institutions may not acquit wrongdoers from formal criminal responsibility, they permit the mitigation of the wrongdoing because of the remorse shown by the wrongdoers. Thus, at least some of the wrongdoers are able to demonstrate that they are sufficiently moral to be capable of personal change. See, e.g., David, "In Exchange for Truth."

To be sure, reconciliatory models are not without controversy. Indeed, the Polish elites fought a fierce battle for every inch of their lustration law and almost every lustration case. But, in doing so, the Poles learned about the communist past from individual biographies and they know why the communist regime was wrong. In comparison to the Czech Republic, the transformed ex-communists and enlightened citizens made Poland more resistant and more united in face of the Russian propaganda, which uses communism as a vehicle in the pursuit of its foreign interests. Unlike Czechs, Poles were remarkably united about Russia's annexation of Crimea from Ukraine. See Roman David, "Różne drogi Europy Środkowej," interview by Patrycja Bukalska, *Tygodnik Powszechny*, Sprawiedliwosc w Panstwach Prawa (June 14, 2015), 12–13.

18. Robert Merton, *Social Theory and Social Structure* (New York: Free Press, 1968).

19. This theorization underpinned my previous book, *Lustration and Transitional Justice*, although it was not explicitly formulated as a theory.

20. See Miller, *Eye for an Eye*.

21. The interventions in restorative justice and transitional justice spheres are different. While the former centers around mediation, the latter works with a variety of measures, such as retributive, revelatory, reparatory, and reconciliatory measures. In general, transitional justice is broader and deeper. See David and Choi, "Getting Even or Getting Equal?"

22. Tom R. Tyler, "Social Justice: Outcome and Procedure," *International Journal of Psychology* 35, no. 2 (2000): 117–25; Tom R. Tyler and S. L. Blader, "The Group Engagement Model: Procedural Justice, Social Identity, and Cooperative Behavior," *Personality and Social Psychology Review* 7, no. 4 (2003): 349–61.

23. The restoration of relationships would be an ideal solution. Restorative justice works on the assumption that there was a relationship, which was broken by the crime. To be sure, in many criminal cases, victims and offenders know each other. The problem is that this may

not apply in political and nonpolitical contexts. There may not have been any previous relationship. In such cases, the only way is an abstract restoration of relations, which encompasses a minimal degree of trust. However, the prospect for such restoration would still depend on the transformative status of the persons concerned.

24. I previously hypothesized that the choice of transitional justice is a function of the perception about the tainted as well as the perception by the tainted. Seeing others as tainted leads to the demand for retributive measures (in order to purify them). Being tainted also leads to demands for retribution (blaming others to purify oneself). David, *Lustration and Transitional Justice*, 93–130.

Bibliography

Aguilar, Paloma, Laia Balcells, and Hector Cebolla-Boado. "Determinants of Attitudes Toward Transitional Justice: An Empirical Analysis of the Spanish Case." *Comparative Political Studies* 44, no. 10 (2011): 1397–430.

Akhavan, Payam. "Beyond Impunity: Can International Criminal Justice Prevent Future Atrocities?" *American Journal of International Law* 95 (2001): 7–31.

Akhavan, Payam. "Justice in the Hague, Peace in the Former Yugoslavia? A Commentary on the United Nations War Crimes Tribunal." *Human Rights Quarterly* 20, no. 4 (1998): 737–816.

Alexander, Cheryl S., and Henry J. Becker. "The Use of Vignettes in Survey Research." *Public Opinion Quarterly* 42, no. 1 (1978): 93–104.

Appel, Hilary. *A New Capitalist Order: Privatization and Ideology in Russia and Eastern Europe*. Pittsburgh: University of Pittsburgh Press, 2004.

Backer, David. "*Overcoming Apartheid: Can Truth Reconcile a Divided Nation?* by James Gibson." *Comparative Political Studies* 39, no. 8 (2006): 1157–61.

Backer, David. "Watching the Bargain Unravel? A Panel Study of Victims' Attitudes About Transitional Justice in Cape Town, South Africa." *International Journal of Transitional Justice* 4, no. 3 (2010): 443–56.

Bartková, Magdaléna. "Historical Names of Streets and Places in Opava." B.A. diss., Palacky University, 2009.

Bartošek, Karel. *Český vězeň: Svědectví politických vězeňkyň a vězňů let padesátých, šedesátých a sedmdesátých*. Prague: Paseka, 2001.

Başoğlu, Metin, Maria Livanou, Cvetana Crnobarić, Tanja Frančišković, Enra Suljić, Dijana Đurić, and Melin Vranešić. "Psychiatric and Cognitive Effects of War in Former Yugoslavia: Association of Lack of Redress for Trauma and Posttraumatic Stress Reactions." *Journal of the American Medical Association* 294, no. 5 (2005): 580–90.

Batson, Charles D. *The Altruism Question: Toward a Social Psychological Answer*. Hillsdale, N.J.: Erlbaum, 1991.

Bazyler, Michael L. "The Holocaust Restitution Movement in Comparative Perspective." *Berkeley Journal of International Law* 20 (2002): 11–34.

Becker, David, Elizabeth Lira, María Isabel Castillo, Elena Gómez, and Juana Kovalskys. "Therapy with Victims of Political Repression in Chile: The Challenge of Social Reparation." *Journal of Social Issues* 46 (1990): 133–49.

Bideleux, Robert, and Ian Jeffries. *A History of Eastern Europe: Crisis and Change.* 2nd ed. New York: Routledge, 2007.

Biggar, Nigel. "Making Peace or Doing Justice: Must We Choose?" In *Burying the Past: Making Peace and Doing Justice After Civil Conflict*, ed. Nigel Biggar. Washington, D.C.: Georgetown University Press, 2003.

Biko, Nkosinathi. "Amnesty and Denial." In *Looking Back, Reaching Forward: Reflections on the Truth and Reconciliation Commission of South Africa*, ed. Charles Villa-Vicencio and Wilhelm Verwoerd. London: Zed, 2000.

Bílek, Jiří, and Karel Kaplan. *Pomocné Technické Prapory 1950–1954. Tábory nucené práce v Československu 1948–1954.* Prague: ÚSD, 1992.

Bílek, Jiří, and Vladimír Pilát. "Závodní, Dělnické a Lidové milice v Československu." *Historie a vojenství* 44, no. 3 (1995): 79–106.

Biro, Miklos, Dean Ajduković, Dinka Corkalo, Dino Djipa, Petar Milin, and Harvey M Weinstein. "Attitudes Toward Justice and Social Reconstruction in Bosnia and Herzegovina." In *My Neighbor, My Enemy*, ed. Eric Stover and Harvey M. Weinstein. Cambridge: Cambridge University Press, 2004. 183–205.

Blatz, Craig W., Karina Schumann, and Michael Ross. "Government Apologies for Historical Injustices." *Political Psychology* 30, no. 2 (2009): 219–41.

Bolton, Jonathan. *Worlds of Dissent: Charter 77, the Plastic People of the Universe, and Czech Culture Under Communism.* Cambridge, Mass.: Harvard University Press, 2010.

Bond, Robert M., et al. "A 61-Million-Person Experiment in Social Influence and Social Mobilization." *Nature* 489 (2012): 295–98.

Booth, James W. " 'From This Far Place': On Justice and Absence." *American Political Science Review* 105 (2001): 750–64.

Braithwaite, John. *Crime, Shame and Reintegration.* Cambridge: Cambridge University Press, 1989.

Brown, Archie. *The Rise and Fall of Communism.* New York: HarperCollins, 2009.

Brown, Rupert. "Social Identity Theory: Past Achievements, Current Problems, and Future Challenges." *European Journal of Social Psychology* 30 (2000): 745–78.

Brzezinski, Zbigniew, and Carl J. Friedrich. *Totalitarian Dictatorship and Autocracy.* Cambridge, Mass.: Harvard University Press, 1956.

Cepl, Vojtěch. "The Transformation of Hearts and Minds in Eastern Europe." *Cato Journal* 17, no. 2 (1997): 229–34.

Cepl, Vojtěch, and Mark Gillis. "Making Amends After Communism." *Journal of Democracy* 7 (1996): 118–24.

Český statistický úřad. "Výsledky voleb a referend." Available at volby.cz (accessed on August 22, 2017).

Chang, Iris. *The Rape of Nanking: The Forgotten Holocaust of World War II.* New York: Penguin, 1997.

Chapman, Audrey R., and Patrick Ball. "The Truth of Truth Commissions: Comparative Lessons from Haiti, South Africa, and Guatemala." *Human Rights Quarterly* 23, no. 1 (2001): 1–43.

Choi, Susanne Y. P., and Roman David. "Lustration Systems and Trust: Evidence from Survey Experiments in the Czech Republic, Hungary, and Poland." *American Journal of Sociology* 117, no. 4 (2012): 1172–201.

Cibulka, Petr. *Cibulkovy seznamy spolupracovníku StB.* Olomouc: Votobia, 1999.

Cohen, Stanley. *States of Denial: Knowing About Atrocities and Suffering*. Cambridge: Polity Press, 2001.

Collins, Cath, and Claudio Fuentes Saavedra. "Chile." In Stan and Nedelsky, *Encyclopedia*, vol. 2, pp. 98–106.

Corkalo, Dinka, Dean Ajdukovic, Harvey M. Weinstein, Eric Stover, Dino Djipa, and Miklos Biro. "Neighbors Again? Intercommunity Relations After Ethnic Cleansing." In *My Neighbor, My Enemy*, ed. Eric Stover and Harvey M. Weinstein. Cambridge: Cambridge University Press, 2004. 143–61.

Cottingham, John. "Varieties of Retribution." *Philosophical Quarterly* 29 (1978): 238–46.

Cronin-Furman, Kate. "Managing Expectations: International Criminal Trials and the Prospects for Deterrence of Mass Atrocity." *International Journal of Transitional Justice* 7, no. 3 (2013): 434–54.

Cullinan, Sarah. *Torture Survivors' Perceptions of Reparation*. London: Redress, 2001.

CVVM. "Dvacet pět let od Sametové revoluce očima občanů ČR a SR." Prague: CVVM, 2014.

Danieli, Yael. "Preliminary Reflections from a Psychological Perspective." In *The Right to Restitution, Compensation and Rehabilitation for Victims of Gross Violations of Human Rights and Fundamental Freedom*, ed. Theo C. van Boven et al. Netherlands Institute of Human Rights. Special issue no. 12 (1992): 196–213.

David, Roman. "Czech Republic." In Stan and Nedelsky, eds., *Encyclopedia*, vol. 2, 131–38.

David, Roman. "In Exchange for Truth: The Polish Lustration and the South African Amnesty Process." *Politikon* 32, no. 1 (2006): 81–99.

David, Roman. "International Criminal Tribunals and the Perception of Justice: The Effect of the ICTY in Croatia." *International Journal of Transitional Justice* 8, no. 3 (2014): 476–95.

David, Roman. "Lustration and Justice." Unpublished manuscript.

David, Roman. *Lustration and Transitional Justice*. Philadelphia: University of Pennsylvania Press, 2011.

David, Roman. "Lustration Laws in Action: The Motives and Evaluation of Lustration Policy in the Czech Republic and Poland (1989–2001)." *Law and Social Inquiry* 28, no. 2 (2003): 387–439.

David, Roman. "The Past or the Politics of the Present? Dealing with the Japanese Occupation of South Korea." *Contemporary Politics* 22, no. 1 (2016): 57–76.

David, Roman. "Situace bývalých politických vězňů." Machine-readable data file, 2000 (on file with the author).

David, Roman. "Symbolic Meaning of Historical Injustices: The Attitudes of South Korean Students to Japan's Policy of Dealing with the Past." *Proceedings of the Conference "Regional Peace Building: The Korean Peninsula and North-east Asia."* Hong Kong: Lingnan University, 2010. 7–18.

David, Roman. "Transitional Injustice? Criteria for Conformity of Lustration to the Right to Political Expression." *Europe-Asia Studies* 56, no. 6 (2004): 789–812.

David, Roman. "Transitional Justice and Changing Memories of the Past in Central Europe." *Government and Opposition* 50, no. 1 (2015): 24–44.

David, Roman. "Transitional Justice Effects in the Czech Republic." In *Post-Communist Transitional Justice: Lessons from Twenty-Five Years of Experience*, ed. Lavinia Stan and Nadya Nedelsky. New York: Cambridge University Press, 2015. 97–121.

David, Roman. "Twenty-Five Years of Dealing with the Past." Machine-readable data file, 2015 (on file with the author).

David, Roman. "Twenty Years of Dealing with the Past." Machine-readable data file, 2010 (on file with the author).

David, Roman. "Twenty Years of Transitional Justice in the Czech Lands." *Europe-Asia Studies* 64, no. 4 (2012): 761–84.

David, Roman. "What We Know About Transitional Justice: Survey and Experimental Evidence." *Advances in Political Psychology* (2017): 151–77.

David, Roman, and Susanne Y. P. Choi. "Forgiveness and Transitional Justice." *Journal of Conflict Resolution* 50, no. 3 (2006): 339–67.

David, Roman, and Susanne Y. P. Choi. "Getting Even or Getting Equal? Retributive Desires and Transitional Justice." *Political Psychology* 30 (2009): 161–92.

David, Roman, and Susanne Y. P. Choi. "Victims on Transitional Justice: Reparations of Victims of Human Rights Abuses in the Czech Republic." *Human Rights Quarterly* 27, no. 2 (2005): 392–435.

David, Zdeněk V. *Realism, Tolerance, and Liberalism in the Czech National Awakening: Legacies of the Bohemian Reformation.* Washington, D.C.: Woodrow Wilson Center Press with Johns Hopkins University Press, 2010.

De Greiff, Pablo, ed. *The Handbook of Reparations.* Oxford: Oxford University Press, 2006.

de Jong, Joop T. V. M., et al. "Lifetime Events and Posttraumatic Stress Disorder in Four Post-conflict Settings." *Journal of the American Medical Association* 286, no. 5 (2001): 555–62.

Druckman, James N., Donald P. Green, James H. Kuklinski, and Arthur Lupia. "The Growth and Development of Experimental Research in Political Science." *American Political Science Review* 100, no. 4 (2006): 627–36.

Edgell, Stephen. *Class: Key Concept in Sociology.* New York: Routledge, 1993.

Elster, Jon. *Closing the Books. Transitional Justice in Historical Perspective.* Cambridge: Cambridge University Press, 2004.

Eyal, Gil. "Antipolitics and the Spirit of Capitalism: Dissidents, Monetarists, and the Czech Transition to Capitalism." *Theory and Society* 29, no. 1 (2000): 49–92.

Eyal, Gil, Iván Szeléneyi, and Elizabeth Townsley. *Making Capitalism Without Capitalists: The New Ruling Elites in Eastern Europe.* London: Verso, 1998.

Fazekas, Zoltán, and Levente Littvay. "The Importance of Context in the Genetic Transmission of U.S. Party Identification." *Political Psychology* 36, no. 4 (2015): 361–77.

Feldman, Lily Gardner. "The Principle and Practice of 'Reconciliation' in German Foreign Policy: Relations with France, Israel, Poland and the Czech Republic." *International Affairs* 75, no. 2 (1999): 333–56.

Fiala, Petr, and Miroslav Mareš. "Konstituování systému politických stran v České republice (1989–1992)." *Politologický časopis* 1 (1997): 104–26.

Fiala, Petr, and Miroslav Mareš. "Vývoj systému politických stran v České republice (1992–1996)." *Politologický časopis* 3 (1997): 305–16.

Fishbein, Martin, and Icek Ajzen, *Belief, Attitude, Intention, and Behavior: An Introduction to Theory and Research.* Reading, Mass.: Addison-Wesley, 1975.

Fletcher, Laurel E., and Harvey M. Weinstein. "Violence and Social Repair: Rethinking the Contribution of Justice to Reconciliation." *Human Rights Quarterly* 24 (2002): 573–639.

Fletcher, Laurel E., Harvey M. Weinstein, and Jamie Rowen. "Context, Timing and the Dynamics of Transitional Justice: A Historical Perspective." *Human Rights Quarterly* 31 (2009): 163–220.

Gadourek, Ivan. *The Political Control of Czechoslovakia.* 2nd ed. Leiden: Greenwood, 1974.

Gaďourek, Ivan, and Jiří Nehněvajsa. *Žalářovaní, pronásledovaní a zneuznaní: Svědectví ještě žijících obětí stalinismu v českých zemích*. Brno: Masaryk University Press, 1997.

Gebauer, Fratišek, Karel Kaplan, František Koudelka, and Rudolf Vyhnálek, eds. *Soudní perzekuce politické povahy v Československu 1948–1989: Statistický přehled*. Prague: ÚSD, 1993.

Gerber, Alan S., Donald P. Green, and Christopher W. Larimer. "Social Pressure and Voter Turnout: Evidence from a Largescale Field Experiment." *American Political Science Review* 102, no. 1 (2008): 33–48.

Gerber, Monica M., and Jonathan Jackson. "Retribution as Revenge and Retribution as Just Deserts." *Social Justice Research* 26, no. 1 (2013): 61–80.

Gibson, James L. "Does Truth Lead to Reconciliation? Testing the Causal Assumptions of the South African Truth and Reconciliation Process." *American Journal of Political Science* 48, no. 2 (2004): 201–17.

Gibson, James L. "Social Networks, Civil Society, and the Prospects for Consolidating Russia's Democratic Transition." *American Journal of Political Science* 45, no. 1 (2001): 51–68.

Gibson, James L. "Truth, Justice, and Reconciliation: Judging the Fairness of Amnesty in South Africa." *American Journal of Political Science* 46, no. 3 (2002): 540–56.

Gibson, James L. "Truth, Reconciliation, and the Creation of Human Rights Culture in South Africa." *Law and Society Review* 38, no. 1 (2004): 5–40.

Gibson, James L., and Amanda Gouws. *Overcoming Political Intolerance in South Africa: Experiments in Democratic Persuasion*. Cambridge: Cambridge University Press, 2003.

Gibson, James L., and Amanda Gouws. "Truth and Reconciliation in South Africa: Attributions of Blame and the Struggle over Apartheid." *American Political Science Review* 93 (1999): 501–17.

Giddens, Anthony. *Sociology*. Cambridge: Polity Press, 2003.

Gobodo-Madikizela, Pumla. *A Human Being Died That Night: A South African Story of Forgiveness*. New York: Houghton Mifflin, 2003.

Goldstein, Jeffrey H. *Social Psychology*. New York: Academic Press, 2013.

Goldstein, Robert J. *Political Repression in 19th Century Europe*. London: Routledge, 1983.

Goldstone, Richard J. "Peace Versus Justice." *Nevada Law Journal* 6 (2005–6): 421–24.

Gready, Paul, and Simon Robins. "From Transitional to Transformative Justice: A New Agenda for Practice." University of York, Centre for Applied Human Rights Briefing Note TFJ-01 (June 2014).

Gula, Marián. "Vývoj typů spolupracovníků kontrarozvědky StB ve směrnicích pro agenturní práci." *Securitas imperii: Sborník k problematice bezpečnostních služeb* 1 (1994): 6–17.

Halpern, Jodi, and Harvey M. Weinstein. "Rehumanizing the Other: Empathy and Reconciliation." *Human Rights Quarterly* 26, no. 3 (2004): 561–83.

Hanley, Seán. *The New Right in the New Europe: Czech Transformation and Right-Wing Politics, 1989–2006*. New York: Routledge, 2008.

Hašek, Jaroslav. *The Good Soldier Svejk and His Fortunes in the World War*. London: Penguin Classics, 2000.

Hatemi, Peter, and Rose McDermott. "The Genetics of Politics: Discovery, Challenges, and Progress." *Trends in Genetics* 28, no. 10 (2012): 525–33.

Hatzfeld, Jean. *Life Laid Bare: The Survivors in Rwanda Speak*. New York: Other Press, 2007.

Hatzfeld, Jean. *Machete Season: The Killers in Rwanda Speak*. New York: Farrar, Straus and Giroux, 2005.

Havel, Václav. *Living in Truth*. Ed. Jan Vladislav; trans. Paul Wilson. London: Faber and Faber, 1986.

Havel, Václav. *Prosím Stručně*. Prague: Gallery, 2006.

Hayner, Priscilla B. *Unspeakable Truths: Confronting State Terror and Atrocity*. New York: Routledge, 2001.

Holý, Ladislav. *The Little Czech and the Great Czech Nation*. Cambridge: Cambridge University Press, 1996.

Horne, Cynthia M. "International Legal Rulings on Lustration Policies in Central and Eastern Europe: Rule of Law in Historical Context." *Law and Social Inquiry* 34, no. 3 (2009): 713–44.

Horne, Cynthia M. "Lustration, Transitional Justice, and Social Trust in Post-Communist Countries: Repairing or Wrestling the Ties That Bind?" *Europe-Asia Studies* 66, no. 2 (2014): 225–54.

Humphrey, Michael, and Estela Valverde. "Uruguay." In Stan and Nedelsky, *Encyclopedia*, vol. 2, pp. 497–503.

Huntington, Samuel P. *The Third Wave: Democratization in the Late Twentieth Century*. Norman: University of Oklahoma Press, 1991.

Hvížďala, Karel. "Oběť je projevem nejvyššího sociálního výkonu: S Vladimírem Čermákem o soudcích za totality, Ústavním soudu a Václavu Klausovi." In *Vladimír Čermák: Člověk—filozof—soudce*, ed. Jiří Baroš. Brno: Masaryk University Press, 2009. 201–10.

Jarolímek, Petr. "Zákony o navrácení majetku KSČ a SSM lidu." *Časopis soudobé dějiny* 9, no. 1 (2002): 65–81.

Jones, Owen. *Chavs: The Demonization of the Working Class*. London: Verso, 2012.

Judt, Tony. *Postwar: A History of Europe Since 1945*. New York: Penguin, 2006.

Kabele, Jiří. "Ďábelský koktejl sametové revoluce." In *Otevřená minulost: Autobiografická sociologie státního socialismu*, ed. Zdeněk Konopásek et al. Prague: Karolinum, 1999. 205–16.

Kabele, Jiří, et al. "Rekonstrukce komunistického vládnuti na konci osmdesátých let: Dědictví komunistické vlady V." *Sociological Papers* SP03, no. 10 (2003): 51.

Kalinová. Lenka, et al., eds. *K proměnám sociální struktury v Československu 1918–1968*. Prague: UPSV, 1993.

Kaminer, Debra, Dan J. Stein, Irene Mbanga, and Nompumelelo Zungu-Dirwayi. "The Truth and Reconciliation Commission in South Africa: Relation to Psychiatric Status and Forgiveness Among Survivors of Human Rights Abuses." *British Journal of Psychiatry* 178 (2001): 373–77.

Kaplan, Karel. *Nebezpečná bezpečnost: Státní bezpečnost 1948–1956*. Brno: Doplnek, 1999.

Kaplan, Karel. *Political Persecution in Czechoslovakia 1948–1972*. Cologne: Index, 1983.

Kiss, Elizabeth. "Moral Ambitions Within and Beyond Political Constraints." In *Truth v. Justice: The Morality of Truth Commissions*, ed. Robert I. Rotberg and Dennis Thompson. Princeton, N.J.: Princeton University Press, 2000. 68–98.

Kocian, Jiří, ed. *Slovníková příručka k Československým dějinám 1948–1989*. Prague: ÚSD, 2006.

Konopásek, Zdeněk, et al., eds. *Otevřená minulost: Autobiografická sociologie státního socialismu*. Prague: Karolinum, 1999.

Korbel, Josef. *Twentieth Century Czechoslovakia*. New York: Columbia University Press, 1977.

Krejčí, Jaroslav, and Pavel Machonin, *Czechoslovakia 1918–92*. London: Macmillan, 1996.

Ku, Julian, and Jide Nzelibe. "Do International Criminal Tribunals Deter or Exacerbate Humanitarian Atrocities?" *Washington University Law Review* 84 (2006): 777–833.

Kundera, Milan. *The Joke: Definitive Version.* New York: HarperCollins, 1993.

Kundera, Milan. *The Unbearable Lightness of Being.* New York: Harper and Row, 1984.

Kunštát, Daniel. *Za rudou oponou: Komunisté a jejich voliči po roce 1989.* Prague: Slon, 2013.

Lambourne, Wendy. "Transitional Justice and Peacebuilding After Mass Violence." *International Journal of Transitional Justice* 3, no. 1 (2009): 28–48.

Leebaw, Bronwyn Anne. "The Irreconcilable Goals of Transitional Justice." *Human Rights Quarterly* 30, no. 1 (2008): 95–118.

Lenin, Vladimir. *The State and Revolution.* https://www.marxists.org/archive/lenin/works/1917/staterev.

Letki, Natalia. "Lustration and Consolidation of Democracy." *Europe-Asia Studies* 54 (2002): 529–52.

Levitsky, Steven, and Lucan A. Way. *Competitive Authoritarianism: Hybrid Regimes After the Cold War.* Cambridge: Cambridge University Press, 2010.

Lewandowsky, Stephan, et al. "Misinformation and Its Correction: Continued Influence and Successful Debiasing." *Psychological Science in the Public Interest* 13, no. 3 (2012): 106–31.

Lijphart, Arend, and Carlos H. Waisman, eds. *Institutional Design in New Democracies: Eastern Europe and Latin America.* Boulder, Colo.: Westview, 1996.

Liška, Otakar, et al. *Vykonané tresty smrti: Československo 1918–1989.* Prague: ÚDV, 2000.

Loewenstein, Karl. "Militant Democracy and Fundamental Rights." Part I. *American Political Science Review* 31, no. 3 (1937): 417–32.

Loewenstein, Karl. "Militant Democracy and Fundamental Rights." Part II. *American Political Science Review* 31, no. 4 (1937): 638–58.

Łoś, Maria. *Communist Ideology, Law, and Crime.* New York: St. Martin's, 1988.

Łoś, Maria. "Lustration and Truth Claims: Unfinished Revolutions in Central Europe." *Law and Social Inquiry* 20, no. 1 (1995): 117–61.

Łoś, Maria, and Andrzej Zybertowicz. *Privatizing the Police-State: The Case of Poland.* New York: Palgrave, 2000.

Macionis, John J. *Sociology.* 14th ed. Boston: Pearson, 2012.

Malamud-Goti, Jaime E. *Game Without End: State Terror and the Politics of Justice.* Norman: University of Oklahoma Press, 1996.

Maňák, Jiří."Čistky v Komunistické straně Československa 1969–1970." *Sešity Ústavu pro soudobé dějiny,* AV ČR 28 (1997): 45.

Mannheim, Karl. "The Problem of Generations." In *Essays on the Sociology of Knowledge by Karl Mannheim,* ed. P. Kecskemeti. New York: Routledge and Kegan Paul, 1952.

Markovits, Inga. "Selective Memory: How the Law Affects What We Remember and Forget About the Past: The Case of East Germany." *Law and Society Review* 35, no. 3 (2001): 513–63.

Mateju, Petr, and Blanka Rehakova. "Turning Left or Class Realignment." *East European Politics and Societies* 11 (1997): 507–41.

McCullough, Michael E., Kenneth I. Pargament, and Carl E. Thoresen. *Forgiveness: Theory, Research and Practice.* New York: Guilford, 2000.

Meernik, James. "Justice and Peace? How the International Criminal Tribunal Affects Societal Peace in Bosnia." *Journal of Peace Research* 42, no. 3 (2005): 271–89.

Mendeloff, David. "Truth-seeking, Truth-telling, and Postconflict Peacebuilding: Curb the Enthusiasm?" *International Studies Review* 6, no. 3 (2004): 355–80.

Merton, Robert K. *Social Theory and Social Structure.* New York: Free Press, 1968.

Miller, William I. *Eye for an Eye.* Cambridge: Cambridge University Press, 2006.

Minow, Martha. *Between Vengeance and Forgiveness.* Boston: Beacon, 1998.

Miron, Anca M., Nyla R. Branscombe, and Monica Biernat. "Motivated Shifting of Justice Standards." *Personality and Social Psychology Bulletin* 36 (2010): 768–79.

Moran, John P. "The Communist Torturers of Eastern Europe: Prosecute and Punish or Forgive and Forget?" *Communist and Post-Communist Studies* 27, no. 1 (1994): 95–109.

Murphy, Jeffrie. *Getting Even: Forgiveness and Its Limits.* Oxford: Oxford University Press, 2003.

Mutua, Dean Makau, ed. "Transitional Justice: Does It Have a Future? A Special Issue." *International Journal of Transitional Justice* 9, no. 1 (2015): 1–169.

Nedelsky, Nadya. "Czechoslovakia, and the Czech and Slovak Republics." In *Transitional Justice in Eastern Europe and the Former Soviet Union: Reckoning with the Communist Past*, ed. Lavinia Stan. New York: Routledge, 2009.

Nedelsky, Nadya. "Divergent Responses to a Common Past: Transitional Justice in the Czech Republic and Slovakia," *Theory and Society* 33 (2004): 65–115.

Nedelsky, Nadya. "Slovak Republic." In Stan and Nedelsky eds., *Encyclopedia*, vol. 2, 433–39.

Neuman, Lawrence W. *Social Research Methods: Qualitative and Quantitative Approaches.* Boston: Allyn and Bacon, 2000.

O'Donnell, Guillermo, Phillipe Schmitter, and Laurence Whitehead, eds. *Transitions from Authoritarian Rule.* Baltimore: Johns Hopkins University Press, 1986.

Olsen, Tricia D., Leigh A. Payne, and Andrew G. Reiter. "The Justice Balance: When Transitional Justice Improves Human Rights and Democracy." *Human Rights Quarterly* 32 (2010): 980–1007.

Orentlicher, Diane F. *Shrinking the Space for Denial: The Impact of the ICTY in Serbia.* New York: Open Society Justice Initiative, 2008.

Orr, Wendy. "Reparation Delayed Is Healing Retarded." In *Looking Back, Reaching Forward: Reflections on the Truth and Reconciliation Commission of South Africa*, ed. Charles Villa-Vicencio and Wilhelm Verwoerd. London: Zed, 2000. 240–41.

Pham, Phuong, Patrick Vinck, Eric Stover, Andrew Moss, Marieke Wierda, and Richard Bailey. "When the War Ends: A Population-Based Survey on Attitudes About Peace, Justice, and Social Reconstruction in Northern Uganda." Human Rights Center, University of California, Berkeley; Payson Center for International Development, Tulane University; and International Center for Transitional Justice, 2007.

Pham, Phuong N., Harvey M. Weinstein, and Timothy Longman. "Trauma and PTSD Symptoms in Rwanda: Implications for Attitudes Toward Justice and Reconciliation." *Journal of the American Medical Association* 292, no. 5 (2004): 602–12.

Pithart, Petr. *Osmašedesátý.* 3rd ed. Prague: Rozmluvy, 1990.

Pulec, Martin. *Organizace a činnost ozbrojených pohraničních složek. Seznamy osob usmrcených na státních hranicích 1945–1989.* Prague: Úřad dokumentace a vyšetřování zločinů komunismu, 2006.

Rice, Condoleezza. *The Soviet Union and the Czechoslovak Army, 1948–1983: Uncertain Allegiance.* Princeton, N.J.: Princeton University Press, 1984.

Rotberg, Robert I., and Dennis Thompson, eds. *Truth v. Justice: The Morality of Truth Commissions.* Princeton, N.J.: Princeton University Press, 2000.

Salivarová-Škvorecká, Zdena. *Osočení: Pravdivé příběhy lidí z "Cibulkova seznamu."* Brno: Host, 2000.

Schabas, William A. "Amnesty, the Sierra Leone Truth and Reconciliation Commission and the Special Court for Sierra Leone." *U.C. Davis Journal of International Law and Policy* (2004): 145–69.

Schelling, Thomas. *Micromotives and Macrobehavior.* New York: W. W. Norton, 1978.

Schudson, Michael. *Watergate in American Memory: How We Remember, Forget, and Reconstruct the Past.* New York: Basic Books, 1992.

Schuman, Howard, and Jacqueline Scott. "Generations and Collective Memories." *American Sociological Review* 54, no. 3 (1989): 359–81.

Sikkink, Kathryn. *The Justice Cascade: How Human Rights Prosecutions Are Changing World Politics.* New York: W. W. Norton, 2011.

Šimečka, Milan. *Obnovení pořádku.* London: Edice Rozmluvy, 1984. Cited in Holý, *Little Czech*, 23.

Šimková, Dagmar. *Byly jsme tam taky.* Prague: Orbis, 1991.

Škutina, Vladimír. *Presidentův vězeň.* 2nd ed. Prague: Středočeské nakladatelství a knihkupectví, 1990.

Sniderman, Paul M., and Douglas Grob. "Innovations in Experimental Design in General Population Attitude Surveys." *Annual Review of Sociology* 22 (1996): 377–99.

Sonis, Jeffrey, James L. Gibson, Joop T. V. M. de Jong, Nigel P. Field, Sokhom Hean, and Ivan Komproe. "Probable Posttraumatic Stress Disorder and Disability in Cambodia: Associations with Perceived Justice, Desire for Revenge, and Attitudes Toward the Khmer Rouge Trials." *Journal of the American Medical Association* 302, no. 5 (2009): 527–36.

Stan, Lavinia, ed. *Transitional Justice in Eastern Europe and the Former Soviet Union: Reckoning with the Communist Past.* New York: Routledge, 2009.

Stan, Lavinia, and Nadya Nedelsky, eds. *Encyclopedia of Transitional Justice.* New York: Cambridge University Press, 2013.

Stan, Lavinia, and Nadya Nedelsky, eds. *Post-Communist Transitional Justice: Lessons from Twenty-Five Years of Experience.* New York: Cambridge University Press, 2015.

Staniszkis, Jadwiga. "'Political Capitalism' in Poland." *East European Politics and Societies* 5, no. 1 (1990): 127–41.

Staniszkis, Jadwiga. *Postkomunizm: Próba Opisu.* Gdańsk: Wydawnictwo Słowo, 2001.

Stinchcombe, Arthur. "Lustration as a Problem of the Social Basis of Constitutionalism." *Law and Social Inquiry* 20, no. 1 (1995): 245–73.

Stover, Eric, and Harvey M. Weinstein, eds. *My Neighbor, My Enemy: Justice and Community in the Aftermath of Mass Atrocity.* Cambridge: Cambridge University Press, 2004.

Strelan, Peter, and Jan-Willem van Prooijen. "Retribution and Forgiveness : The Healing Effect of Punishment for Just Desserts." *European Journal of Social Psychology* 43, no. 6 (2013): 544–553.

Szczygiel, Mariusz. *Gottland: Mostly True Stories from Half of Czechoslovakia.* New York: Melville House, 2014.

Tarrant, Mark, Nyla R. Branscombe, Ruth H. Warner, and Dale Weston. "Social Identity and Perceptions of Torture: It's Moral When We Do It." *Journal of Experimental Social Psychology* 48 (2012): 513–18.

Tavuchis, Nicholas. *Mea Culpa: A Sociology of Apology and Reconciliation*. Stanford, Calif.: Stanford University Press, 1991.

Teich, Mikuláš, ed. *Bohemia in History*. Cambridge: Cambridge University Press, 1998.

Teitel, Ruti G. *Transitional Justice*. Oxford: Oxford University Press, 2000.

Thompson, S. Harrison. *Czechoslovakia in European History*. 2nd ed. London: Frank Cass, 1965.

Tigrid, Pavel. *Dnešek je váš, zítřek je náš: Dělnické revolty v komunistických zemích*. Prague: Vokno, 1990.

Tóka, Gábor, et al. "The Development of Party Systems and Electoral Alignments in East Central Europe." Machine-readable data files. Budapest: Central European University, 1992–96.

Torpey, John. "'Making Whole What Has Been Smashed': Reflections on Reparations." *Journal of Modern History* 73 (2001): 333–58.

Tucker, Aviezer. "Reproducing Incompetence: The Constitution of Czech Higher Education." *East European Constitutional Review* 9, no. 3 (2000): 94–99.

Tutu, Desmond M. *No Future Without Forgiveness*. New York: Doubleday, 1999.

Tyler, Tom R. "Social Justice: Outcome and Procedure." *International Journal of Psychology* 35, no. 2 (2000): 117–25.

Tyler, Tom R., and S. L. Blader. "The Group Engagement Model: Procedural Justice, Social Identity, and Cooperative Behavior." *Personality and Social Psychology Review* 7, no. 4 (2003): 349–61.

Vachudová, Milada A. *Europe Undivided: Democracy, Leverage, and Integration After Communism*. Oxford: Oxford University Press, 2005.

van Boven, Theo. "Study Concerning the Right to Restitution, Compensation and Rehabilitation for Victims of Gross Violations of Human Rights and Fundamental Freedoms." Excerpted in *Transitional Justice: How Emerging Democracies Reckon with Former Regimes*, vol. 1, ed. Neil J. Kritz. Washington, D.C.: United States Institute of Peace, 1995.

van der Merwe, Hugo. "Editorial Note." *International Journal of Transitional Justice* 7 (2013): 1–7.

Vinck, Patrick, Phuong N. Pham, Eric Stover, and Harvey M. Weinstein. "Exposure to War Crimes and Implications for Peace Building in Northern Uganda." *Journal of the American Medical Association* 298, no. 5 (2007): 543–54.

Vinjamuri, Leslie, and Jack Snyder. "Advocacy and Scholarship in the Study of International War Crime Tribunals and Transitional Justice." *Annual Review of Political Science* 7 (2004): 345–62.

Wasilewski, Jacek. *Elita polityczna 1998*. Warsaw: ISP PAN, 1999.

Williams, Kieran, and Dennis Deletant. *Security Intelligence Services in New Democracies: The Czech Republic, Slovakia and Romania*. New York: Palgrave, 2001.

Wilson, Richard A. *The Politics of Truth and Reconciliation in South Africa: Legitimizing the Post-Apartheid State*. Cambridge: Cambridge University Press, 2001.

Wuthnow, Robert. *Meaning and Moral Order: Explorations in Cultural Analysis*. Berkeley: University of California Press, 1987.

Žáček, Pavel. *Přísně tajné! Státní bezpečnost za normalizace*. Prague: Votobia, 2001.

Zakaria, Fareed. *The Future of Freedom: Illiberal Democracy at Home and Abroad*. New York: W. W. Norton, 2003.

Zehr, Howard. *Changing Lenses: A New Focus for Crime and Justice*. 3rd ed. Scottdale, Pa.: Herald Press, 2005.

Index

Acknowledgments

This book was written under the auspices of Lingnan University in Hong Kong. Nevertheless, I also conducted the research for this book while at Newcastle University, United Kingdom, and at Charles University in the Czech Republic. My research was funded by grants from the British Academy and Lingnan University. I would like to thank Dr. Jiří Vinopal and Ms. Naděžda Čadová at CVVM for the administration of my surveys; Ms. Veronika Hřebenářová, Ms. Lenka Chudomelová, Ms. Markéta Těthalová, and Ms. Renáta Topinková for their assistance in conducting interviews; Ms. Ying Zhang for statistical assistance, consultancy, and analysis; Ms. Kamila Krygier for her comments on the first version of the manuscript; and Mrs. Glenda Webster for editing it. I am indebted to two anonymous referees for their insightful and detailed comments. I would like to thank to Susanne Choi, Sláva Sládeček, and Peter Agree for hammering out the title of the book with me; and Erica Ginsburg and other members of the University of Pennsylvania Press for their work on the book's production. I would especially like to thank Susanne Choi for her comments and insights, and Susanne Choi, Jan David, and Antonin David for bearing with me while I was writing it.

Chapter 3, on victims, is largely adapted from an article entitled "Victims on Transitional Justice: Reparation of Former Political Prisoners in the Czech Republic," which I coauthored with Susanne Choi. It was first published in *Human Rights Quarterly* 27, no. 2 (2005): 392–435, copyright © 2005 The Johns Hopkins University Press, reprinted by permission of The Johns Hopkins University Press. It was, however, statistically reanalyzed, and its qualitative sections updated by the analyses of focus-group sessions held in 2006 and 2014. Most survey datasets and interviews used in this book are from my original research.